Joseph Butler, Samuel Hallifax

The Works of the Right Reverend Father in God Joseph Butler

To which is prefixed a preface, giving some account of the character and writings of

the author. Vol. 1

Joseph Butler, Samuel Hallifax

The Works of the Right Reverend Father in God Joseph Butler
To which is prefixed a preface, giving some account of the character and writings of the author. Vol. 1

ISBN/EAN: 9783337424770

Printed in Europe, USA, Canada, Australia, Japan

Cover: Foto ©Lupo / pixelio.de

More available books at **www.hansebooks.com**

THE WORKS

OF THE

RIGHT REVEREND FATHER IN GOD,

JOSEPH BUTLER, D.C.L.

LATE LORD BISHOP OF DURHAM.

TO WHICH IS PREFIXED,

A PREFACE, GIVING SOME ACCOUNT OF THE CHARACTER
AND WRITINGS OF THE AUTHOR.

BY SAMUEL HALIFAX, D.D.

LATE LORD BISHOP OF GLOUCESTER.

IN TWO VOLUMES.

VOL. I.

OXFORD:

AT THE CLARENDON PRESS.

MDCCCLXXIV.

THE

ANALOGY OF RELIGION,

NATURAL AND REVEALED,

TO THE

CONSTITUTION AND COURSE OF NATURE.

TO WHICH ARE ADDED

TWO BRIEF DISSERTATIONS.

I. OF PERSONAL IDENTITY.
II. OF THE NATURE OF VIRTUE.

BY JOSEPH BUTLER, D.C.L.

LATE LORD BISHOP OF DURHAM.

Ejus [Analogiæ] hæc vis est, ut id quod dubium est ad aliquid simile, de quo non quæritur, referat; ut incerta certis probet.   QUINTIL. i. 6.

WITH A PREFACE,

GIVING SOME ACCOUNT OF THE CHARACTER AND WRITINGS OF THE AUTHOR,

BY SAMUEL HALIFAX, D.D.

LATE LORD BISHOP OF GLOUCESTER.

OXFORD:
AT THE CLARENDON PRESS.
MDCCCLXXIV.

TO

THE REVEREND

DR. THOMAS BALGUY,

ARCHDEACON AND PREBENDARY OF WINCHESTER, &c.

DEAR SIR,

I TRUST you will excuse the liberty I have taken of prefixing your name to the following sheets; the latter part of which, I am confident, will not be thought undeserving of your approbation; and of the former part you will commend the intention at least, if not the execution. In vindicating the character of Bishop Butler from the aspersions thrown upon it since his death, I have but discharged a common duty of humanity, which survivors owe to those who have deserved well of mankind by their lives or writings, when they are past the power of appearing in their own defence. And if what I have added, by way of opening the general design of the Works of this great Prelate, be of use in exciting the younger class of Students in our Universities to read, and so to read as to understand, the Two Volumes prepared and published by the Author himself; I flatter myself I shall have done no inconsiderable service to Morality and Religion. Your time and studies have been long successfully devoted to the support of the same great cause: and in what you have lately given to the world, both as an Author and an Editor, you have largely contributed to the defence of our common Christianity, and of what was esteemed by One, who was perfectly competent to judge, its best establishment, the Church of England. In the present publication I consider myself as a fellow-labourer with You in the same design, and tracing the path You have trod before, but at great distance, and with unequal paces. When, by His Majesty's goodness, I was raised to that station of eminence in the Church, to which You had been first named, and which, on account of the infirmity of your health, You had desired to decline; it was honour enough for Me on such an occasion to have been thought of next to You: and I know of no better rule by which to govern my conduct, so as not to discredit the Royal Hand which conferred on me so signal and unmerited a favour, than in cases of difficulty to put the question to myself, How You would probably have acted in the same situation. You see, Sir, I still look up to You, as I have been wont, both as my Superior and my Example. That I may long reap the benefit of your advice and friendship; and that such a measure of health and strength may be continued to You, as may enable You to pass the evening of your days with comfort, and enjoy the blessings of the life you love; is the cordial wish of,

> Dear Sir,
> Your very affectionate
> and faithful Servant,
> S. GLOUCESTER.

Dartmouth Street, Westminster,
12th May, 1786.

PREFACE

BY

THE EDITOR.

"When I consider how light a matter very often subjects the best established characters to the suspicions of posterity, posterity often as malignant to virtue as the age that saw it was envious of its glory; and how ready a remote age is to catch at a low revived slander, which the times that brought it forth saw despised and forgotten almost in its birth; I cannot but think it a matter that deserves attention."—*Letter to the Editor of the Letters on the Spirit of Patriotism*, &c. by BISHOP WARBURTON. See his Works, vol. vii. p. 547.

THE Charge to the Clergy of the Diocese of Durham, which is placed immediately after the Sermons, was printed and published in the year 1751, by the learned Prelate whose name it bears; and, together with the Sermons and Analogy of the same writer, both too well known to need a more particular description, completes the collection of his Works. It has long been considered as a matter of curiosity, on account of its scarceness; and it is equally curious on other accounts—its subject, and the calumny to which it gave occasion, of representing the Author as *addicted to superstition*, as *inclined to Popery*, and as *dying in the communion of the Church of Rome*. The improved edition of the *Biographia Britannica*, published under the care of Dr. Kippis, having unavoidably brought this calumny again into notice, it may not be unseasonable to offer a few reflections in this place, by way of obviating any impressions that may hence arise to the disadvantage of so great a character as that of the late Bishop Butler; referring those, who desire a more particular account of his life, to the third volume of the same entertaining work, printed in 1784, art. BUTLER (Joseph)*.

I. The principal design of the Bishop in his Charge is, to exhort his Clergy to "do their part towards reviving a practical sense of religion amongst the people committed to their care;" and, as one way of effecting this, to "instruct them in the *Importance of External Religion*," or the usefulness of outward observances in promoting inward piety. Now, from the compound nature of man, consisting of two parts, the body and the mind, together with the influence which these are found to have on one another, it follows, that the religious regards of such a creature ought to be so framed, as to be in some way properly accommodated to both. A religion which is purely spiritual, stripped of every thing that may affect the senses, and considered only as a divine philosophy of the mind, if it do not mount up into enthusiasm, as has frequently been the case, often sinks, after a few short fervors, into indifference: an abstracted invisible object, like that which natural religion offers, ceases to move or interest the heart; and something further is wanting to bring it nearer, and render it more present to our view, than merely an intellectual contemplation. On the other hand, when, in order to remedy this inconvenience, recourse is had to instituted forms and ritual injunctions, there is always danger lest men be tempted to rest entirely on these, and persuade themselves that a painful attention to such observances will atone for the want of genuine piety and virtue. Yet surely there is a way of steering safely between these two extremes; of so consulting both the parts of our constitution, that the body and the mind may concur in rendering our religious services acceptable to God, and at the same time useful to ourselves. And what way can this be, but precisely that which is recommended in the Charge; such a cultivation of outward as well as inward religion, that from both may result, what is the point chiefly to be laboured, and at all events to be secured, a correspondent temper and behaviour;

---

* The account here alluded to is subjoined to this preface.

or, in other words, such an application of the forms of godliness, as may be subservient in promoting the power and spirit of it? No man, who believes the Scriptures of the Old and New Testament, and understands what he believes, but must know, that external religion is as much enjoined, and constitutes as real a part of revelation, as that which is internal. The many ceremonies in use among the Jews, in consequence of a Divine command; the baptism of water, as an emblem of moral purity; the eating and drinking of bread and wine, as symbols and representations of the body and blood of Christ, required of Christians, are proofs of this. On comparing these two parts of religion together, one, it is immediately seen, is of much greater importance than the other; and, whenever they happen to interfere, is always to be preferred: but does it follow from hence, that therefore that other is of little or no importance, and, in cases where there is no competition, may entirely be neglected? Or rather is not the legitimate conclusion directly the reverse, that nothing is to be looked upon as of little importance, which is of any use at all in preserving upon our minds a sense of the Divine authority, which recalls to our remembrance the obligations we are under, and helps to keep us, as the Scripture expresses it, "in the fear of the Lord all the day long[b]?" If, to adopt the instance mentioned in the Charge, the sight of a church should remind a man of some sentiment of piety; if, from the view of a material building dedicated to the service of God, he should be led to regard himself, his own body, as a living "temple of the Holy Ghost[c]," and therefore no more than the other to be profaned or desecrated by any thing that defileth or is impure; could it be truly said of such a one, that he was superstitious, or mistook the means of religion for the end? If, to use another, and what has been thought a more obnoxious instance, taken from the Bishop's practice, a cross, erected in a place of public worship[d], should cause us to reflect on Him who died on a cross for our salvation, and on the necessity of our "own dying to sin[e]," and of "crucifying the flesh with its affections and

[b] Prov. xxiii. 17.
[d] See Note A, at the end of this preface.
[c] 1 Cor. vi. 19.
[e] Rom. vi. 11.

lusts [f];" would any worse consequences follow from such sentiments so excited, than if the same sentiments had been excited by the view of a picture, of the crucifixion suppose, such as is commonly placed, and with this very design, in foreign churches, and indeed in many of our own? Both the instances here adduced, it is very possible, may be far from being approved, even by those who are under the most sincere convictions of the importance of true religion: and it is easy to conceive how open to scorn and censure they must be from others, who think they have a talent for ridicule, and have accustomed themselves to regard all pretensions to piety as hypocritical or superstitious. But "Wisdom is justified of her children [g]." Religion is what it is, "whether men will hear, or whether they will forbear [h];" and whatever in the smallest degree promotes its interests, and assists us in performing its commands, whether that assistance be derived from the medium of the body or the mind, ought to be esteemed of great weight, and deserving of our most serious attention.

However, be the danger of superstition what it may, no one was more sensible of that danger, or more in earnest in maintaining, that external acts of themselves are nothing, and that moral holiness, as distinguished from bodily observances of every kind, is that which constitutes the essence of religion, than Bishop Butler. Not only the Charge itself, the whole intention of which is plainly nothing more than to enforce the necessity of *practical religion*, the reality as well as form, is a demonstration of this, but many passages besides to the same purpose, selected from his other writings. Take the two following as specimens. In his Analogy he observes thus: "Though mankind have, in all ages, been greatly prone to place their religion in peculiar positive rites, by way of equivalent for obedience to moral precepts; yet, without making any comparison at all between them, and consequently without determining which is to have the preference, the nature of the thing abundantly shews all notions of that kind to be utterly subversive of true religion: as they are, moreover, contrary to the whole general tenor of Scripture; and likewise to the most express particular declarations of it, that nothing can render us accepted of God, without moral virtue[i]." And to the same purpose in his Sermon, preached before the Society for the Propagation of the Gospel, in Feb. 1738-9. " Indeed, amongst creatures naturally formed for religion, yet so much under the power of imagination as men are, superstition is an evil, which can never be out of sight. But even against this, true religion is a great security, and the only one. True religion takes up that place in the mind, which superstition would usurp, and so leaves little room for it; and likewise lays us under the strongest obligations to oppose it. On the contrary, the danger of superstition cannot but be increased by the prevalence of irreligion; and, by its general prevalence, the evil will be unavoidable. For the common people, wanting a religion, will of course take up with almost any superstition which is thrown in their way: and in process of time, amidst the infinite vicissitudes of the political world, the leaders of parties will certainly be able to serve themselves of that superstition, whatever it be, which is getting ground; and will not fail to carry it to the utmost length their occasions require. The general nature of the thing shews this; and history and fact confirm it. It is therefore wonderful, those people who seem to think there is but one evil in life, that of superstition, should not see that atheism and profaneness must be the introduction of it [k]."

He who can think and write in such a manner, can never be said to mistake the nature of real religion: and he, who, after such proofs to the contrary, can persist in asserting of so discreet and learned a person, that he was *addicted to superstition*, must himself be much a stranger both to truth and charity.

And here it may be worth our while to observe, that the same excellent prelate, who by one set of men was suspected of *superstition*, on account of his Charge, has by another been represented as leaning to the opposite extreme of *enthusiasm*, on account of his two discourses *On the Love of God*. But both opinions are equally without foundation. He was neither superstitious, nor an enthusiast: his mind was much too

---

[i] Analogy, part II. chap. i.   [k] Serm. xvi.

strong, and his habits of thinking and reasoning much too strict and severe, to suffer him to descend to the weaknesses of either character. His piety was at once fervent and rational. When impressed with a generous concern for the declining cause of religion, he laboured to revive its dying interests; nothing he judged would be more effectual to that end, among creatures so much engaged with bodily things, and so apt to be affected with whatever strongly solicits the senses, as men are, than a religion of such a frame as should in its exercise require the joint exertions of the body and the mind. On the other hand, when penetrated with the dignity and importance of "the first and great commandment [l]," love to God, he set himself to inquire, what those movements of the heart are, which are due to Him, the Author and Cause of all things; he found, in the coolest way of consideration, that God is the natural object of the *same* affections of gratitude, reverence, fear, desire of approbation, trust, and dependence, the same affections in *kind*, though doubtless in a very disproportionate *degree*, which any one would feel from contemplating a perfect character in a creature, in which goodness, with wisdom and power, are supposed to be the predominant qualities, with the further circumstance, that this creature was also his governor and friend. This subject is manifestly a real one; there is nothing in it fanciful or unreasonable: this way of being affected towards God is piety, in the strictest sense: this is religion, considered as a habit of mind; a religion, suited to the nature and condition of man [m].

II. From superstition to *Popery* the transition is easy: no wonder then, that, in the progress of detraction, the simple imputation of the former of these, with which the attack on the character of our Author was opened, should be followed by the more aggravated imputation of the latter. Nothing, I think, can fairly be gathered in support of such a suggestion from the Charge, in which Popery is barely mentioned, and occasionally only, and in a sentence or two; yet even there, it should be remarked, the Bishop takes care to describe the peculiar observances required by it, "some as in themselves

---

[l] Matt. xxii. 38.   [m] See Note B, at the end of this preface.

wrong and superstitious, and others of them as being made subservient to the purposes of superstition." With respect to his other writings, any one at all conversant with them needs not to be told, that the matters treated of both in his Sermons and his Analogy did none of them directly lead him to consider, and much less to combat, the opinions, whether relating to faith or worship, which are peculiar to the Church of Rome: it might therefore have happened, yet without any just conclusion arising from thence, of being himself inclined to favour those opinions, that he had never mentioned, so much as incidentally, the subject of Popery at all. But fortunately for the reputation of the Bishop, and to the eternal disgrace of his calumniators, even this poor resource is wanting to support their malevolence. In his Sermon at St. Bride's before the Lord Mayor in 1740, after having said that "our laws and whole constitution go more upon supposition of an equality amongst mankind, than the constitution and laws of other countries;" he goes on to observe, that "this plainly requires, that more particular regard should be had to the education of the lower people here, than in places where they are born slaves of power, and to be made *slaves of superstition*[n]:" meaning evidently in this place, by the general term *superstition*, the particular errors of the Romanists. This is something: but we have a still plainer indication what his sentiments concerning Popery really were, from another of his additional Sermons, I mean that before the House of Lords on June the 11th, 1747, the anniversary of his late Majesty's accession. The passage alluded to is as follows; and my readers will not be displeased that I give it them at length. "The value of our religious Establishment ought to be very much heightened in our esteem, by considering what it is a security from; I mean that great corruption of Christianity, Popery, which is ever hard at work to bring us again under its yoke. Whoever will consider the Popish claims, to the disposal of the whole earth, as of Divine right, to dispense with the most sacred engagements, the claims to supreme absolute authority in religion; in short, the general claims which the Canonists express by the words *plenitude of power*

[n] Serm. xvii.

—whoever, I say, will consider Popery as it is professed at Rome, may see, that it is manifest, open usurpation of all human and Divine authority. But even in those Roman Catholic countries where these monstrous claims are not admitted, and the civil power does, in many respects, restrain the papal; yet persecution is professed, as it is absolutely enjoined by what is acknowledged to be their highest authority, a general council, so called, with the Pope at the head of it; and is practised in all of them, I think without exception, where it can be done safely. Thus they go on to substitute force instead of argument; and external profession made by force, instead of reasonable conviction. And thus corruptions of the grossest sort have been in vogue, for many generations, in many parts of Christendom; and are so still, even where Popery obtains in its least absurd form: and their antiquity and wide extent are insisted upon as proofs of their truth; a kind of proof, which at best can only be presumptive, but which loses all its little weight in proportion as the long and large prevalence of such corruptions have been obtained by force[o]." In another part of the same Sermon, where he is again speaking of our ecclesiastical constitution, he reminds his audience that it is to be valued, "not because it leaves us at liberty to have as little religion as we please, without being accountable to human judicatories; but because it exhibits to our view, and enforces upon our consciences, genuine Christianity, free from the superstitions with which it is defiled in other countries; which superstitions, he observes, "naturally tend to abate its force." The date of this Sermon should here be attended to. It was preached in June, 1747; that is, four years before the delivery and publication of the Charge, which was in the year 1751; and exactly five years before the author died, which was in June, 1752. We have then, in the passages now laid before the reader, a clear and unequivocal proof, brought down to within a few years of Bishop Butler's death, that Popery was held by him in the utmost abhorrence, and that he regarded it in no other light, than as *the great corruption of Christianity*, and a *manifest open usurpation of all human and Divine authority*. The argu-

[o] Serm. xx.

ment is decisive; nor will any thing be of force to invalidate it, unless from some *after-act* during the short remainder of the Bishop's life, *besides* that of delivering and printing his Charge, (which, after what I have said here, and in the notes added to this Preface and to the Charge, I must have leave to consider as affording no evidence at all of his inclination to Papistical doctrines or ceremonies,) the contrary shall incontrovertibly appear.

III. One such after-act however has been alleged, which would effectually demolish all that we have urged in behalf of our Prelate, were it true, as is pretended, that he *died in the communion of the Church of Rome*. Had a story of this sort been invented and propagated by Papists, the wonder might have been less:

Hoc Ithacus velit, et magno mercentur Atridæ.

But to the reproach of Protestantism, the fabrication of this calumny, for such we shall find it, originated from among ourselves. It is pretty remarkable, that a circumstance so extraordinary should never have been divulged till the year 1767, fifteen years after the Bishop's decease. At that time Dr. Thomas Secker was Archbishop of Canterbury; who of all others was the most likely to know the truth or falsehood of the fact asserted, having been educated with our Author in his early youth, and having lived in a constant habit of intimacy with him to the very time of his death. The good Archbishop was not silent on this occasion: with a virtuous indignation he stood forth to protect the posthumous character of his friend; and in a public newspaper, under the signature of *Misopseudes*, called upon his accuser to support what he had advanced, by whatever proofs he could. No proof, however, nor any thing like a proof, appeared in reply; and every man of sense and candour at that time was perfectly convinced the assertion was entirely groundless [p]. As a further confirmation of the rectitude of this judgment, it may not be amiss to mention, there is yet in existence a strong *presumptive* argument at least in its favour, drawn from the testimony of those who attended our Author in the sickness of which he died. The last days of this excellent

[p] See Note C, at the end of this preface.

Prelate were passed at Bath; Dr. Nathanael Forster, his chaplain, being continually with him; and for one day, and at the very end of his illness, Dr. Martin Benson also, the then Bishop of Gloucester, who shortened his own life in his pious haste to visit his dying friend. Both these persons constantly wrote letters to Dr. Secker, then Bishop of Oxford, containing accounts of Bishop Butler's declining health, and of the symptoms and progress of his disorder, which, as was conjectured, soon terminated in his death. These letters, which are still preserved in the Lambeth library [q], I have read; and not the slenderest argument can be collected from them, in justification of the ridiculous slander we are here considering. If at that awful season the Bishop was not known to have expressed any opinion tending to shew his *dislike* to Popery, neither was he known to have said any thing, that could at all be construed in *approbation* of it: and the natural presumption is, that whatever sentiments he had formerly entertained concerning that corrupt system of religion, he continued to entertain them to the last. The truth is, neither the word nor the idea of Popery seems once to have occurred either to the Bishop himself, or to those who watched his parting moments: their thoughts were otherwise engaged. His disorder had reduced him to such debility, as to render him incapable of speaking much or long on any subject: the few bright intervals that occurred were passed in a state of the utmost tranquillity and composure; and in that composure he expired. "Mark the perfect man, and behold the upright: for the end of that man is peace[r]." "Let me die the death of the righteous, and let my last end be like his[s]!"

Out of pure respect for the virtues of a man, whom I had never the happiness of knowing, or even of seeing, but from whose writings I have received the greatest benefit and illumination, and which I have reason to be thankful to Providence for having early thrown in my way, I have adventured, in what I have now offered to the public, to step forth in his defence, and to vindicate his honest fame from the attacks of those, who, with the vain hope of bringing down

[q] See Note D, at the end of this preface.   [r] Ps. xxxvii. 37.   [s] Numb. xxiii. 10.

superior characters to their own level, are for ever at work in detracting from their just praise. For the literary reputation of Bishop Butler, it stands too high in the opinion of the world, to incur the danger of any diminution: but this in truth is the least of his excellencies. He was more than a good writer, he was a good man; and, what is an addition even to this eulogy, he was a sincere Christian. His whole study was directed to the knowledge and practice of sound morality and true religion: these he adorned by his life, and has recommended to future ages in his writings; in which, if my judgment be of any avail, he has done essential service to both, as much, perhaps, as any single person since the extraordinary gifts of "the word of wisdom and the word of knowledge[t]" have been withdrawn.

In what follows I propose to give a short account of the Bishop's *moral and religious systems*, as these are collected from his works.

I. His way of treating the subject of *morals* is to be gathered from the volume of his Sermons, and particularly from the three first, and from the preface to that volume.

"There is," as our Author with singular sagacity has observed, "a much more exact correspondence between the natural and moral world, than we are apt to take notice of[u]." The inward frame of man answers to his outward condition; the several propensities, passions, and affections, implanted in our hearts by the Author of nature, are in a peculiar manner adapted to the circumstances of life in which he hath placed us. This general observation, properly pursued, leads to several important conclusions. The original internal constitution of man, compared with his external condition, enables us to discern what course of action and behaviour that constitution leads to, what is our duty respecting that condition, and furnishes us besides with the most powerful arguments to the practice of it.

What the inward frame and constitution of man is, is a

[t] 1 Cor. xii. 8.   [u] Serm. vi.

question of fact; to be determined, as other facts are, from experience, from our internal feelings and external senses, and from the testimony of others. Whether human nature, and the circumstances in which it is placed, might not have been ordered otherwise, is foreign to our inquiry, and none of our concern: our province is, taking both of these as they are, and viewing the connexion between them, from that connexion to discover, if we can, what course of action is fitted to that nature and those circumstances. From contemplating the bodily senses, and the organs or instruments adapted to them, we learn that the eye was given to see with, the ear to hear with. In like manner, from considering our inward perceptions and the final causes of them, we collect that the feeling of shame, for instance, was given to prevent the doing of things shameful; compassion, to carry us to relieve others in distress; anger, to resist sudden violence offered to ourselves. If, continuing our inquiries in this way, it should at length appear, that the nature, the whole nature, of man leads him to and is fitted for that particular course of behaviour which we usually distinguish by the name of virtue, we are authorized to conclude, that virtue is the law we are born under, that it was so intended by the Author of our being; and we are bound by the most intimate of all obligations, a regard to our own highest interest and happiness, to conform to it in all situations and events.

Human nature is not simple and uniform, but made up of several parts; and we can have no just idea of it as a system or constitution, unless we take into our view the respects and relations which these parts have to each other. As the body is not one member, but many; so our inward structure consists of various instincts, appetites, and propensions. Thus far there is no difference between human creatures and brutes. But besides these common passions and affections, there is another principle, peculiar to mankind, that of conscience, moral sense, reflection, call it what you please, by which they are enabled to review their whole conduct, to approve of some actions in themselves, and to disapprove of others. That this principle will of course have *some* influence on our behaviour, at least at times, will hardly be disputed: but the particular influence which it *ought* to have, the precise degree of power in the regulating of our internal frame that is assigned it by Him who placed it there, is a point of the utmost consequence in itself, and on the determination of which the very hinge of our Author's Moral System turns. If the faculty here spoken of be, indeed, what it is asserted to be, in nature and kind *superior* to every other passion and affection; if it be given, not merely that it may exert its force occasionally, or as our present humour or fancy may dispose us, but that it may at all times exercise an uncontrollable authority and government over all the rest; it will then follow, that, in order to complete the idea of human nature, as a system, we must not only take in each particular bias, propension, instinct, which are seen to belong to it, but we must add besides the principle of conscience, together with the subjection that is due to it from all the other appetites and passions: just as the idea of a civil constitution is formed, not barely from enumerating the several members and ranks of which it is composed, but from these considered as acting in various degrees of subordination to each other, and all under the direction of the same supreme authority, whether that authority be vested in one person or more.

The view here given of the internal constitution of man, and of the supremacy of conscience, agreeably to the conceptions of Bishop Butler, enables us to comprehend the force of that expression, common to him and the ancient moralists, that virtue consists in *following nature*. The meaning cannot be, that it consists in acting agreeably to that propensity of our nature which happens to be the strongest; or which propels us towards certain objects, without any regard to the methods by which they are to be obtained: but the meaning must be, that virtue consists in the due regulation and subjection of all the other appetites and affections to the superior faculty of conscience; from a conformity to which alone our actions are properly *natural*, or correspondent to the nature, to the whole nature, of such an agent as man. From hence too it appears, that the Author of our frame is by no means indifferent to virtue and vice, or has left us at liberty to act at random, as humour or appetite may prompt us; but that every man has the rule of right within him; a rule attended in the very notion of it with authority, and such as has the force of a direction and a command from Him who made us what we are, what course of behaviour is suited to our nature, and which he expects that we should follow. This moral faculty implies also a presentiment and apprehension, that the judgment which passes on our actions, considered as of good or ill-desert, will hereafter be confirmed by the unerring judgment of God; when virtue and happiness, vice and misery, whose ideas are now so closely connected, shall be indissolubly united, and the Divine government be found to correspond in the most exact proportion to the nature he has given us. Lastly, this just prerogative or supremacy of conscience it is, which Mr. Pope has described in his Universal Prayer, though perhaps he may have expressed it rather *too* strongly, where he says,

> "What conscience dictates to be done,
> Or warns me not to do,
> This teach me *more than* hell to shun,
> That *more than* heaven pursue."

The reader will observe, that this way of treating the subject of morals, by an appeal to *facts*, does not at all interfere with that other way, adopted by Dr. Samuel Clarke and others, which begins with inquiring into the *relations* and *fitnesses of things*, but rather illustrates and confirms it. That there are essential differences in the qualities of human actions, established by nature, and that this *natural* difference of things, prior to and independent of all *will*, creates a natural *fitness* in the agent to act agreeably to it, seems as little to be denied, as that there is the *moral* difference before explained, from which we approve and feel a pleasure in what is right, and conceive a distaste to what is wrong. Still, however, when we are endeavouring to establish either this moral or that natural difference, it ought never to be forgotten, or rather it will require to be distinctly shewn, that both of these, when traced up to their source, suppose an intelligent Author of nature and moral Ruler of the world; who originally appointed these differences, and by such an appointment has signified his *will* that we should conform to them, as the only effectual method of securing our *happiness* on the whole under his government[x]. And of this consideration our Prelate himself was not unmindful; as may be collected from many expressions in different parts of his writings, and particularly from the following passages in his eleventh Sermon. "It may be allowed, without any prejudice to the cause of virtue and religion, that our ideas of happiness and misery are of all our ideas the nearest and most important to us; that they will, nay, if you please, that they ought to prevail over those of order, and beauty, and harmony, and proportion, if there should ever be, as it is impossible there ever should be, any inconsistence between them." And again, "Though virtue or moral rectitude does indeed consist in affection to and pursuit of what is right and good, as such; yet, when we sit down in a cool hour, we can neither justify to ourselves this or any other pursuit, till we are convinced that it will be for our happiness, or at least not contrary to it[y]."

Besides the general system of morality opened above, our Author in his volume of Sermons has stated with accuracy the difference between self-love and benevolence; in opposition to those who, on the one hand, make the whole of virtue to consist in benevolence[z], and to those who, on the other, assert that every particular affection and action is resolvable into self-love. In combating these opinions, he has shewn, I think unanswerably, that there are the same kind of indications in human nature, that we were made to promote the happiness of others, as that we were made to promote our own: that it is no just objection to this, that we have dispositions to do *evil* to *others* as well as good; for we have also dispositions to do *evil* as well as good to *ourselves*, to our own most important interests even in this life, for the sake of gratifying a present passion: that the thing to be lamented is, not that men have too great a regard to their own real good, but that they have not enough: that benevolence is not more at variance with or unfriendly to self-love, than any other particular affection is: and that by consulting

---

[x] See Note E, at the end of this preface.   [y] Serm. xi.

[z] See the second dissertation "On the Nature of Virtue," at the end of the Analogy.

the happiness of others a man is so far from *lessening* his own, that the very endeavour to do so, though he should fail in the accomplishment, is a source of the highest satisfaction and peace of mind[a]. He has also, in passing, animadverted on the philosopher of Malmesbury, who in his book "Of Human Nature" has advanced, as discoveries in moral science, that benevolence is only the love of power, and compassion the fear of future calamity to ourselves. And this our Author has done, not so much with the design of exposing the false reasoning of Mr. Hobbes, but because on so perverse an account of human nature he has raised a system, subversive of all justice and honesty[b].

II. The religious system of Bishop Butler is chiefly to be collected from the treatise, entitled, "The Analogy of Religion, Natural and Revealed, to the Constitution and Course of Nature."

"All things are double one against another, and God hath made nothing imperfect[c]." On this single observation of the Son of Sirach, the whole fabric of our Prelate's defence of religion, in his Analogy, is raised. Instead of indulging to idle speculations, how the world might possibly have been better than it is; or, forgetful of the difference between hypothesis and fact, attempting to explain the Divine economy with respect to intelligent creatures, from preconceived notions of his own; he first inquires what the constitution of nature, as made known to us in the way of experiment, actually is; and from this, now seen and acknowledged, he endeavours to form a judgment of that larger constitution, which religion discovers to us. If the dispensation of Providence we are now under, considered as inhabitants of this world, and having a temporal interest to secure in it, be found, on examination, to be analogous to, and of a piece with, that further dispensation, which relates to us as designed for another world, in which we have an eternal interest, depending on our behaviour here; if both may be traced up to the same general laws, and appear to be carried on according to the same plan of administration; the fair presumption is, that both proceed from one

[a] See Serm. i. and xi. and the preface to the volume of Sermons.
[b] See the notes to Serm. i. and v.   [c] Ecclus. xlii. 24.

and the same Author. And if the principal parts objected to in this latter dispensation be similar to and of the same kind with what we certainly experience under the former; the objections, being clearly inconclusive in one case, because contradicted by plain fact, must, in all reason, be allowed to be inconclusive also in the other.

This way of arguing from what is acknowledged to what is disputed, from things known to other things that resemble them, from that part of the Divine establishment which is exposed to our view to that more important one which lies beyond it, is on all hands confessed to be just. By this method Sir Isaac Newton has unfolded the system of nature; by the same method Bishop Butler has explained the system of grace; and thus, to use the words of a writer, whom I quote with pleasure, " has formed and concluded a happy alliance between faith and philosophy[d]."

And although the argument from analogy be allowed to be imperfect, and by no means sufficient to solve all difficulties respecting the government of God, and the designs of his providence with regard to mankind; (a degree of knowledge, which we are not furnished with faculties for attaining, at least in the present state;) yet surely it is of importance to learn from it, that the natural and moral world are intimately connected, and parts of one stupendous whole or system; and that the chief objections which are brought against religion may be urged with equal force against the constitution and course of nature, where they are certainly false in fact. And this information we may derive from the work before us; the proper design of which, it may be of use to observe, is not to prove the truth of religion, either natural or revealed, but to confirm that proof, already known, by considerations from analogy.

After this account of the method of reasoning employed by our Author, let us now advert to his manner of applying it, first to the subject of Natural Religion, and secondly to that of Revealed.

1. The foundation of all our hopes and fears is a future life; and with this the treatise begins. Neither the reason

---

[d] Mr. Mainwaring's Dissertation, prefixed to his volume of Sermons.

of the thing, nor the analogy of nature, according to Bishop Butler, give ground for imagining, that the unknown event, death, will be our destruction. The states in which we have formerly existed, in the womb and in infancy, are not more different from each other than from that of mature age in which we now exist: therefore, that we shall continue to exist hereafter, in a state as different from the present as the present is from those through which we have passed already, is a presumption favoured by the analogy of nature. All that we know from reason concerning death, is the effects it has upon animal bodies: and the frequent instances among men of the intellectual powers continuing in high health and vigour, at the very time when a mortal disease is on the point of putting an end to all the powers of sensation, induce us to hope that it may have no effect at all on the human soul, not even so much as to suspend the exercise of its faculties; though, if it have, the suspension of a power by no means implies its extinction, as sleep or a swoon may convince us[e].

The probability of a future state once granted, an important question arises, How best to secure our interest in that state. We find from what passes daily before us, that the constitution of nature admits of misery as well as happiness; that both of these are the consequences of our own actions; and these consequences we are enabled to foresee. Therefore, that our happiness or misery in a future world may depend on our own actions also, and that rewards or punishments hereafter may follow our good or ill behaviour here, is but an appointment of the same sort with what we experience under the Divine government, according to the regular course of nature[f].

This supposition is confirmed from another circumstance, that the natural government of God, under which we now live, is also moral; in which rewards and punishments are the consequences of actions, considered as virtuous and vicious. Not that every man is rewarded or punished here in exact proportion to his desert; for the essential tendencies of virtue and vice, to produce happiness and the contrary, are often hindered from taking effect from accidental causes. However, there are plainly the rudiments and beginnings of a righteous

[e] Part I. chap. i.   [f] Chap. ii.

administration to be discerned in the constitution of nature: from whence we are led to expect, that these accidental hinderances will one day be removed, and the rule of distributive justice obtain completely in a more perfect state[g].

The moral government of God, thus established, implies in the notion of it some sort of trial, or a moral possibility of acting wrong as well as right, in those who are the subjects of it. And the doctrine of religion, that the present life is in fact a state of probation for a future one, is rendered credible, from its being analogous throughout to the general conduct of Providence towards us with respect to this world; in which prudence is necessary to secure our temporal interest, just as we are taught that virtue is necessary to secure our eternal interest; and both are trusted to ourselves[h].

But the present life is not merely a state of probation, implying in it difficulties and danger; it is also a state of discipline and improvement; and that both in our temporal and religious capacity. Thus childhood is a state of discipline for youth; youth for manhood; and that for old age. Strength of body, and maturity of understanding, are acquired by degrees; and neither of them without continual exercise and attention on our part, not only in the beginning of life, but through the whole course of it. So again with respect to our religious concerns, the present world is fitted to be, and to good men is in event, a state of discipline and improvement for a future one. The several passions and propensions implanted in our hearts incline us, in a multitude of instances, to forbidden pleasures: this inward infirmity is increased by various snares and temptations, perpetually occurring from without: hence arises the necessity of recollection and self-government, of withstanding the calls of appetite, and forming our minds to habits of piety and virtue; habits, of which we are capable, and which, to creatures in a state of moral imperfection, and fallen from their original integrity, must be of the greatest use, as an additional security, over and above the principle of conscience, from the dangers to which we are exposed [i].

Nor is the credibility here given, by the analogy of nature,

[g] Chap. iii.   [h] Chap. iv.   [i] Part I. chap. v.

to the general doctrine of religion, destroyed or weakened by any notions concerning necessity. Of itself it is a mere word, the sign of an abstract idea; and as much requires an agent, that is, a necessary agent, in order to effect any thing, as freedom requires a free agent. Admitting it to be speculatively true, if considered as influencing practice, it is the same as false: for it is matter of experience, that, with regard to our present interest, and as inhabitants of this world, we are treated as if we were free; and therefore the analogy of nature leads us to conclude, that, with regard to our future interest, and as designed for another world, we shall be treated as free also. Nor does the opinion of necessity, supposing it possible, at all affect either the general proof of religion, or its external evidence [k].

Still objections may be made against the wisdom and goodness of the Divine government, to which analogy, which can only shew the truth or credibility of facts, affords no answer. Yet even here analogy is of use, if it suggest that the Divine government is a scheme or system, and not a number of unconnected acts, and that this system is also above our comprehension. Now the government of the natural world appears to be a system of this kind; with parts, related to each other, and together composing a whole: in which system, ends are brought about by the use of means, many of which means, before experience, would have been suspected to have had a quite contrary tendency; which is carried on by general laws, similar causes uniformly producing similar effects: the utility of which general laws, and the inconveniences which would probably arise from the occasional or even secret suspension of them, we are in some sort enabled to discern [l]; but of the whole we are incompetent judges, because of the small part which comes within our view. Reasoning then from what we know, it is highly credible, that the government of the moral world is a system also, carried on by general laws, and in which ends are accomplished by the intervention of means; and that both constitutions, the natural and the moral, are so connected,

[k] Chap. vi. [l] See a Treatise on Divine Benevolence, by Dr. Thomas Balguy, part ii.

as to form together but one scheme. But of this scheme, as of that of the natural world taken alone, we are not qualified to judge, on account of the mutual respect of the several parts to each other and to the whole, and our own incapacity to survey the whole, or, with accuracy, any single part. All objections therefore to the wisdom and goodness of the Divine government may be founded merely on our ignorance[m]; and to such objections our ignorance is the proper, and a satisfactory answer[n].

2. The chief difficulties concerning Natural Religion being now removed, our Author proceeds, in the next place, to that which is Revealed; and as an introduction to an inquiry into the Credibility of Christianity, begins with the consideration of its Importance.

The Importance of Christianity appears in two respects. First, in its being a republication of Natural Religion, in its native simplicity, with authority, and with circumstances of advantage; ascertaining, in many instances of moment, what before was only probable, and particularly confirming the doctrine of a future state of rewards and punishments[o]. Secondly, as revealing a new dispensation of Providence, originating from the pure love and mercy of God, and conducted by the mediation of his Son, and the guidance of his Spirit, for the recovery and salvation of mankind, represented in a state of apostasy and ruin. This account of Christianity being admitted to be just, and the distinct offices of these three Divine persons being once discovered to us, we are as much obliged in point of duty to acknowledge the relations we stand in to the Son and Holy Ghost, as our Mediator and Sanctifier, as we are obliged in point of duty to acknowledge the relation we stand in to God the Father; although the two former of these relations be learnt from Revelation only, and in the last we are instructed by the light of nature; the obligation in either case arising from the offices themselves, and not at all depending on the manner in which they are made known to us[p].

The presumption against Revelation in general are, that

[m] See Note F, at the end of this preface.
[o] See Note G, at the end of this preface.
[n] Part I. chap. vii.
[p] Part II. chap. i.

it is not discoverable by reason, that it is unlike to what is so discovered, and that it was introduced and supported by miracles. But in a scheme so large as that of the universe, unbounded in extent and everlasting in duration, there must of necessity be numberless circumstances which are beyond the reach of our faculties to discern, and which can only be known by Divine illumination. And both in the natural and moral government of the world, under which we live, we find many things unlike one to another, and therefore ought not to wonder if the same unlikeness obtain between things visible and invisible; although it be far from true, that revealed religion is entirely unlike the constitution of nature, as analogy may teach us. Nor is there any thing incredible in Revelation, considered as miraculous; whether miracles be supposed to have been performed at the beginning of the world, or after a course of nature has been established. Not *at the beginning of the world;* for then there was either no course of nature at all, or a power must have been exerted totally different from what that course is at present: all men and animals cannot have been born, as they are now; but a pair of each sort must have been produced at first, in a way altogether unlike to that in which they have been since produced; unless we affirm, that men and animals have existed from eternity in an endless succession: one miracle therefore at least there must have been at the beginning of the world, or at the time of man's creation. Not *after the settlement of a course of nature*, on account of miracles being contrary to that course, or, in other words, contrary to experience; for, in order to know whether miracles, worked in attestation of a Divine religion, be contrary to experience or not, we ought to be acquainted with other cases, similar or parallel to those, in which miracles are alleged to have been wrought. But where shall we find such similar or parallel cases? The world which we inhabit affords none: we know of no extraordinary revelations from God to man, but those recorded in the Old and New Testament; all of which were established by miracles: it cannot therefore be said, that miracles are incredible, because contrary to experience, when all the experience we have is in favour of miracles, and on the side of religion ^q. Besides, in reasoning concerning miracles, they ought not to be compared with common natural events, but with uncommon appearances, such as comets, magnetism, electricity; which, to one acquainted only with the usual phenomena of nature, and the common powers of matter, must, before proof of their actual existence, be thought incredible^r.

The presumptions against Revelation in general being despatched, objections against the Christian Revelation in particular, against the scheme of it, as distinguished from objections against its evidence, are considered next. Now, supposing a revelation to be really given, it is highly probable beforehand, that it must contain many things appearing to us liable to objections. The acknowledged dispensation of nature is very different from what we should have expected: reasoning then from analogy, the revealed dispensation, it is credible, would be also different. Nor are we in any sort judges at what time, or in what degree, or manner, it is fit or expedient for God to instruct us, in things confessedly of the greatest use, either by natural reason, or by supernatural information. Thus, arguing on speculation only, and without experience, it would seem very unlikely that so important a remedy as that provided by Christianity, for the recovery of mankind from a state of ruin, should have been for so many ages withheld; and, when at last vouchsafed, should be imparted to so few; and, after it has been imparted, should be attended with obscurity and doubt. And just so we might have argued, before experience, concerning the remedies provided in nature for bodily diseases, to which by nature we are exposed: for many of these were unknown to mankind for a number of ages; are known but to few now; some important ones probably not discovered yet; and those which are, neither certain in their application, nor universal in their use: and the same mode of reasoning that would lead us to expect they should have been so, would lead us to expect that the necessity of them should have been superseded, by there being no diseases; as the necessity of the Christian scheme, it may be thought, might also have been

^q See Note H, at the end of this preface.   ^r Chap. ii.

superseded, by preventing the fall of man, so that he should not have stood in need of a Redeemer at all [s].

As to objections against the wisdom and goodness of Christianity, the same answer may be applied to them as was to the like objections against the constitution of nature. For here also, Christianity is a scheme or economy, composed of various parts, forming a whole; in which scheme means are used for the accomplishing of ends; and which is conducted by general laws, of all of which we know as little as we do of the constitution of nature. And the seeming want of wisdom or goodness in this system is to be ascribed to the same cause, as the like appearances of defects in the natural system; our inability to discern the whole scheme, and our ignorance of the relation of those parts which are discernible to others beyond our view.

The objections against Christianity as a matter of fact, and against the wisdom and goodness of it, having been obviated together, the chief of them are now to be considered distinctly. One of these, which is levelled against the entire system itself, is of this sort: the restoration of mankind, represented in Scripture as the great design of the Gospel, is described as requiring a long series of means and persons and dispensations, before it can be brought to its completion; whereas the whole ought to have been effected at once. Now every thing we see in the course of nature shews the folly of this objection. For in the natural course of Providence, ends are brought about by means, not operating immediately and at once, but deliberately and in a way of progression; one thing being subservient to another, this to somewhat further. The change of seasons, the ripening of fruits, the growth of vegetable and animal bodies, are instances of this. And therefore, that the same progressive method should be followed in the dispensation of Christianity, as is observed in the common dispensation of Providence, is a reasonable expectation, justified by the analogy of nature [t].

Another circumstance objected to in the Christian scheme is the appointment of a Mediator, and the saving of the world through him. But the visible government of God

[s] Chap. iii.   [t] Chap. iv.

being actually administered in this way, or by the mediation and instrumentality of others, there can be no general presumption against an appointment of this kind, against his invisible government being exercised in the same manner. We have seen already, that with regard to ourselves this visible government is carried on by rewards and punishments; for happiness and misery are the consequences of our own actions, considered as virtuous and vicious; and these consequences we are enabled to foresee. It might have been imagined, before consulting experience, that after we had rendered ourselves liable to misery by our own ill conduct, sorrow for what was past, and behaving well for the future, would, alone and of themselves, have exempted us from deserved punishment, and restored us to the Divine favour. But the fact is otherwise; and real reformation is often found to be of no avail, so as to secure the criminal from poverty, sickness, infamy, and death, the never-failing attendants on vice and extravagance, exceeding a certain degree. By the course of nature then it appears, God does not always pardon a sinner on his repentance. Yet there is provision made, even in nature, that the miseries, which men bring on themselves by unlawful indulgences, may in many cases be mitigated, and in some removed; partly by extraordinary exertions of the offender himself, but more especially and frequently by the intervention of others, who voluntarily, and from motives of compassion, submit to labour and sorrow, such as produce long and lasting inconveniences to themselves, as the means of rescuing another from the wretched effects of former imprudences. Vicarious punishment, therefore, or one person's sufferings contributing to the relief of another, is a providential disposition in the economy of nature[a]: and it ought not to be matter of surprise, if by a method analogous to this we be redeemed from sin and misery, in the economy of grace. That mankind at present are in a state of degradation, different from that in which they were originally created, is the very ground of the Christian revelation, as contained in the Scriptures. Whether we acquiesce in the account, that our being placed in such a

[a] See Note I, at the end of this preface.

state is owing to the crime of our first parents, or choose to ascribe it to any other cause, it makes no difference as to our condition: the vice and unhappiness of the world are still there, notwithstanding all our suppositions; nor is it Christianity that hath put us into this state. We learn also from the same Scriptures, what experience and the use of expiatory sacrifices from the most early times might have taught us, that repentance alone is not sufficient to prevent the fatal consequences of past transgressions: but that still there is room for mercy, and that repentance shall be available, though not of itself, yet through the mediation of a Divine person, the Messiah; who, from the sublimest principles of compassion, when we were *dead in trespasses and sins*[x], suffered and died, the innocent for the guilty, *the just for the unjust*[y], that *we might have redemption through his blood, even the forgiveness of sins*[z]. In what way the death of Christ was of that efficacy it is said to be, in procuring the reconciliation of sinners, the Scriptures have not explained: it is enough that the doctrine is revealed; that it is not contrary to any truths which reason and experience teach us; and that it accords in perfect harmony with the usual method of the Divine conduct in the government of the world[a].

Again it hath been said, that if the Christian revelation were true, it must have been universal, and could not have been left upon doubtful evidence. But God, in his natural providence, dispenses his gifts in great variety, not only among creatures of the same species, but to the same individuals also at different times. Had the Christian revelation been universal at first, yet, from the diversity of men's abilities, both of mind and body, their various means of improvement, and other external advantages, some persons must soon have been in a situation, with respect to religious knowledge, much superior to that of others, as much perhaps as they are at present: and all men will be equitably dealt with at last; and to whom little is given, of him little will be required. Then as to the evidence for religion being left doubtful, difficulties of this sort, like difficulties in practice, afford scope and opportunity for a virtuous exercise of the

[x] Ephes. ii. 1. [y] 1 Pet. iii. 18. [z] Coloss. i. 14. [a] Chap. v.

understanding, and dispose the mind to acquiesce and rest satisfied with any evidence that is real. In the daily commerce of life, men are obliged to act upon great uncertainties, with regard to success in their temporal pursuits; and the case with regard to religion is parallel. However, though religion be not intuitively true, the proofs of it which we have are amply sufficient in reason to induce us to embrace it; and dissatisfaction with those proofs may possibly be men's own fault[b].

Nothing remains but to attend to the positive evidence there is for the truth of Christianity. Now, besides its direct and fundamental proofs, which are miracles and prophecies, there are many collateral circumstances, which may be united into one view, and all together may be considered as making up one argument. In this way of treating the subject, the revelation, whether real or otherwise, may be supposed to be wholly historical: the general design of which appears to be, to give an account of the condition of religion, and its professors, with a concise narration of the political state of things, as far as religion is affected by it, during a great length of time, near six thousand years of which are already past. More particularly it comprehends an account of God's entering into covenant with one nation, the Jews, that he would be their God, and that they should be his people; of his often interposing in their affairs; giving them the promise, and afterwards the possession, of a flourishing country; assuring them of the greatest national prosperity, in case of their obedience, and threatening the severest national punishment, in case they forsook him, and joined in the idolatry of their Pagan neighbours. It contains also a prediction of a particular person to appear in the fulness of time, in whom all the promises of God to the Jews were to be fulfilled: and it relates, that, at the time expected, a person did actually appear, assuming to be the Saviour foretold; that he worked various miracles among them, in confirmation of his Divine authority; and, as was foretold also, was rejected and put to death by the very people who had long desired and waited for his coming; but that his religion, in spite of all opposition,

[b] Chap. vi.

was established in the world by his disciples, invested with supernatural powers for that purpose; of the fate and fortunes of which religion there is a prophetical description, carried down to the end of time. Let any one now, after reading the above history, and not knowing whether the whole were not a fiction, be supposed to ask, Whether all that is here related be true? and instead of a direct answer, let him be informed of the several acknowledged facts, which are found to correspond to it in real life; and then let him compare the history and facts together, and observe the astonishing coincidence of both: such a joint review must appear to him of very great weight, and to amount to evidence somewhat more than human. And unless the whole series, and every particular circumstance contained in it, can be thought to have arisen from accident, the truth of Christianity is proved[c].

The view here given of the moral and religious systems of Bishop Butler, it will immediately be perceived, is chiefly intended for younger students, especially for students in Divinity; to whom it is hoped it may be of use, so as to encourage them to peruse, with proper diligence, the original works of the Author himself. For it may be necessary to observe, that neither of the volumes of this excellent Prelate are addressed to those who read for amusement, or curiosity, or to get rid of time. All subjects are not to be comprehended with the same ease; and morality and religion, when

---

[c] Chap. vii. To the Analogy are subjoined two Dissertations, both originally inserted in the body of the work. One on *Personal Identity*, in which are contained some strictures on Mr. Locke, who asserts that consciousness makes or constitutes personal identity; whereas, as our Author observes, consciousness makes only personality, or is necessary to the idea of a person, i.e. a thinking intelligent being, but presupposes, and therefore cannot constitute, personal identity; just as knowledge presupposes truth, but does not constitute it. Consciousness of past actions does indeed shew us the identity of ourselves, or gives us a certain assurance that we are the same persons or living agents now, which we were at the time to which our remembrance can look back : but still we should be the same persons as we were, though this consciousness of what is past were wanting, though all that had been done by us formerly were forgotten; unless it be true, that no person has existed a single moment beyond what he can remember. The other Dissertation is *On the Nature of Virtue*, which properly belongs to the moral system of our Author, already explained.

treated as sciences, each accompanied with difficulties of its own, can neither of them be understood as they ought, without a very peculiar attention. But morality and religion are not merely to be studied as sciences, or as being speculatively true; they are to be regarded in another and higher light, as the rule of life and manners, as containing authoritative directions by which to regulate our faith and practice. And in this view, the infinite importance of them considered, it can never be an indifferent matter whether they be received or rejected. For both claim to be the voice of God; and whether they be so or not, cannot be known, till their claims be impartially examined. If they indeed come from Him, we are bound to conform to them at our peril: nor is it left to our choice, whether we will submit to the obligations they impose upon us or not; for submit to them we must, in such a sense, as to incur the punishments denounced by both against wilful disobedience to their injunctions.

NOTES

TO THE

PREFACE BY THE EDITOR.

Page ix. A.

Dr. BUTLER, when Bishop of Bristol, put up a cross, a plain piece of marble inlaid, in the chapel of his episcopal house. This, which was intended by the blameless Prelate merely as a sign or memorial, that true Christians are to bear their cross, and not to be ashamed of following a crucified Master, was considered as affording a presumption that he was secretly inclined to Popish forms and ceremonies, and had no great dislike to Popery itself. And, on account of the offence it occasioned, both at the time and since, it were to be wished, in prudence, it had not been done.

Page xii. B.

Many of the sentiments, in these Two Discourses of Bishop Butler, concerning the sovereign good of man; the impossibility of procuring it in the present life; the unsatisfactoriness of earthly enjoyments; together with the somewhat beyond and above them all, which once attained, there will rest nothing further to be wished or hoped; and which is then only to be expected, when we shall have put off this mortal body, and our union with God shall be complete; occur in *Hooker's Ecclesiastical Polity*, book I. §. 11.

Page xv. C.

When the first edition of this Preface was published, I had in vain endeavoured to procure a sight of the papers, in which Bishop Butler was accused of having died a Papist, and Archbishop Secker's replies to them; though I well remembered to have read both, when they first appeared in the public prints. But a learned Professor in the University of Oxford has furnished me with the whole controversy in its original form; a brief history of which it may not be unacceptable to offer here to the curious reader.

The attack was opened in the year 1767, in an anonymous pamphlet, entitled, "The Root of Protestant Errors examined;" in which the author asserted, that, "by an anecdote lately given him, "that same Prelate" (who at the bottom of the page is called B—p of D—m) "is said to have died in the communion of a Church, that "makes much use of saints, saints' days, and all the trumpery of "saint worship." When this remarkable fact, now first divulged, came to be generally known, it occasioned, as might be expected, no little alarm; and intelligence of it was no sooner conveyed to Archbishop Secker, than in a short letter, signed *Misopseudes*, and printed in the St. James's Chronicle of May 9, he called upon the writer to produce his authority for publishing "so gross and scan- "dalous a falsehood." To this challenge an immediate answer was returned by the author of the pamphlet, who, now assuming the name of *Phileleutheros*, informed *Misopseudes*, through the channel of the same paper, that "such anecdote had been given him; and "that he was yet of opinion that there was nothing improbable in "it, when it is considered that the same Prelate put up the Popish "*insignia* of the *cross* in his chapel, when at Bristol; and in his "last Episcopal Charge has squinted very much towards that super- "stition." Here we find the accusation not only repeated, but supported by reasons, such as they are, of which it seemed necessary that some notice should be taken: nor did the Archbishop conceive it unbecoming his own dignity to stand up on this occasion, as the vindicator of innocence against the calumniator of the helpless dead. Accordingly, in a second letter in the same newspaper of May 23, and subscribed *Misopseudes* as before; after reciting from Bishop Butler's Sermon before the Lords the very passage here printed in the Preface, and observing, that, "there are, in the same Sermon, "declarations as strong as can be made against temporal punishments "for. heresy, schism, or even for idolatry;" his Grace expresses himself thus: "Now he" (Bishop Butler) "was universally esteemed, "throughout his life, a man of strict piety and honesty, as well as "uncommon abilities. He gave all the proofs, public and private, "which his station led him to give, and they were decisive and daily, "of his continuing to the last a sincere member of the Church of "England. Nor had ever any of his acquaintance, or most intimate "friends, nor have they to this day, the least doubt of it." As to putting up a *cross* in his chapel, the Archbishop frankly owns, that for himself he wishes he had not; and thinks that in so doing the Bishop did amiss. But then he asks, "Can that be opposed, as any "proof of Popery, to all the evidence on the other side; or even to "the single evidence of the above mentioned Sermon? Most of "our churches have crosses upon them: are they therefore Popish "churches? The Lutherans have more than crosses in theirs; are "the Lutherans therefore Papists?" And as to the Charge, no Papist, his Grace remarks, would have spoken as Bishop Butler there does, of the observances peculiar to Roman Catholics, some of which he expressly censures as wrong and superstitious, and others, as made subservient to the purposes of superstition, and, on these accounts, abolished at the Reformation. After the publication of this letter, *Phileleutheros* replied in a short defence of his own conduct, but without producing any thing new in confirmation of what he had advanced. And here the controversy, so far as the two principals were concerned, seems to have ended.

But the dispute was not suffered to die away quite so soon. For in the same year, and in the same newspaper of July 21, another letter appeared; in which the author not only contended that the cross in the Episcopal chapel at Bristol, and the Charge to the Clergy of Durham in 1751, amount to full proof of a strong attachment to the idolatrous communion of the Church of Rome, but, with the reader's leave, he would fain account for the Bishop's "ten-"dency this way." And this he attempted to do, " from the natural "melancholy and gloominess of Dr. Butler's disposition; from his " great fondness for the lives of Romish saints, and their books of " mystic piety; from his drawing his notions of teaching men reli-"gion, not from the New Testament, but from philosophical and "political opinions of his own; and above all, from his transition "from a strict Dissenter amongst the Presbyterians to a rigid "Churchman, and his sudden and unexpected elevation to great "wealth and dignity in the Church." The attack, thus renewed, excited the Archbishop's attention a second time, and drew from him a fresh answer, subscribed also *Misopseudes*, in the St. James's Chronicle of August 4. In this letter, our excellent Metropolitan, first of all obliquely hinting at the unfairness of sitting in judgment on the character of a man who had been dead fifteen years; and then reminding his correspondent, that " full proof had been already "published, that Bishop Butler abhorred Popery as a vile corruption "of Christianity, and that it might be proved, if needful, that he "held the Pope to be Antichrist;" (to which decisive testimonies of undoubted aversion from the Romish Church, another is also added in the Postscript, his taking, when promoted to the see of Durham, for his domestic Chaplain, Dr. Nath. Forster, who had published, not four years before, a Sermon, entitled, Popery destructive of the

Evidence of Christianity;) proceeds to observe, "that the natural "melancholy of the Bishop's temper would rather have fixed him "amongst his first friends, than prompted him to the change he "made: that he read books of all sorts, as well as books of mystic "piety, and knew how to pick the good that was in them out of "the bad: that his opinions were exposed without reserve in his "Analogy and his Sermons, and if the doctrine of either be Popish "or unscriptural, the learned world hath mistaken strangely in ad-"miring both: that, instead of being a strict Dissenter, he never "was a communicant in any Dissenting assembly; on the contrary, "that he went occasionally, from his early years, to the established "worship, and became a constant conformist to it when he was "barely of age, and entered himself, in 1714, of Oriel College: "that his elevation to great dignity in the Church, far from being "sudden and unexpected, was a gradual and natural rise, through a "variety of preferments, and a period of thirty-two years: that, as "Bishop of Durham, he had very little authority beyond his bre-"thren, and, in ecclesiastical matters, had none beyond them; a "larger income than most of them he had; but this he employed, "not, as was insinuated, in augmenting the pomp of worship in his "cathedral, where indeed it is no greater than in others, but for the "purposes of charity, and in the repairing of his houses." After these remarks, the letter closes with the following words: "Upon "the whole, few accusations, so entirely groundless, have been so "pertinaciously, I am unwilling to say maliciously, carried on, as the "present: and surely it is high time for the authors and abettors of "it, in mere common prudence, to shew some regard, if not to truth, "at least to shame."

It only remains to be mentioned, that the above letters of Arch-bishop Secker had such an effect on a writer, who signed himself in the St. James's Chronicle of August 25, *A Dissenting Minister*, that he declared it as his opinion, that "the author of the pamphlet, "called, 'The Root of Protestant Errors examined,' and his friends, "were obliged in candour, in justice, and in honour, to retract their "charge, unless they could establish it on much better grounds than "had hitherto appeared:" and he expressed "his hopes that it would "be understood that the Dissenters in general had no hand in the "accusation, and that it had only been the act of two or three "mistaken men." Another person also, "a foreigner by birth," as he says of himself, who had been long an admirer of Bishop Butler, and had perused with great attention all that had been written on both sides in the present controversy, confesses he had been "won-

"derfully pleased with observing, with what candour and temper,
"as well as clearness and solidity, he was vindicated from the
"aspersions laid against him." All the adversaries of our Prelate,
however, had not the virtue or sense to be thus convinced; some of
whom still continued, under the signatures of *Old Martin*, *Latimer*,
An Impartial Protestant, *Paulinus*, *Misonothos*, to repeat their confuted falsehoods in the public prints; as if the curse of calumniators
had fallen upon them, and their memory, by being long a traitor
to truth, had taken at last a severe revenge, and compelled them
to credit their own lie. The first of these gentlemen, *Old Martin*,
who dates from Newcastle, May 29, from the rancour and malignity
with which his letter abounds, and from the particular virulence he
discovers towards the characters of Bishop Butler and his defender,
I conjecture to be no other than the very person who had already
figured in this dispute, so early as the year 1752; of whose work,
entitled, "A Serious Inquiry into the Use and Importance of
"External Religion," the reader will find some account in the notes
subjoined to the Bishop's Charge.

Page xvi. D.

The letters, with a sight of which I was indulged by the favour
of our present most worthy Metropolitan, are all, as I remember,
wrapped together under one cover; on the back of which is written,
in Archbishop Secker's own hand, the following words, or words to
this effect: "Presumptive Arguments that Bishop Butler did not
"die a Papist."

Page xxi. E.

"Far be it from me," says the excellent Dr. T. Balguy[a], "to
"dispute the reality of a *moral* principle in the human heart. I
"*feel* its existence; I clearly discern its use and importance. But
"in no respect is it *more* important, than as it suggests the idea of
"a *moral Governor*. Let this idea be once effaced, and the prin-
"ciple of conscience will soon be found weak and ineffectual. Its
"influence on men's conduct has, indeed, been *too much* under-
"valued by some philosophical inquirers. But be that influence,
"while it lasts, more or less, it is not a *steady* and *permanent* prin-
"ciple of action. Unhappily we always have it in our power to lay
"it *asleep*.—*Neglect* alone will suppress and stifle it, and bring it
"almost into a state of stupefaction. Nor can any thing, less than
"the *terrors* of religion, awaken our minds from this dangerous
"and deadly sleep. It can never be a matter of indifference to a

[a] Discourse IX.

"*thinking* man, whether he is to be happy or miserable beyond the "grave."

Page xxvii. F.

The ignorance of man is a favourite doctrine with Bishop Butler. It occurs in the Second Part of the Analogy; it makes the subject of his Fifteenth Sermon; and we meet with it again in his Charge. Whether sometimes it be not carried to a length which is excessive, may admit of doubt.

Page xxvii. G.

Admirable to this purpose are the words of Dr. T. Balguy, in the Ninth of his Discourses, already referred to, p. xli. "The "doctrine of a *life to come*, some persons will say, is a doctrine of "*natural* religion; and can never therefore be properly alleged to "shew the importance of revelation. They judge perhaps from the "frame of the world, that the present system is *imperfect;* they "see designs in it, not yet *completed;* and they think they have "grounds for expecting *another* state, in which these designs shall "be *farther* carried on, and brought to a conclusion, worthy of "infinite wisdom. I am not concerned to dispute the *justness of* "this reasoning; nor do I wish to dispute it. But how far will it "reach? Will it lead us to the *Christian* doctrine of a judgment to "come? Will it give us the prospect of an *eternity* of happiness? "Nothing of all this. It shews us only, that *death* is not the end "of our being; that we are likely to pass hereafter into other "systems, more favourable than the present to the great ends of "God's providence, the *virtue* and the *happiness* of his intelligent "creatures. But into *what* systems we are to be removed; what "new scenes are to be presented to us, either of pleasure or pain; "what new parts we shall have to act, and to what trials and "temptations we may yet be exposed; on all these subjects we "know just nothing. That our happiness *for ever* depends on our "conduct *here*, is a most important proposition, which we learn *only* "from *revelation.*"

Page xxix. H.

"In the common affairs of life, common *experience* is sufficient "to direct us. But will common experience serve to guide our "judgment concerning the *fall* and *redemption* of mankind? From "what we see every day, can we explain the *commencement*, or "foretell the *dissolution* of the world? To judge of events like "these, we should be conversant in the history of other planets; "should be distinctly informed of God's various dispensations to all "the different orders of rational beings. Instead then of grounding

"our religious opinions on what *we* call *experience*, let us apply
"to a more certain guide, let us hearken to the *testimony* of God
"himself. The credibility of *human testimony*, and the conduct of
"*human agents*, are subjects perfectly within the reach of our natu-
"ral faculties; and we ought to desire no firmer foundation for
"our belief of religion, than for the judgments we form in the
"common affairs of life: where we see a little plain testimony
"easily outweighs the most specious conjectures, and not seldom
"even strong probabilities." Dr. Balguy's Fourth Charge. See
also an excellent pamphlet, entitled, "Remarks on Mr. Hume's
"Essay on the Natural History of Religion," §. 5; and the Sixth
of Dr. Powell's Discourses.

Page xxxi. I.

Dr. Arthur Ashley Sykes, from whose writings some good may
be collected out of a multitude of things of a contrary tendency, in
what he is pleased to call "The Scripture Doctrine of Redemption[b],"
opposes what is here advanced by Bishop Butler; quoting his words,
but without mentioning his name. If what is said above be not
thought a sufficient answer to the objections of this author, the
reader may do well to consult a Charge "On the Use and Abuse
"of Philosophy in the Study of Religion," by the late Dr. Powell:
who seems to me to have had the observations of Dr. Sykes in his
view, where he is confuting the reasonings of certain philosophizing
Divines against the doctrine of the Atonement. Powell's Discourses,
Charge III. p. 342—348.

[b] See the observations on the texts cited in his first chapter, and also in chapters the fifth and sixth.

The following Epitaph, said to be written by Dr. Nathanael Forster, is inscribed on a flat marble stone, in the cathedral church of Bristol, placed over the spot where the remains of Bishop Butler are deposited; and which, as it is now almost obliterated, it may be worth while here to preserve.

H. S.

Reverendus admodum in Christo Pater

JOSEPHUS BUTLER, LL.D.

Hujusce primo Diœceseos

Deinde Dunelmensis Episcopus.

Qualis quantusque Vir erat

Sua libentissime agnovit ætas:

Et si quid Præsuli aut Scriptori ad famam valent

Mens altissima,

Ingenii perspicacis et subacti Vis,

Animusque pius, simplex, candidus, liberalis,

Mortui haud facile evanescet memoria.

Obiit Bathoniæ 16 Kalend. Julii,

A.D. 1752.

Annos natus 60.

THE LIFE OF DR. BUTLER.

DR. JOSEPH BUTLER, a Prelate of the most distinguished character and abilities, was born at Wantage, in Berkshire, in the year 1692. His father, Mr. Thomas Butler, who was a substantial and reputable shopkeeper in that town, observing in his son Joseph[a] an excellent genius and inclination for learning, determined to educate him for the ministry, among the Protestant Dissenters of the Presbyterian denomination. For this purpose, after he had gone through a proper course of grammatical literature, at the free grammar school of his native place, under the care of the Rev. Mr. Philip Barton, a clergyman of the Church of England, he was sent to a Dissenting academy, then kept at Gloucester, but which was soon afterwards removed to Tewkesbury. The principal tutor of this academy was Mr. Jones, a man of uncommon abilities and knowledge, who had the honour of training up several scholars, who became of great eminence, both in the Established Church and among the Dissenters. At Tewkesbury Mr. Butler made an extraordinary progress in the study of Divinity; of which he gave a remarkable proof, in the letters addressed by him, while he resided at Tewkesbury, to Dr. Samuel Clarke, laying before him the doubts that had arisen in his mind, concerning the conclusiveness of some arguments in the Doctor's demonstration of the being and attributes of God. The first of these letters was dated the 4th of November, 1713; and the sagacity and depth of thought displayed in it immediately excited Dr. Clarke's particular notice. This condescension encouraged Mr. Butler to address the Doctor again upon the same subject, which

[a] He was the youngest of eight children.

likewise was answered by him; and the correspondence being carried on in three other letters, the whole was annexed to the celebrated treatise before mentioned, and the collection has been retained in all the subsequent editions of that work. The management of this correspondence was entrusted by Mr. Butler to his friend and fellow-pupil, Mr. Secker, who, in order to conceal the affair, undertook to convey the letters to the post-office at Gloucester, and to bring back Dr. Clarke's answers. When Mr. Butler's name was discovered to the Doctor, the candour, modesty, and good sense, with which he had written, immediately procured him the friendship of that eminent and excellent man. Our young student was not, however, during his continuance at Tewkesbury, solely employed in metaphysical speculations and inquiries. Another subject of his serious consideration was, the propriety of his becoming a Dissenting minister. Accordingly, he entered into an examination of the principles of non-conformity; the result of which was, such a dissatisfaction with them, as determined him to conform to the Established Church. This intention was, at first, disagreeable to his father, who endeavoured to divert him from his purpose; and, with that view, called in the assistance of some eminent Presbyterian Divines; but finding his son's resolution to be fixed, he at length suffered him to be removed to Oxford, where he was admitted a commoner of Oriel College, on the 17th of March, 1714. At what time he took Orders doth not appear, nor who the Bishop was by whom he was ordained; but it is certain that he entered into the Church soon after his admission at Oxford, if it be true, as is asserted, that he sometimes assisted Mr. Edward Talbot in the divine service, at his living of Hendred, near Wantage. With this gentleman, who was the second son of Dr. William Talbot, successively Bishop of Oxford, Salisbury, and Durham, Mr. Butler formed an intimate friendship at Oriel College; which friendship laid the foundation of all his subsequent preferments, and procured for him a very honourable situation when he was only twenty-six years of age. For it was in 1718 that, at the recommendation of Mr. Talbot, in conjunction with that of Dr. Clarke, he was appointed by Sir Joseph Jekyll to be preacher at the

Rolls. This was three years before he had taken any degree at the University, where he did not go out Bachelor of Law till the 10th of June 1721, which, however, was as soon as that degree could suitably be conferred upon him. Mr. Butler continued at the Rolls till 1726; in the beginning of which year he published, in one volume octavo, "Fifteen Sermons "preached at that Chapel." In the meanwhile, by the patronage of Dr. Talbot, Bishop of Durham, to whose notice he had been recommended (together with Mr. Benson and Mr. Secker) by Mr. Edward Talbot, on his death-bed, our Author had been presented first to the rectory of Haughton, near Darlington, and afterwards to that of Stanhope, in the same diocese. The benefice of Haughton was given to him in 1722, and that of Stanhope in 1725. At Haughton there was a necessity for rebuilding a great part of the parsonage-house, and Mr. Butler had neither money nor talents for that work. Mr. Secker, therefore, who had always the interest of his friends at heart, and acquired a very considerable influence with Bishop Talbot, persuaded that Prelate to give Mr. Butler, in exchange for Haughton, the rectory of Stanhope, which was not only free from any such incumbrance, but was likewise of much superior value, being indeed one of the richest parsonages in England. Whilst our Author continued preacher at the Rolls Chapel, he divided his time between his duty in town and country; but when he quitted the Rolls, he resided, during seven years, wholly at Stanhope, in the conscientious discharge of every obligation appertaining to a good parish priest. This retirement, however, was too solitary for his disposition, which had in it a natural cast of gloominess. And though his recluse hours were by no means lost, either to private improvement or public utility, yet he felt at times, very painfully, the want of that select society of friends to which he had been accustomed, and which could inspire him with the greatest cheerfulness. Mr. Secker, therefore, who knew this, was extremely anxious to draw him out into a more active and conspicuous scene, and omitted no opportunity of expressing this desire to such as he thought capable of promoting it. Having himself been appointed King's Chaplain in 1732, he took occasion, in a conversation which he had the honour of holding with Queen

Caroline, to mention to her his friend Mr. Butler. The Queen said she thought he had been dead. Mr. Secker assured her he was not. Yet her Majesty afterwards asked Archbishop Blackburn if he was not dead; his answer was, "No, Madam; "but he is buried." Mr. Secker continuing his purpose of endeavouring to bring his friend out of his retirement, found means, upon Mr. Charles Talbot's being made Lord Chancellor, to have Mr. Butler recommended to him for his Chaplain. His Lordship accepted, and sent for him; and this promotion calling him to Town, he took Oxford in his way, and was admitted there to the degree of Doctor of Law, on the 8th of December, 1733. The Lord Chancellor, who gave him also a prebend in the Church of Rochester, had consented that he should reside at his parish of Stanhope one half of the year.

Dr. Butler being thus brought back into the world, his merits and his talents soon introduced him to particular notice, and paved the way for his rising to those high dignities which he afterwards enjoyed. In 1736 he was appointed Clerk of the Closet to Queen Caroline; and, in the same year, he presented to her Majesty a copy of his excellent Treatise, entitled, "The "Analogy of Religion, Natural and Revealed, to the Constitu- "tion and Course of Nature." His attendance upon his Royal Mistress, by her especial command, was from seven to nine in the evening every day: and though this particular relation to that excellent and learned Queen was soon determined by her death in 1737, yet he had been so effectually recommended by her, as well as by the late Lord Chancellor Talbot, to his Majesty's favour, that in the next year he was raised to the highest order of the Church, by a nomination to the bishopric of Bristol; to which see he was consecrated on the 3rd of December 1738. King George II, not being satisfied with this proof of his regard to Dr. Butler, promoted him, in 1740, to the Deanery of St. Paul's, London; into which he was in- stalled on the 24th of May in that year. Finding the demands of this dignity to be incompatible with his parish duty at Stanhope, he immediately resigned that rich benefice. Besides our Prelate's unremitted attention to his peculiar obligations, he was called upon to preach several discourses on public occasions, which were afterwards separately printed, and have since been annexed to the latter editions of the Sermons at the Rolls Chapel. In 1746, upon the death of Dr. Egerton, Bishop of Hereford, Dr. Butler was made Clerk of the Closet to the King; and on the 16th of October, 1750, he received another distinguished mark of his Majesty's favour, by being translated to the see of Durham. This was on the 16th of October in that year, upon the decease of Dr. Edward Chandler. Our Prelate being thus appointed to preside over a diocese with which he had long been connected, delivered his first, and indeed his last Charge to his Clergy, at his primary visitation in 1751. The principal object of it was "External Religion." The Bishop having observed, with deep concern, the great and growing neglect of serious piety in the kingdom, insisted strongly on the usefulness of outward forms and institutions, in fixing and preserving a sense of devotion and duty in the minds of men. In doing this, he was thought by several persons to speak too favourably of Pagan and Popish ceremonies, and to countenance, in a certain degree, the cause of superstition. Under that apprehension, an able and spirited writer, who was understood to be a Clergyman of the Church of England, published, in 1752, a pamphlet, entitled, "A serious Inquiry into the Use and Importance of External Religion: occasioned by some Passages in the Right Rev. the Lord Bishop of Durham's Charge to the Clergy of that Diocese;—Humbly addressed to his Lordship." Many persons, however, and we believe the greater part of the Clergy of the diocese, did not think our Prelate's Charge so exceptionable as it appeared to this author. The Charge, being printed at Durham, and having never been annexed to any of Dr. Butler's other works, is now become extremely scarce; and it is observable, that it is the only one of his publications which ever produced him a direct literary antagonist.

By this promotion, our worthy Bishop was furnished with ample means of exerting the virtue of charity; a virtue which eminently abounded in him, and the exercise of which was his highest delight. But this gratification he did not long enjoy. He had been but a short time seated in his new bishopric, when his health began visibly to decline; and having been complimented, during his indisposition, upon account of his great resignation to the Divine will, he is said to have expressed some regret, that he should be taken from the present world so soon after he had been rendered capable of becoming much more useful in it. In his last illness he was carried to Bristol, to try the waters of that place; but these proving ineffectual, he removed to Bath, where, being past recovery, he died on the 16th of June, 1752. His corpse was conveyed to Bristol, and interred in the Cathedral there, where a monument, with an inscription, is erected to his memory.

On the greatness of Bishop Butler's character we need not enlarge; for his profound knowledge, and the prodigious strength of his mind, are amply displayed in his incomparable writings. His piety was of the most serious and fervent, and, perhaps, somewhat of the ascetic kind. His benevolence was warm, generous, and diffusive. Whilst he was Bishop of Bristol, he expended, in repairing and improving the episcopal palace, four thousand pounds, which is said to have been more than the whole revenues of the bishopric amounted to during his continuance in that see. Besides his private benefactions, he was a contributor to the infirmary at Bristol, and a subscriber to three of the hospitals at London. He was likewise a principal promoter, though not the first founder, of the infirmary at Newcastle, in Northumberland. In supporting the hospitality and dignity of the rich and powerful diocese of Durham, he was desirous of imitating the spirit of his patron, Bishop Talbot. In this spirit he set apart three days every week for the reception and entertainment of the principal gentry of the country. Nor were even the Clergy who had the poorest benefices neglected by him. He not only occasionally invited them to dine with him, but condescended to visit them at their respective parishes. By his will he left five hundred pounds to the Society for propagating the Gospel in Foreign Parts, and some legacies to his friends and domestics. His executor and residuary legatee was his Chaplain, the Rev. Dr. Nathanael Foster, a divine of distinguished literature. Bishop Butler was never married. Soon after his decease, the following lines, by way of epitaph, were written concerning him; and were printed first, if we recollect aright, in the London Magazine.

DR. BUTLER.

Beneath this marble Butler lies entomb'd,
   Who, with a soul inflam'd by love divine,
His life in presence of his God consum'd,
   Like the bright lamps before the holy shrine.
His aspect pleasing, mind with learning fraught :
   His eloquence was like a chain of gold,
   That the wild passions of mankind controll'd ;
Merit, wherever to be found, he sought.
Desire of transient riches he had none ;
   These he, with bounteous hand, did well dispense ;
   Bent to fulfil the ends of Providence ;
His heart still fixed on an immortal crown.
   His heart a mirror was, of purest kind,
   Where the bright image of his Maker shin'd ;
Reflecting faithful to the throne above,
Th' irradiant glories of the Mystic Dove.

TO THE

RIGHT HONOURABLE

CHARLES, LORD TALBOT,

BARON OF HENSOL,

LORD HIGH CHANCELLOR OF GREAT BRITAIN,

THE FOLLOWING TREATISE

IS, WITH ALL RESPECT, INSCRIBED,

IN ACKNOWLEDGMENT OF THE HIGHEST OBLIGATIONS

TO

THE LATE LORD BISHOP OF DURHAM,

AND TO HIMSELF,

BY HIS LORDSHIP'S MOST DUTIFUL,

MOST DEVOTED,

AND MOST HUMBLE SERVANT,

JOSEPH BUTLER.

THE

ANALOGY OF RELIGION,

NATURAL AND REVEALED,

TO THE

CONSTITUTION AND COURSE OF NATURE.

ADVERTISEMENT

PREFIXED TO THE FIRST EDITION.

IF the reader should meet here with any thing which he had not before attended to, it will not be in the observations upon the constitution and course of nature, these being all obvious; but in the application of them: in which, though there is nothing but what appears to me of some real weight, and therefore of great importance; yet he will observe several things, which will appear to him of very little, if he can think things to be of little importance, which are of any real weight at all, upon such a subject as religion. However, the proper force of the following Treatise lies in the whole general analogy considered together.

It is come, I know not how, to be taken for granted, by many persons, that Christianity is not so much as a subject of inquiry; but that it is, now at length, discovered to be fictitious. And accordingly they treat it, as if, in the present age, this were an agreed point among all people of discernment; and nothing remained, but to set it up as a principal subject of mirth and ridicule, as it were by way of reprisals, for its having so long interrupted the pleasures of the world. On the contrary, thus much, at least, will be here found, not taken for granted, but proved, that any reasonable man, who will thoroughly consider the matter, may be as much assured, as he is of his own being, that it is not, however, so clear a case, that there is nothing in it. There is, I think, strong evidence of its truth; but it is certain no one can, upon principles of reason, be satisfied of the contrary. And the practical consequence to be drawn from this is not attended to by every one who is concerned in it.

May, 1736.

CONTENTS.

INTRODUCTION 1

PART I.
OF NATURAL RELIGION.

CHAP. I.
Of a Future Life 13

CHAP. II.
Of the Government of God by Rewards and Punishments; and particularly of the latter 34

CHAP. III.
Of the Moral Government of God 47

CHAP. IV.
Of a State of Probation, as implying Trial, Difficulties, and Danger 75

CHAP. V.
Of a State of Probation, as intended for moral Discipline and Improvement 81

CHAP. VI.
Of the Opinion of Necessity, considered as influencing Practice 111

CHAP. VII.
Of the Government of God, considered as a Scheme or Constitution, imperfectly comprehended 129

CONCLUSION 142

PART II.

OF REVEALED RELIGION.

CHAP. I.
Of the Importance of Christianity 151

CHAP. II.
Of the supposed Presumption against a Revelation, considered as miraculous 171

CHAP. III.
Of our Incapacity of judging, what were to be expected in a Revelation; and the Credibility, from Analogy, that it must contain Things appearing liable to Objections 179

CHAP. IV.
Of Christianity, considered as a Scheme or Constitution imperfectly comprehended 196

CHAP. V.
Of the particular System of Christianity; the Appointment of a Mediator, and the Redemption of the World by him 205

CHAP. VI.
Of the Want of Universality in Revelation: and of the supposed Deficiency in the Proof of it 227

CHAP. VII.
Of the particular Evidence for Christianity 250

CHAP. VIII.
Of the Objections which may be made against arguing from the Analogy of Nature to Religion 292

CONCLUSION 306

DISSERTATION I.
Of Personal Identity 319

DISSERTATION II.
Of the Nature of Virtue 328

INTRODUCTION.

PROBABLE evidence is essentially distinguished from demonstrative by this, that it admits of degrees; and of all variety of them, from the highest moral certainty, to the very lowest presumption. We cannot indeed say a thing is probably true upon one very slight presumption for it; because, as there may be probabilities on both sides of a question, there may be some against it: and though there be not, yet a slight presumption does not beget that degree of conviction, which is implied in saying a thing is probably true. But that the slightest possible presumption is of the nature of a probability, appears from hence; that such low presumption, often repeated, will amount even to moral certainty. Thus a man's having observed the ebb and flow of the tide to-day, affords some sort of presumption, though the lowest imaginable, that it may happen again to-morrow: but the observation of this event for so many days, and months, and ages together, as it has been observed by mankind, gives us a full assurance that it will.

That which chiefly constitutes Probability is expressed in the word Likely, i. e. like some truth [a], or true event; like it, in itself, in its evidence, in some more or fewer of its circumstances. For when we

[a] Verisimile.

determine a thing to be probably true, suppose that an event has or will come to pass, it is from the mind's remarking in it a likeness to some other event, which we have observed has come to pass. And this observation forms, in numberless daily instances, a presumption, opinion, or full conviction, that such event has or will come to pass; according as the observation is, that the like event has sometimes, most commonly, or always so far as our observation reaches, come to pass at like distances of time, or place, or upon like occasions. Hence arises the belief, that a child, if it lives twenty years, will grow up to the stature and strength of a man; that food will contribute to the preservation of its life, and the want of it for such a number of days be its certain destruction. So likewise the rule and measure of our hopes and fears concerning the success of our pursuits; our expectations that others will act so and so in such circumstances; and our judgment that such actions proceed from such principles; all these rely upon our having observed the like to what we hope, fear, expect, judge; I say upon our having observed the like, either with respect to others or ourselves. And thus, whereas the prince [b] who had always lived in a warm climate, naturally concluded in the way of analogy, that there was no such thing as water's becoming hard, because he had always observed it to be fluid and yielding: we, on the contrary, from analogy conclude, that there is no presumption at all against this: that it is supposable there may be frost in England any given day in January next; probable that there will on some day of the month; and that there is a moral certainty, i. e. ground for an expectation with-

[b] The story is told by Mr. Locke in the chapter of Probability.

out any doubt of it, in some part or other of the winter.

Probable evidence, in its very nature, affords but an imperfect kind of information; and is to be considered as relative only to beings of limited capacities. For nothing which is the possible object of knowledge, whether past, present, or future, can be probable to an infinite Intelligence; since it cannot but be discerned absolutely as it is in itself, certainly true, or certainly false. But to Us, probability is the very guide of life.

From these things it follows, that in questions of difficulty, or such as are thought so, where more satisfactory evidence cannot be had, or is not seen; if the result of examination be, that there appears upon the whole, any the lowest presumption on one side, and none on the other, or a greater presumption on one side, though in the lowest degree greater; this determines the question, even in matters of speculation; and in matters of practice, will lay us under an absolute and formal obligation, in point of prudence and of interest, to act upon that presumption or low probability, though it be so low as to leave the mind in very great doubt which is the truth. For surely a man is as really bound in prudence, to do what upon the whole appears, according to the best of his judgment, to be for his happiness, as what he certainly knows to be so. Nay further, in questions of great consequence, a reasonable man will think it concerns him to remark lower probabilities and presumptions than these; such as amount to no more than shewing one side of a question to be as supposable and credible as the other: nay, such as but amount to much less even than this. For numberless instances might be mentioned respecting the common pursuits of life, where a man would be thought, in a literal sense, distracted, who would not act, and with great application too, not only upon an even chance, but upon much less, and where the probability or chance was greatly against his succeeding [c].

It is not my design to inquire further into the nature, the foundation, and measure of probability; or whence it proceeds that *likeness* should beget that presumption, opinion, and full conviction, which the human mind is formed to receive from it, and which it does necessarily produce in every one; or to guard against the errors, to which reasoning from analogy is liable. This belongs to the subject of Logic; and is a part of that subject which has not yet been thoroughly considered. Indeed I shall not take upon me to say, how far the extent, compass, and force, of analogical reasoning, can be reduced to general heads and rules; and the whole be formed into a system. But though so little in this way has been attempted by those who have treated of our intellectual powers, and the exercise of them; this does not hinder but that we may be, as we unquestionably are, assured, that analogy is of weight, in various degrees, towards determining our judgment and our practice. Nor does it in any wise cease to be of weight in those cases, because persons, either given to dispute, or who require things to be stated with greater exactness than our faculties appear to admit of in practical matters, may find other cases in which it is not easy to say, whether it be, or be not, of any weight; or instances of seeming analogies, which are really of none. It is enough to the present purpose to observe, that this general way of arguing is

[c] See chap. vi. part II.

evidently natural, just, and conclusive. For there is no man can make a question, but that the sun will rise to-morrow, and be seen, where it is seen at all, in the figure of a circle, and not in that of a square.

Hence, namely from analogical reasoning, Origen [d] has with singular sagacity observed, that *he who believes the Scripture to have proceeded from him who is the Author of Nature, may well expect to find the same sort of difficulties in it, as are found in the constitution of Nature.* And in a like way of reflexion it may be added, that he who denies the Scripture to have been from God upon account of these difficulties, may, for the very same reason, deny the world to have been formed by him. On the other hand, if there be an analogy or likeness between that system of things and dispensation of Providence, which Revelation informs us of, and that system of things and dispensation of Providence, which Experience together with Reason informs us of, i.e. the known course of Nature; this is a presumption, that they have both the same author and cause; at least so far as to answer objections against the former's being from God, drawn from any thing which is analogical or similar to what is in the latter, which is acknowledged to be from him; for an Author of Nature is here supposed.

Forming our notions of the constitution and government of the world upon reasoning, without foundation for the principles which we assume, whether from the attributes of God, or any thing else, is building a world upon hypothesis, like Des

---

[d] Χρὴ μέν τοι γε τὸν ἅπαξ παραδεξάμενον τοῦ κτίσαντος τὸν κόσμον εἶναι ταύτας τὰς γραφὰς πεπεῖσθαι, ὅτι ὅσα περὶ τῆς κτίσεως ἀπαντᾷ τοῖς ζητοῦσι τὸν περὶ αὐτῆς λόγον, ταῦτα καὶ περὶ τῶν γραφῶν. Philocal. p. 23. ed. Cant.

Cartes. Forming our notions upon reasoning from principles which are certain, but applied to cases to which we have no ground to apply them, (like those who explain the structure of the human body, and the nature of diseases and medicines from mere mathematics without sufficient *data*,) is an error much akin to the former: since what is assumed in order to make the reasoning applicable, is Hypothesis. But it must be allowed just, to join abstract reasonings with the observation of facts, and argue from such facts as are known, to others that are like them; from that part of the Divine government over intelligent creatures which comes under our view, to that larger and more general government over them which is beyond it; and from what is present, to collect, what is likely, credible, or not incredible, will be hereafter.

This method then of concluding and determining being practical, and what, if we will act at all, we cannot but act upon in the common pursuits of life; being evidently conclusive, in various degrees, proportionable to the degree and exactness of the whole analogy or likeness; and having so great authority for its introduction into the subject of religion, even revealed religion; my design is to apply it to that subject in general, both natural and revealed: taking for proved, that there is an intelligent Author of Nature, and natural Governor of the world. For as there is no presumption against this prior to the proof of it: so it has been often proved with accumulated evidence; from this argument of analogy and final causes; from abstract reasonings; from the most ancient tradition and testimony; and from the general consent of mankind. Nor does it appear, so far as I can find, to be denied by the generality of those who profess themselves dissatisfied with the evidence of religion.

As there are some, who, instead of thus attending to what is in fact the constitution of Nature, form their notions of God's government upon hypothesis: so there are others, who indulge themselves in vain and idle speculations, how the world might possibly have been framed otherwise than it is; and upon supposition that things might, in imagining that they should, have been disposed and carried on after a better model, than what appears in the present disposition and conduct of them. Suppose now a person of such a turn of mind, to go on with his reveries, till he had at length fixed upon some particular plan of Nature, as appearing to him the best.——One shall scarce be thought guilty of detraction against human understanding, if one should say, even beforehand, that the plan which this speculative person would fix upon, though he were the wisest of the sons of men, probably would not be the very best, even according to his own notions of *best*; whether he thought that to be so, which afforded occasions and motives for the exercise of the greatest virtue, or which was productive of the greatest happiness, or that these two were necessarily connected, and run up into one and the same plan. However, it may not be amiss once for all to see, what would be the amount of these emendations and imaginary improvements upon the system of nature, or how far they would mislead us. And it seems there could be no stopping, till we came to some such conclusions as these: that all creatures should at first be made as perfect and as happy as they were capable of ever being: that nothing, to be sure, of hazard or danger should be put upon them to do; some indolent persons would perhaps think nothing at all: or certainly, that effectual care should be taken, that they should, whether necessarily or not, yet eventually and in fact, always do what was right and most conducive to happiness, which would be thought easy for infinite power to effect; either by not giving them any principles which would endanger their going wrong; or by laying the right motive of action in every instance before their minds continually in so strong a manner, as would never fail of inducing them to act conformably to it: and that the whole method of government by punishments should be rejected as absurd; as an awkward roundabout method of carrying things on; nay, as contrary to a principal purpose, for which it would be supposed creatures were made, namely, happiness.

Now, without considering what is to be said in particular to the several parts of this train of folly and extravagance; what has been above intimated, is a full direct general answer to it, namely, that we may see beforehand that we have not faculties for this kind of speculation. For though it be admitted, that, from the first principles of our nature, we unavoidably judge or determine some ends to be absolutely in themselves preferable to others, and that the ends now mentioned, or if they run up into one, that this one is absolutely the best; and consequently that we must conclude the ultimate end designed, in the constitution of Nature and conduct of Providence, is the most virtue and happiness possible: yet we are far from being able to judge what particular disposition of things would be most friendly and assistant to virtue; or what means might be absolutely necessary to produce the most happiness in a system of such extent as our own world may be, taking in all that is past and to come, though we should suppose it detached from the whole of things. Indeed we are so far from being able to judge of this, that we are not judges what may be the necessary means of raising and conducting one person to the highest perfection and happiness of his nature. Nay, even in the little affairs of the present life, we find men of different educations and ranks are not competent judges of the conduct of each other. Our whole nature leads us to ascribe all moral perfection to God, and to deny all imperfection of him. And this will for ever be a practical proof of his moral character, to such as will consider what a practical proof is; because it is the voice of God speaking in us. And from hence we conclude, that virtue must be the happiness, and vice the misery, of every creature; and that regularity and order and right cannot but prevail finally in a universe under his government. But we are in no sort judges, what are the necessary means of accomplishing this end.

Let us then, instead of that idle and not very innocent employment of forming imaginary models of a world, and schemes of governing it, turn our thoughts to what we experience to be the conduct of Nature with respect to intelligent creatures; which may be resolved into general laws or rules of administration, in the same way as many of the laws of Nature respecting inanimate matter may be collected from experiments. And let us compare the known constitution and course of things with what is said to be the moral system of Nature; the acknowledged dispensations of Providence, or that government which we find ourselves under, with what religion teaches us to believe and expect; and see whether they are not analogous and of a piece. And upon such a comparison it will, I think, be found, that they are very much so : that both may be traced up to the same general laws, and resolved into the same principles of divine conduct.

The analogy here proposed to be considered is of pretty large extent, and consists of several parts, in some, more, in others, less, exact. In some few instances perhaps it may amount to a real practical proof; in others not so. Yet in these it is a confirmation of what is proved other ways. It will undeniably shew, what too many want to have shewn them, that the system of Religion, both natural and revealed, considered only as a system, and prior to the proof of it, is not a subject of ridicule, unless that of nature be so too. And it will afford an answer to almost all objections against the system both of natural and revealed Religion; though not perhaps an answer in so great a degree, yet in a very considerable degree, an answer to the objections against the evidence of it: for objections against a proof, and objections against what is said to be proved, the reader will observe are different things.

Now the divine government of the world, implied in the notion of religion in general and of Christianity, contains in it; that mankind is appointed to live in a future state[e]; that there, every one shall be rewarded or punished[f]; rewarded or punished respectively for all that behaviour here, which we comprehend under the words, virtuous or vicious, morally good or evil[g]: that our present life is a probation, a state of trial[h]; and of discipline[i], for

[e] Ch. i.   [f] Ch. ii.   [g] Ch. iii.   [h] Ch. iv.   [i] Ch. v.

INTRODUCTION.

that future one; notwithstanding the objections, which men may fancy they have, from notions of Necessity, against there being any such moral plan as this at all[k]; and whatever objections may appear to lie against the wisdom and goodness of it, as it stands so imperfectly made known to us at present[l]: that this world being in a state of apostasy and wickedness, and consequently of ruin, and the sense both of their condition and duty being greatly corrupted amongst men, this gave occasion for an additional dispensation of Providence; of the utmost importance[m]; proved by miracles[n]; but containing in it many things appearing to us strange, and not to have been expected[o]; a dispensation of Providence, which is a scheme or system of things[p]; carried on by the mediation of a divine person, the Messiah, in order to the recovery of the world[q]; yet not revealed to all men, nor proved with the strongest possible evidence to all those to whom it is revealed; but only to such a part of mankind, and with such particular evidence, as the wisdom of God thought fit[r]. The design then of the following Treatise will be to shew, that the several parts principally objected against in this moral and Christian dispensation, including its scheme, its publication, and the proof which God has afforded us of its truth; that the particular parts principally objected against in this whole dispensation, are analogous to what is experienced in the constitution and course of Nature, or Providence; that the chief objections themselves which are alleged against the former, are no other than what may be alleged with like justness against the latter, where they are found in fact to be in-

[k] Ch. vi. [l] Ch. vii. [m] Part II. ch. i. [n] Ch. ii.
[o] Ch. iii. [p] Ch. iv. [q] Ch. v. [r] Ch. vi. vii.

conclusive; and that this argument from analogy is in general unanswerable, and undoubtedly of weight on the side of religion[s], notwithstanding the objections which may seem to lie against it, and the real ground which there may be for difference of opinion, as to the particular degree of weight which is to be laid upon it. This is a general account of what may be looked for in the following Treatise. And I shall begin it with that which is the foundation of all our hopes and of all our fears; all our hopes and fears, which are of any consideration; I mean a Future Life.

[s] Ch. viii.

THE
ANALOGY OF RELIGION
TO THE
CONSTITUTION AND COURSE OF NATURE.

PART I.
OF NATURAL RELIGION.

CHAP. I.

Of a future life.

STRANGE difficulties have been raised by some concerning personal identity, or the sameness of living agents, implied in the notion of our existing now and hereafter, or in any two successive moments; which whoever thinks it worth while, may see considered in the first Dissertation at the end of this Treatise. But without regard to any of them here, let us consider what the analogy of nature, and the several changes which we have undergone, and those which we know we may undergo without being destroyed, suggest, as to the effect which death may, or may not, have upon us; and whether it be not from thence probable, that we may survive this change, and exist in a future state of life and perception.

I. From our being born into the present world in the helpless imperfect state of infancy, and having arrived from thence to mature age, we find it to be a general law of nature in our own species, that the same creatures, the same individuals, should exist in degrees of life and perception, with capacities of action, of enjoyment and suffering, in one period of their being, greatly different from those appointed them in another period of it. And in other creatures the same law holds. For the difference of their capacities and states of life at their birth (to go no higher) and in maturity; the change of worms into flies, and the vast enlargement of their locomotive powers by such change: and birds and insects bursting the shell their habitation, and by this means entering into a new world, furnished with new accommodations for them, and finding a new sphere of action assigned them; these are instances of this general law of nature. Thus all the various and wonderful transformations of animals are to be taken into consideration here. But the states of life in which we ourselves existed formerly in the womb and in our infancy, are almost as different from our present in mature age, as it is possible to conceive any two states or degrees of life can be. Therefore, that we are to exist hereafter in a state as different (suppose) from our present, as this is from our former, is but according to the analogy of nature; according to a natural order or appointment of the very same kind, with what we have already experienced.

II. We know we are endued with capacities of action, of happiness and misery: for we are conscious of acting, of enjoying pleasure and suffering pain. Now that we have these powers and capacities before death, is a presumption that we shall retain them through and after death; indeed a probability of it abundantly sufficient to act upon, unless there be some positive reason to think that death is the destruction of those living powers : because there is in every case a probability, that all things will continue as we experience they are, in all respects, except those in which we have some reason to think they will be altered. This is that *kind* [a] of presumption or probability from analogy, expressed in the very word *continuance*, which seems our only natural reason for believing the course of the world will continue to-morrow, as it has done so far as our experience or knowledge of history can carry us back. Nay it seems our only reason for believing, that any one substance now existing will continue to exist a moment longer ; the self-existent substance only excepted. Thus if men were assured that the unknown event, death, was not the destruction of our faculties of perception and of action, there would be no apprehension, that any other power or event, unconnected with this of death, would destroy these faculties just at the instant of each creature's death ; and therefore no doubt but that they would remain after it : which shews the high probability that our living powers will continue after death, unless there be some ground to think that death is their destruction[b]. For, if it

---

[a] I say *kind* of presumption or probability ; for I do not mean to affirm that there is the same *degree* of conviction, that our living powers will continue after death, as there is, that our substances will.

[b] *Destruction of living powers* is a manner of expression unavoidably ambiguous; and may signify either *the destruction of a living being, so as that the same living being shall be uncapable of ever perceiving or acting again at all;* or *the destruction of those means and instruments by which it is capable of its present life, of its present state of perception and of action.* It is here used in the former sense. When it is used in the latter, the epithet *present* is added. The loss of a man's eye is a destruction of living powers in

would be in a manner certain that we should survive death, provided it were certain that death would not be our destruction, it must be highly probable we shall survive it, if there be no ground to think death will be our destruction.

Now though I think it must be acknowledged, that prior to the natural and moral proofs of a future life commonly insisted upon, there would arise a general confused suspicion, that in the great shock and alteration which we shall undergo by death, we, i.e. our living powers, might be wholly destroyed; yet even prior to those proofs, there is really no particular distinct ground or reason for this apprehension at all, so far as I can find. If there be, it must arise either from *the reason of the thing*, or from *the analogy of nature.*

But we cannot argue from *the reason of the thing*, that death is the destruction of living agents, because we know not at all what death is in itself; but only some of its effects, such as the dissolution of flesh, skin, and bones. And these effects do in no wise appear to imply the destruction of a living agent. And besides, as we are greatly in the dark, upon what the exercise of our living powers depends, so we are wholly ignorant what the powers themselves depend upon; the powers themselves as distinguished, not only from their actual exercise, but also from the present capacity of exercising them; and as opposed to their destruction: for sleep, or however a swoon, shews us, not only that these

the latter sense. But we have no reason to think the destruction of living powers, in the former sense, to be possible. We have no more reason to think a being endued with living powers, ever loses them during its whole existence, than to believe that a stone ever acquires them.

powers exist when they are not exercised, as the passive power of motion does in inanimate matter; but shews also that they exist, when there is no present capacity of exercising them: or that the capacities of exercising them for the present, as well as the actual exercise of them, may be suspended, and yet the powers themselves remain undestroyed. Since then we know not at all upon what the existence of our living powers depends, this shews further, there can no probability be collected from the reason of the thing, that death will be their destruction: because their existence may depend, upon somewhat in no degree affected by death; upon somewhat quite out of the reach of this king of terrors. So that there is nothing more certain, than that *the reason of the thing* shews us no connection between death, and the destruction of living agents. Nor can we find any thing throughout the whole *analogy of nature*, to afford us even the slightest presumption, that animals ever lose their living powers; much less, if it were possible, that they lose them by death: for we have no faculties wherewith to trace any beyond or through it, so as to see what becomes of them. This event removes them from our view. It destroys the *sensible* proof, which we had before their death, of their being possessed of living powers, but does not appear to afford the least reason to believe that they are, then, or by that event, deprived of them.

And our knowing, that they were possessed of these powers, up to the very period to which we have faculties capable of tracing them, is itself a probability of their retaining them, beyond it. And this is confirmed, and a sensible credibility is given to it, by observing the very great and astonishing changes which we have experienced; so great, that our existence in another state of life, of perception and of action, will be but according to a method of providential conduct, the like to which has been already exercised even with regard to ourselves; according to a course of nature, the like to which, we have already gone through.

However, as one cannot but be greatly sensible, how difficult it is to silence imagination enough to make the voice of reason even distinctly heard in this case; as we are accustomed, from our youth up, to indulge that forward delusive faculty, ever obtruding beyond its sphere; of some assistance indeed to apprehension, but the author of all error: as we plainly lose ourselves in gross and crude conceptions of things, taking for granted that we are acquainted with, what indeed we are wholly ignorant of; it may be proper to consider the imaginary presumptions, that death will be our destruction, arising from these kinds of early and lasting prejudices; and to shew how little they can really amount to, even though we cannot wholly divest ourselves of them. And,

I. All presumption of death's being the destruction of living beings, must go upon supposition that they are. compounded; and so, discerptible. But since consciousness is a single and indivisible power, it should seem that the subject in which it resides must be so too. For were the motion of any particle of matter absolutely one and indivisible, so as that it should imply a contradiction to suppose part of this motion to exist, and part not to exist, i.e. part of this matter to move, and part to be at rest; then its power of motion would be indivisible; and so also would the subject in which the power inheres, namely, the particle of matter: for if this could be divided into two, one part might be moved and the other at rest, which is contrary to the supposition. In like manner it has been argued[c], and, for any thing appearing to the contrary, justly, that since the perception or consciousness, which we have of our own existence, is indivisible, so as that it is a contradiction to suppose one part of it should be here and the other there; the perceptive power, or the power of consciousness, is indivisible too: and consequently the subject in which it resides; i.e. the conscious being. Now upon supposition that living agent each man calls himself, is thus a single being, which there is at least no more difficulty in conceiving than in conceiving it to be a compound, and of which there is the proof now mentioned; it follows, that our organized bodies are no more ourselves or part of ourselves, than any other matter around us. And it is as easy to conceive, how matter, which is no part of ourselves, may be appropriated to us in the manner which our present bodies are; as how we can receive impressions from, and have power over any matter. It is as easy to conceive, that we may exist out of bodies, as in them; that we might have animated bodies of any other organs and senses wholly different from these now given us, and that we may hereafter animate these same or new bodies variously modified and organized; as to conceive how we can animate such bodies as our present. And lastly, the dissolution of all these several organized bodies, supposing ourselves to have successively animated them, would have no more conceivable tendency to destroy the living beings ourselves, or deprive us of living faculties, the faculties

[c] See Dr. Clarke's Letter to Mr. Dodwell, and the defences of it.

of perception and of action, than the dissolution of any foreign matter, which we are capable of receiving impressions from, and making use of for the common occasions of life.

II. The simplicity and absolute oneness of a living agent cannot indeed, from the nature of the thing, be properly proved by experimental observations. But as these *fall in* with the supposition of its unity, so they plainly lead us to *conclude* certainly, that our gross organized bodies, with which we perceive the objects of sense, and with which we act, are no part of ourselves; and therefore shew us, that we have no reason to believe their destruction to be ours: even without determining whether our living substances be material or immaterial. For we see by experience, that men may lose their limbs, their organs of sense, and even the greatest part of these bodies, and yet remain the same living agents. And persons can trace up the existence of themselves to a time, when the bulk of their bodies was extremely small, in comparison of what it is in mature age: and we cannot but think, that they might then have lost a considerable part of that small body, and yet have remained the same living agents; as they may now lose great part of their present body, and remain so. And it is certain, that the bodies of all animals are in a constant flux, from that never-ceasing attrition, which there is in every part of them. Now things of this kind unavoidably teach us to distinguish, between these living agents ourselves, and large quantities of matter, in which we are very nearly interested: since these may be alienated, and actually are in a daily course of succession, and changing their owners; whilst we are assured, that each living agent remains one and the same permanent being[d]. And this general observation leads us on to the following ones.

First, That we have no way of determining by experience, what is the certain bulk of the living being each man calls himself: and yet, till it be determined that it is larger in bulk than the solid elementary particles of matter, which there is no ground to think any natural power can dissolve, there is no sort of reason to think death to be the dissolution of it, of the living being, even though it should not be absolutely indiscerptible.

Secondly, From our being so nearly related to and interested in certain systems of matter, suppose our flesh and bones, and afterwards ceasing to be at all related to them, the living agents ourselves remaining all this while undestroyed notwithstanding such alienation; and consequently these systems of matter not being ourselves: it follows further, that we have no ground to conclude any other, suppose *internal systems* of matter, to be the living agents ourselves; because we can have no ground to conclude this, but from our relation to and interest in such other systems of matter: and therefore we can have no reason to conclude, what befalls those systems of matter at death, to be the destruction of the living agents. We have already several times over lost a great part or perhaps the whole of our body, according to certain common established laws of nature; yet we remain the same living agents: when we shall lose as great a part, or the whole, by another common established law of nature, death; why may we not also remain the same? That the alienation has been gradual in one case, and in the

[d] See Dissertation I.

other will be more at once, does not prove any thing to the contrary. We have passed undestroyed through those many and great revolutions of matter, so peculiarly appropriated to us ourselves; why should we imagine death will be so fatal to us? Nor can it be objected, that what is thus alienated or lost, is no part of our original solid body, but only adventitious matter; because we may lose entire limbs, which must have contained many solid parts and vessels of the original body: or if this be not admitted, we have no proof, that any of these solid parts are dissolved or alienated by death. Though, by the way, we are very nearly related to that extraneous or adventitious matter, whilst it continues united to and distending the several parts of our solid body. But after all; the relation a person bears to those parts of his body, to which he is the most nearly related; what does it appear to amount to but this, that the living agent, and those parts of the body, mutually affect each other? And the same thing, the same thing in kind though not in degree, may be said of *all foreign* matter, which gives us ideas, and which we have any power over. From these observations the whole ground of the imagination is removed, that the dissolution of any matter, is the destruction of a living agent, from the interest he once had in such matter.

Thirdly, If we consider our body somewhat more distinctly, as made up of organs and instruments of perception and of motion, it will bring us to the same conclusion. Thus the common optical experiments shew, and even the observation how sight is assisted by glasses shews, that we see with our eyes in the same sense as we see with glasses. Nor is there any reason to believe, that we see with them in any other sense; any other, I mean, which would lead us to think the eye itself a percipient. The like is to be said of hearing: and our feeling distant solid matter by means of somewhat in our hand, seems an instance of the like kind, as to the subject we are considering. All these are instances of foreign matter, or such as is no part of our body, being instrumental in preparing objects for, and conveying them to, the perceiving power, in a manner similar or like to the manner in which our organs of sense prepare and convey them. Both are in a like way instruments of our receiving such ideas from external objects, as the Author of nature appointed those external objects to be the occasions of exciting in us. However, glasses are evidently instances of this; namely of matter which is no part of our body, preparing objects for and conveying them towards the perceiving power, in like manner as our bodily organs do. And if we see with our eyes only in the same manner as we do with glasses, the like may justly be concluded, from analogy, of all our other senses. It is not intended, by any thing here said, to affirm, that the whole apparatus of vision, or of perception by any other of our senses, can be traced, through all its steps, quite up to the living power of seeing, or perceiving: but that so far as it can be traced by experimental observations, so far it appears, that our organs of sense prepare and convey on objects, in order to their being perceived, in like manner as foreign matter does, without affording any shadow of appearance, that they themselves perceive. And that we have no reason to think our organs of sense percipients, is confirmed by instances of persons losing some of them, the living beings themselves, their former occupiers, remaining unimpaired. It is confirmed also by the experience of dreams; by which we find we are at present possessed of a latent, and, what would otherwise be, an unimagined unknown power of perceiving sensible objects, in as strong and lively a manner without our external organs of sense as with them.

So also with regard to our power of moving, or directing motion by will and choice: upon the destruction of a limb, this active power remains, as it evidently seems, unlessened; so as that the living being, who has suffered this loss, would be capable of moving as before, if it had another limb to move with. It can walk by the help of an artificial leg; just as it can make use of a pole or a lever, to reach towards itself and to move things, beyond the length and the power of its natural arm: and this last it does in the same manner as it reaches and moves, with its natural arm, things nearer and of less weight. Nor is there so much as any appearance of our limbs being endued with a power of moving or directing themselves; though they are adapted, like the several parts of a machine, to be the instruments of motion to each other; and some parts of the same limb, to be instruments of motion to other parts of it.

Thus a man determines, that he will look at such an object through a microscope; or being lame suppose, that he will walk to such a place with a staff a week hence. His eyes and his feet no more determine in these cases, than the microscope and the staff. Nor is there any ground to think they any more put the determination in practice; or that his eyes are the seers or his feet the movers, in any other sense than as the microscope and the staff are. Upon the whole then, our organs of sense and our limbs are certainly instruments, which the living persons ourselves make use of to perceive and move with : there is not any probability, that they are any more ; nor consequently, that we have any other kind of relation to them, than what we may have to any other foreign matter formed into instruments of perception and motion, suppose into a microscope or a staff; (I say any other kind of relation, for I am not speaking of the degree of it ;) nor consequently is there any probability, that the alienation or dissolution of these instruments is the destruction of the perceiving and moving agent.

And thus our finding, that the dissolution of matter, in which living beings were most nearly interested, is not their dissolution ; and that the destruction of several of the organs and instruments of perception and of motion belonging to them, is not their destruction ; shews demonstratively, that there is no ground to think that the dissolution of any other matter, or destruction of any other organs and instruments, will be the dissolution or destruction of living agents, from the like kind of relation. And we have no reason to think we stand in any other kind of relation to any thing which we find dissolved by death.

But it is said these observations are equally applicable to brutes : and it is thought an insuperable difficulty, that they should be immortal, and by consequence capable of everlasting happiness. Now this manner of expression is both invidious and weak : but the thing intended by it, is really no difficulty at all, either in the way of natural or moral consideration. For first, suppose the invidious thing, designed in such a manner of expression, were really implied, as it is not in the least, in the natural immortality of brutes; namely, that they must arrive at great attainments, and become rational and moral agents; even this would be no difficulty: since we know not what latent powers and capacities they may be endued with. There was once, prior to experience, as great presumption against human creatures, as there is against the brute creatures, arriving at that degree of understanding, which we have in mature age. For we can trace up our own existence to the same original with theirs. And we find it to be a general law of nature, that creatures endued with capacities of virtue and religion should be placed in a condition of being, in which they are altogether without the use of them, for a considerable length of their duration; as in infancy and childhood. And great part of the human species go out of the present world, before they come to the exercise of these capacities in any degree at all. But then, secondly, the natural immortality of brutes does not in the least imply, that they are endued with any latent capacities of a rational or moral nature. And the economy of the universe might require, that there should be living creatures without any capacities of this kind. And all difficulties as to the manner how they are to be disposed of are so apparently and wholly founded in our ignorance, that it is wonderful they should be insisted upon by any, but such as are weak enough to think they are acquainted with the whole system of things. There is then absolutely nothing at all in this objection, which is so rhetorically urged, against the greatest part of the natural proofs or presumptions of the immortality of human minds: I say the greatest part; for it is less applicable to the following observation, which is more peculiar to mankind:

III. That as it is evident our *present* powers and capacities of reason, memory, and affection, do not depend upon our gross body in the manner in which perception by our organs of sense does; so they do not appear to depend upon it at all in any such manner, as to give ground to think, that the dissolution of this body will be the destruction of these our *present* powers of reflection, as it will of our powers of sensation; or to give ground to conclude, even that it will be so much as a suspension of the former.

Human creatures exist at present in two states of life and perception, greatly different from each other : each of which has its own peculiar laws, and its own peculiar enjoyments and sufferings. When any of our senses are affected or appetites gratified with the objects of them, we may be said to exist or live in a state of sensation. When none of our senses are affected or appetites gratified, and yet we perceive, and reason, and act; we may be said to exist or live in a state of reflection. Now it is by no means certain, that any thing which is dissolved by death, is any way necessary to the living being in this its state of reflection, after ideas are gained. For, though, from our present constitution and condition of being, our external organs of sense are necessary for conveying in ideas to our reflecting powers, as carriages, and levers, and scaffolds are in architecture : yet when these ideas are brought in, we are capable of reflecting in the most intense degree, and of enjoying the greatest pleasure, and feeling the greatest pain, by means of that reflection, without any assistance from our senses; and without any at all, which we know of, from that body, which will be dissolved by death. It does not appear then, that the relation of this gross body to the reflecting being, is, in any degree, necessary to thinking; to our intellectual enjoyments or sufferings: nor, consequently, that the dissolution or alienation of the former by death, will be the destruction of those present powers, which render us capable of this state of reflection. Further, there are instances of mortal diseases, which do not at all affect our present intellectual powers; and this affords a presumption, that those diseases will not destroy these present powers. Indeed, from the observations made above [c], it appears, that there is no presumption, from their mutually affecting each other, that the dissolution of the body is the destruction of the living agent. And by the same reasoning, it must appear too, that there is no presumption, from their mutually affecting each other, that the dissolution of the body is the destruction of our present reflecting powers: but instances of their not affecting each other, afford a presumption of the contrary. Instances of mortal diseases not impairing our present reflecting powers, evidently turn our thoughts even from imagining such diseases to be the destruction of them. Several things indeed greatly affect all our living powers, and at length suspend the exercise of them; as for instance drowsiness, increasing till it ends in sound sleep: and from hence we might have imagined it would destroy them, till we found by experience the weakness of this way of judging. But in the diseases now mentioned, there is not so much as this shadow of probability, to lead us to any such conclusion, as to the reflecting powers which we have at present. For in those diseases, persons the moment before death appear to be in the highest

[e] P. 21, 22.

vigour of life. They discover apprehension, memory, reason, all entire; with the utmost force of affection; sense of a character, of shame and honour; and the highest mental enjoyments and sufferings, even to the last gasp: and these surely prove even greater vigour of life than bodily strength does. Now what pretence is there for thinking, that a progressive disease when arrived to such a degree, I mean that degree which is mortal, will destroy those powers, which were not impaired, which were not affected by it, during its whole progress quite up to that degree? And if death by diseases of this kind is not the destruction of our present reflecting powers, it will scarce be thought that death by any other means is.

It is obvious that this general observation may be carried on further: and there appears so little connexion between our bodily powers of sensation, and our present powers of reflection, that there is no reason to conclude, that death, which destroys the former, does so much as suspend the exercise of the latter, or interrupt our *continuing* to exist in the like state of reflection which we do now. For suspension of reason, memory, and the affections which they excite, is no part of the idea of death, nor is implied in our notion of it. And our daily experiencing these powers to be exercised, without any assistance, that we know of, from those bodies, which will be dissolved by death; and our finding often, that the exercise of them is so lively to the last; these things afford a sensible apprehension, that death may not perhaps be so much as a discontinuance of the exercise of these powers, nor of the enjoyments and sufferings which it implies [f]. So

[f] There are three distinct questions, relating to a future life, here considered: Whether death be the destruction of living agents; if

that our posthumous life, whatever there may be in it additional to our present, yet may not be entirely beginning anew; but going on. Death may, in some sort, and in some respects, answer to our birth; which is not a suspension of the faculties which we had before it, or a total change of the state of life in which we existed when in the womb; but a continuation of both, with such and such great alterations.

Nay, for ought we know of ourselves, of our present life and of death; death may immediately, in the natural course of things, put us into a higher and more enlarged state of life, as our birth does [g]; a state in which our capacities, and sphere of perception and of action, may be much greater than at present. For as our relation to our external organs of sense, renders us capable of existing in our present state of sensation; so it may be the only natural hinderance to our existing, immediately and of course, in a higher state of reflection. The truth is, reason does not at all shew us, in what state death naturally leaves us. But were we sure, that it would suspend all our perceptive and active powers; yet the sus-

---

not, Whether it be the destruction of their *present* powers of reflection, as it certainly is the destruction of their present powers of sensation; and if not, Whether it be the suspension, or discontinuance of the exercise, of these present reflecting powers. Now, if there be no reason to believe the last, there will be, if that were possible, less for the next, and less still for the first.

[g] This, according to Strabo, was the opinion of the Brachmans, νομίζειν μὲν γὰρ δὴ τὸν μὲν ἐνθάδε βίον, ὡς ἂν ἀκμὴν κυομένων εἶναι· τὸν δὲ θάνατον, γένεσιν εἰς τὸν ὄντως βίον, καὶ τὸν εὐδαίμονα τοῖς φιλοσοφήσασι. Lib. xv. p. 1039. ed. Amst. 1707. To which opinion perhaps Antoninus may allude in these words, ὡς νῦν περιμένεις, πότε ἔμβρυον ἐκ τῆς γαστρὸς τῆς γυναικός σου ἐξέλθῃ, οὕτως ἐκδέχεσθαι τὴν ὥραν ἐν ᾗ τὸ ψυχάριόν σου τοῦ ἐλύτρου τούτου ἐκπεσεῖται. Lib. ix. c. 3.

pension of a power and the destruction of it, are effects so totally different in kind, as we experience from sleep and a swoon, that we cannot in any wise argue from one to the other; or conclude even to the lowest degree of probability, that the same kind of force which is sufficient to suspend our faculties, though it be increased ever so much, will be sufficient to destroy them.

These observations together may be sufficient to shew, how little presumption there is, that death is the destruction of human creatures. However, there is the shadow of an analogy, which may lead us to imagine it is; the supposed likeness which is observed between the decay of vegetables, and of living creatures. And this likeness is indeed sufficient to afford the poets very apt allusions to the flowers of the field, in their pictures of the frailty of our present life. But in reason, the analogy is so far from holding, that there appears no ground even for the comparison, as to the present question; because one of the two subjects compared is wholly void of that, which is the principal and chief thing in the other, the power of perception and of action; and which is the only thing we are inquiring about the continuance of. So that the destruction of a vegetable is an event not similar or analogous to the destruction of a living agent.

But if, as was above intimated, leaving off the delusive custom of substituting imagination in the room of experience, we would confine ourselves to what we do know and understand; if we would argue only from that, and from that form our expectations; it would appear at first sight, that as no probability of living beings ever ceasing to be so, can be concluded from the reason of the thing: so none can be collected from the analogy of Nature; because we cannot trace any living beings beyond death. But as we are conscious that we are endued with capacities of perception and of action, and are living persons; what we are to go upon is, that we shall continue so, till we foresee some accident or event, which will endanger those capacities, or be likely to destroy us: which death does in no wise appear to be.

And thus, when we go out of this world, we may pass into new scenes, and a new state of life and action, just as naturally as we came into the present. And this new state may naturally be a social one. And the advantages of it, advantages of every kind, may naturally be bestowed, according to some fixed general laws of wisdom, upon every one in proportion to the degrees of his virtue. And though the advantages of that future natural state should not be bestowed, as these of the present in some measure are, by the will of the society; but entirely by his more immediate action, upon whom the whole frame of nature depends: yet this distribution may be just as natural, as their being distributed here by the instrumentality of men. And indeed, though one were to allow any confused undetermined sense, which people please to put upon the word *natural*, it would be a shortness of thought scarce credible, to imagine, that no system or course of things can be so, but only what we see at present[h]: especially whilst the probability of a future life, or the natural immortality of the soul, is admitted upon the evidence of reason; because this is really both admitting and denying at once, a state of being different from the present to be natural. But the only distinct meaning of that word is, *stated, fixed,* or *settled:* since what is natural, as

[h] See part II. chap. ii. and part II. chap. iv.

much requires and presupposes an intelligent agent to render it so, i. e. to effect it continually, or at stated times; as what is supernatural or miraculous does to effect it for once. And from hence it must follow, that persons' notion of what is natural, will be enlarged in proportion to their greater knowledge of the works of God, and the dispensations of his Providence. Nor is there any absurdity in supposing, that there may be beings in the universe, whose capacities, and knowledge, and views, may be so extensive, as that the whole Christian dispensation may to them appear natural, i. e. analogous or conformable to God's dealings with other parts of his creation; as natural as the visible known course of things appears to us. For there seems scarce any other possible sense to be put upon the word, but that only in which it is here used; *similar, stated*, or *uniform*.

This credibility of a future life, which has been here insisted upon, how little soever it may satisfy our curiosity, seems to answer all the purposes of religion, in like manner as a demonstrative proof would. Indeed a proof, even a demonstrative one, of a future life, would not be a proof of religion. For, that we are to live hereafter, is just as reconcilable with the scheme of atheism, and as well to be accounted for by it, as that we are now alive, is: and therefore nothing can be more absurd than to argue from that scheme, that there can be no future state. But as religion implies a future state, any presumption against such a state, is a presumption against religion. And the foregoing observations remove all presumptions of that sort, and prove, to a very considerable degree of probability, one fundamental doctrine of religion; which, if believed, would greatly open and dispose the mind seriously to attend to the general evidence of the whole.

CHAP. II.
Of the government of God by rewards and punishments; and particularly of the latter.

THAT which makes the question concerning a future life to be of so great importance to us, is our capacity of happiness and misery. And that which makes the consideration of it to be of so great importance to us, is the supposition of our happiness and misery Hereafter, depending upon our actions Here. Without this indeed, curiosity could not but sometimes bring a subject, in which we may be so highly interested, to our thoughts; especially upon the mortality of others, or the near prospect of our own. But reasonable men would not take any further thought about Hereafter, than what should happen thus occasionally to rise in their minds, if it were certain that our future interest no way depended upon our present behaviour: whereas on the contrary, if there be ground, either from analogy or any thing else, to think it does; then there is reason also for the most active thought and solicitude, to secure that interest; to behave so as that we may escape that misery, and obtain that happiness in another life, which we not only suppose ourselves capable of, but which we apprehend also is put in our own power. And whether there be ground for this last apprehension, certainly would deserve to be most seriously considered, were there no other proof of a future life and interest, than that presumptive one, which the foregoing observations amount to.

Now in the present state, all which we enjoy, and a great part of what we suffer, *is put in our own power.* For pleasure and pain are the consequences of our actions: and we are endued by the Author of our Nature with capacities of foreseeing these consequences. We find by experience He does not so much as preserve our lives, exclusively of our own care and attention, to provide ourselves with, and to make use of, that sustenance by which he has appointed our lives shall be preserved; and without which, he has appointed, they shall not be preserved at all. And in general we foresee, that the external things, which are the objects of our various passions, can neither be obtained nor enjoyed, without exerting ourselves in such and such manners: but by thus exerting ourselves, we obtain and enjoy these objects, in which our natural good consists; or by this means God gives us the possession and enjoyment of them. I know not, that we have any one kind or degree of enjoyment, but by the means of our own actions. And by prudence and care, we may, for the most part, pass our days in tolerable ease and quiet: or, on the contrary, we may, by rashness, ungoverned passion, wilfulness, or even by negligence, make ourselves as miserable as ever we please. And many do please to make themselves extremely miserable, i. e. to do what they know beforehand will render them so. They follow those ways, the fruit of which they know, by instruction, example, experience, will be disgrace, and poverty, and sickness, and untimely death. This every one observes to be the general course of things; though it is to be allowed, we cannot find by experience, that all our sufferings are owing to our own follies.

Why the Author of Nature does not give his

creatures promiscuously such and such perceptions, without regard to their behaviour; why he does not make them happy without the instrumentality of their own actions, and prevent their bringing any sufferings upon themselves; is another matter. Perhaps there may be some impossibilities in the nature of things, which we are unacquainted with [i]. Or less happiness, it may be, would upon the whole be produced by such a method of conduct, than is by the present. Or perhaps Divine goodness, with which, if I mistake not, we make very free in our speculations, may not be a bare single disposition to produce happiness; but a disposition to make the good, the faithful, the honest man happy. Perhaps an infinitely perfect Mind may be pleased, with seeing his creatures behave suitably to the nature which he has given them; to the relations which he has placed them in to each other; and to that, which they stand in to himself: that relation to himself, which, during their existence, is even necessary, and which is the most important one of all: perhaps, I say, an infinitely perfect Mind may be pleased with this moral piety of moral agents, in and for itself; as well as upon account of its being essentially conducive to the happiness of his creation. Or the whole end, for which God made, and thus governs the world, may be utterly beyond the reach of our faculties: there may be somewhat in it as impossible for us to have any conception of, as for a blind man to have a conception of colours. But however this be, it is certain matter of universal experience, that the general method of Divine administration is, forewarning us, or giving us capacities to foresee, with more or less clearness, that if we act so and so, we

[i] Part I. chap. vii.

shall have such enjoyments, if so and so, such sufferings; and giving us those enjoyments, and making us feel those sufferings, in consequence of our actions.

"But all this is to be ascribed to the general course of nature." True. This is the very thing which I am observing. It is to be ascribed to the general course of nature: i. e. not surely to the words or ideas, *course of nature;* but to him who appointed it, and put things into it: or to a course of operation, from its uniformity or constancy, called natural [k]; and which necessarily implies an operating agent. For when men find themselves necessitated to confess an Author of Nature, or that God is the natural governor of the world; they must not deny this again, because his government is uniform; they must not deny that he does things at all, because he does them constantly; because the effects of his acting are permanent, whether his acting be so or not; though there is no reason to think it is not. In short, every man, in every thing he does, naturally acts upon the forethought and apprehension of avoiding evil or obtaining good: and if the natural course of things be the appointment of God, and our natural faculties of knowledge and experience are given us by him; then the good and bad consequences which follow our actions, are his appointment, and our foresight of those consequences, is a warning given us by him, how we are to act.

"Is the pleasure then, naturally accompanying every particular gratification of passion, intended to put us upon gratifying ourselves in every such particular instance, and as a reward to us for so doing?" No certainly. Nor is it to be said, that our eyes were naturally intended to give us the sight of each

[k] P. 32. 33.

particular object, to which they do or can extend; objects which are destructive of them, or which, for any other reason, it may become us to turn our eyes from. Yet there is no doubt, but that our eyes were intended for us to see with. So neither is there any doubt, but that the foreseen pleasures and pains belonging to the passions, were intended, in general, to induce mankind to act in such and such manners.

Now from this general observation, obvious to every one, that God has given us to understand, he has appointed satisfaction and delight to be the consequence of our acting in one manner, and pain and uneasiness of our acting in another, and of our not acting at all; and that we find the consequences, which we were beforehand informed of, uniformly to follow; we may learn, that we are at present actually under his government in the strictest and most proper sense; in such a sense, as that he rewards and punishes us for our actions. An Author of Nature being supposed, it is not so much a deduction of reason, as a matter of experience, that we are thus under his government: under his government, in the same sense, as we are under the government of civil magistrates. Because the annexing pleasure to some actions, and pain to others, in our power to do or forbear, and giving notice of this appointment beforehand to those whom it concerns; is the proper formal notion of government. Whether the pleasure or pain which thus follows upon our behaviour, be owing to the Author of Nature's acting upon us every moment which we feel it; or to his having at once contrived and executed his own part in the plan of the world; makes no alteration as to the matter before us. For if civil magistrates could make the sanctions of their laws take place, without interposing at all, after they had passed them; without a trial, and the formalities of an execution: if they were able to make their laws execute themselves, or every offender to execute them upon himself; we should be just in the same sense under their government then, as we are now; but in a much higher degree, and more perfect manner. Vain is the ridicule with which, one foresees, some persons will divert themselves, upon finding lesser pains considered as instances of Divine punishment. There is no possibility of answering or evading the general thing here intended, without denying all final causes. For final causes being admitted, the pleasures and pains now mentioned must be admitted too as instances of them. And if they are; if God annexes delight to some actions, and uneasiness to others, with an apparent design to induce us to act so and so; then he not only dispenses happiness and misery, but also rewards and punishes actions. If, for example, the pain which we feel, upon doing what tends to the destruction of our bodies, suppose upon too near approaches to fire, or upon wounding ourselves, be appointed by the Author of Nature to prevent our doing what thus tends to our destruction; this is altogether as much an instance of his punishing our actions, and consequently of our being under his government, as declaring by a voice from heaven, that if we acted so, he would inflict such pain upon us, and inflicting it, whether it be greater or less.

Thus we find, that the true notion or conception of the Author of Nature, is that of a master or governor, prior to the consideration of his moral attributes. The fact of our case, which we find by experience, is, that he actually exercises dominion or government over us at present, by rewarding and punishing us for our actions, in as strict and proper a sense of these words, and even in the same sense, as children, servants, subjects, are rewarded and punished by those who govern them.

And thus the whole analogy of Nature, the whole present course of things, most fully shews, that there is nothing incredible in the general doctrine of religion, that God will reward and punish men for their actions hereafter: nothing incredible, I mean, arising out of the notion of rewarding and punishing. For the whole course of nature is a present instance of his exercising that government over us, which implies in it rewarding and punishing.

BUT as Divine punishment is what men chiefly object against, and are most unwilling to allow; it may be proper to mention some circumstances in the natural course of punishments at present, which are analogous to what religion teaches us concerning a future state of punishment; indeed so analogous, that as they add a farther credibility to it, so they cannot but raise a most serious apprehension of it in those who will attend to them.

It has been now observed, that such and such miseries naturally follow such and such actions of imprudence and wilfulness, as well as actions more commonly and more distinctly considered as vicious; and that these consequences, when they may be foreseen, are properly natural punishments annexed to such actions. For the general thing here insisted upon, is, not that we see a great deal of misery in the world, but a great deal which men bring upon themselves by their own behaviour, which they might have foreseen and avoided. Now the circumstances of these natural punishments, particularly deserving our attention, are such as these: That oftentimes they follow, or are inflicted in consequence of, actions, which procure many present advantages, and are accompanied with much present pleasure; for instance, sickness and untimely death is the consequence of intemperance, though accompanied with the highest mirth and jollity: That these punishments are often much greater, than the advantages or pleasures obtained by the actions, of which they are the punishments or consequences: That though we may imagine a constitution of nature, in which these natural punishments, which are in fact to follow, would follow, immediately upon such actions being done, or very soon after; we find on the contrary in our world, that they are often delayed a great while, sometimes even till long after the actions occasioning them are forgot; so that the constitution of nature is such, that delay of punishment is no sort nor degree of presumption of final impunity: That after such delay, these natural punishments or miseries often come, not by degrees, but suddenly, with violence, and at once: however, the chief misery often does: That as certainty of such distant misery following such actions, is never afforded persons; so perhaps during the actions, they have seldom a distinct full expectation of its following[1]: and many times the case is only thus, that they see in general, or may see, the credibility, that intemperance, suppose, will bring after it diseases; civil crimes, civil punishments; when yet the real probability often is, that they shall escape: but things notwithstanding take their destined course, and the misery inevitably follows at its appointed time, in very many of these cases.

[1] See part II. chap. vi.

Thus also though youth may be alleged as an excuse for rashness and folly, as being naturally thoughtless, and not clearly foreseeing all the consequences of being untractable and profligate; this does not hinder, but that these consequences follow, and are grievously felt, throughout the whole course of mature life. Habits contracted even in that age, are often utter ruin: and men's success in the world, not only in the common sense of worldly success, but their real happiness and misery, depends, in a great degree, and in various ways, upon the manner in which they pass their youth; which consequences they for the most part neglect to consider, and perhaps seldom can properly be said to believe, beforehand. It requires also to be mentioned, that in numberless cases, the natural course of things affords us opportunities for procuring advantages to ourselves at certain times, which we cannot procure when we will; nor ever recall the opportunities, if we have neglected them. Indeed the general course of nature is an example of this. If, during the opportunity of youth, persons are indocile and self-willed; they inevitably suffer in their future life, for want of those acquirements, which they neglected the natural season of attaining. If the husbandman lets his seedtime pass without sowing, the whole year is lost to him beyond recovery. In like manner, though after men have been guilty of folly and extravagance *up to a certain degree*, it is often in their power, for instance, to retrieve their affairs, to recover their health and character; at least in good measure: yet real reformation is, in many cases, of no avail at all towards preventing the miseries, poverty, sickness, infamy, naturally annexed to folly and extravagance *exceeding that degree*.

There is a certain bound to imprudence and misbehaviour, which being transgressed, there remains no place for repentance in the natural course of things. It is further very much to be remarked, that neglects from inconsiderateness, want of attention[m], not looking about us to see what we have to do, are often attended with consequences altogether as dreadful, as any active misbehaviour, from the most extravagant passion. And lastly, civil government being natural, the punishments of it are so too: and some of these punishments are capital: as the effects of a dissolute course of pleasure are often mortal. So that many natural punishments are final[n] to him, who incurs them, if considered

[m] Part II. chap. vi.

[n] The general consideration of a future state of punishment, most evidently belongs to the subject of Natural Religion. But if any of these reflections should be thought to relate more peculiarly to this doctrine, as taught in Scripture; the reader is desired to observe, that Gentile writers, both moralists and poets, speak of the future punishment of the wicked, both as to the duration and degree of it, in a like manner of expression and of description, as the Scripture does. So that all which can positively be asserted to be matter of mere Revelation, with regard to this doctrine, seems to be, that the great distinction between the righteous and the wicked, shall be made at the end of this world; that each shall *then* receive according to his deserts. Reason did, as it well might, conclude that it should, finally and upon the whole, be well with the righteous, and ill with the wicked: but it could not be determined upon any principles of reason, whether human creatures might not have been appointed to pass through other states of life and being, before that distributive justice should finally and effectually take place. Revelation teaches us, that the next state of things after the present is appointed for the execution of this justice; that it shall be no longer delayed; but *the mystery of God*, the great mystery of his suffering vice and confusion to prevail, *shall then be finished;* and he will *take to him his great power, and will reign,* by rendering to every one according to his works.

only in his temporal capacity: and seem inflicted by natural appointment, either to remove the offender out of the way of being further mischievous; or as an example, though frequently a disregarded one, to those who are left behind.

These things are not, what we call accidental, or to be met with only now and then; but they are things of every day's experience: they proceed from general laws, very general ones, by which God governs the world, in the natural course of his providence. And they are so analogous to what Religion teaches us concerning the future punishment of the wicked, so much of a piece with it, that both would naturally be expressed in the very same words, and manner of description. In the book of *Proverbs*[o], for instance, Wisdom is introduced, as frequenting the most public places of resort, and as rejected when she offers herself as the natural appointed guide of human life. *How long*, speaking to those who are passing through it, *how long, ye simple ones, will ye love folly? and the scorners delight in their scorning, and fools hate knowledge? Turn ye at my reproof: behold, I will pour out my spirit upon you, I will make known my words unto you.* But upon being neglected, *Because I have called, and ye refused; I have stretched out my hand, and no man regarded; but ye have set at nought all my counsel, and would none of my reproof: I also will laugh at your calamity; I will mock when your fear cometh; when your fear cometh as desolation, and your destruction cometh as a whirlwind; when distress and anguish cometh upon you. Then shall they call upon me, but I will not answer; they shall seek me early, but they shall not*

[o] Chap. i.

find me. This passage, every one sees, is poetical, and some parts of it are highly figurative; but their meaning is obvious. And the thing intended is expressed more literally in the following words; *For that they hated knowledge, and did not choose the fear of the Lord:—therefore shall they eat of the fruit of their own way, and be filled with their own devices. For the security of the simple shall slay them, and the prosperity of fools shall destroy them.* And the whole passage is so equally applicable, to what we experience in the present world, concerning the consequences of men's actions, and to what Religion teaches us is to be expected in another, that it may be questioned which of the two was principally intended.

Indeed when one has been recollecting the proper proofs of a future state of rewards and punishments, nothing methinks can give one so sensible an apprehension of the latter, or representation of it to the mind; as observing, that after the many disregarded checks, admonitions and warnings, which people meet with in the ways of vice and folly and extravagance; warnings from their very nature; from the examples of others; from the lesser inconveniences which they bring upon themselves; from the instructions of wise and virtuous men: after these have been long despised, scorned, ridiculed: after the chief bad consequences, temporal consequences, of their follies, have been delayed for a great while; at length they break in irresistibly, like an armed force: repentance is too late to relieve, and can serve only to aggravate, their distress: the case is become desperate: and poverty and sickness, remorse and anguish, infamy and death, the effects of their own doings, overwhelm them, beyond possibility of remedy or escape. This is an account of what is in fact the general constitution of nature.

It is not in any sort meant, that according to what appears at present of the natural course of things, men are always uniformly punished in proportion to their misbehaviour: but that there are very many instances of misbehaviour punished in the several ways now mentioned, and very dreadful instances too; sufficient to shew what the laws of the universe may admit; and, if thoroughly considered, sufficient fully to answer all objections against the credibility of a future state of punishments, from any imaginations, that the frailty of our nature and external temptations, almost annihilate the guilt of human vices: as well as objections of another sort; from necessity; from suppositions, that the will of an infinite Being cannot be contradicted; or that he must be incapable of offence and provocation[q].

Reflections of this kind are not without their terrors to serious persons, the most free from enthusiasm, and of the greatest strength of mind; but it is fit things be stated and considered as they really are. And there is, in the present age, a certain fearlessness, with regard to what may be hereafter under the government of God, which nothing but an universally acknowledged demonstration on the side of atheism can justify; and which makes it quite necessary, that men be reminded, and if possible made to feel, that there is no sort of ground for being thus presumptuous, even upon the most sceptical principles. For, may it not be said of any person upon his being born into the world, he may behave so, as to be of no service to it, but by being made an example of the woful effects of vice and

[q] See chap. iv. and vi.

folly? That he may, as any one may, if he will, incur an infamous execution, from the hands of civil justice; or in some other course of extravagance shorten his days; or bring upon himself infamy and diseases worse than death? So that it had been better for him, even with regard to the present world, that he had never been born. And is there any pretence of reason, for people to think themselves secure, and talk as if they had certain proof, that, let them act as licentiously as they will, there can be nothing analogous to this, with regard to a future and more general interest, under the providence and government of the same God?

CHAP. III.

Of the moral government of God.

As the manifold appearances of design and of final causes, in the constitution of the world, prove it to be the work of an intelligent Mind; so the particular final causes of pleasure and pain distributed amongst his creatures, prove that they are under his government; what may be called his natural government of creatures endued with sense and reason. This, however, implies somewhat more than seems usually attended to, when we speak of God's natural government of the world. It implies government of the very same kind with that, which a master exercises over his servants, or a civil magistrate over his subjects. These latter instances of final causes, as really prove an intelligent *Governor* of the world, in the sense now mentioned, and before[a] distinctly treated

[a] Chap. ii.

of; as any other instances of final causes prove an intelligent Maker of it.

But this alone does not appear at first sight to determine any thing certainly, concerning the moral character of the Author of Nature, considered in this relation of governor; does not ascertain his government to be moral, or prove that he is the righteous judge of the world. Moral government consists, not barely in rewarding and punishing men for their actions, which the most tyrannical person may do: but in rewarding the righteous, and punishing the wicked; in rendering to men according to their actions, considered as good or evil. And the perfection of moral government consists in doing this, with regard to all intelligent creatures, in an exact proportion to their personal merits or demerits.

Some men seem to think the only character of the Author of Nature to be that of simple absolute benevolence. This, considered as a principle of action and infinite in degree, is a disposition to produce the greatest possible happiness, without regard to persons' behaviour, otherwise than as such regard would produce higher degrees of it. And supposing this to be the only character of God, veracity and justice in him would be nothing but benevolence conducted by wisdom. Now surely this ought not to be asserted, unless it can be proved; for we should speak with cautious reverence upon such a subject. And whether it can be proved or no, is not the thing here to be inquired into; but whether in the constitution and conduct of the world, a righteous government be not discernibly planned out: which necessarily implies a righteous governor. There may possibly be in the creation, beings, to whom the Author of Nature manifests himself under this most amiable of all characters, this of infinite absolute benevolence; for it is the most amiable, supposing it not, as perhaps it is not, incompatible with justice: but he manifests himself to us under the character of a righteous governor. He may, consistently with this, be simply and absolutely benevolent, in the sense now explained: but he is, for he has given us a proof in the constitution and conduct of the world that he is, a governor over servants, as he rewards and punishes us for our actions. And in the constitution and conduct of it, he may also have given, besides the reason of the thing, and the natural presages of conscience, clear and distinct intimations, that his government is righteous or moral: clear to such as think the nature of it deserving their attention; and yet not to every careless person, who casts a transient reflection upon the subject[b].

But it is particularly to be observed, that the Divine government, which we experience ourselves under in the present state, taken alone, is allowed not to be the perfection of moral government. And yet this by no means hinders, but that there may be somewhat, be it more or less, truly moral in it. A righteous government may plainly appear to be carried on to some degree: enough to give us the apprehension that it shall be completed, or carried on

[b] The objections against Religion, from the evidence of it not being universal, nor so strong as might possibly have been, may be urged against natural Religion, as well as against revealed. And therefore the consideration of them belongs to the first part of this Treatise, as well as the second. But as these objections are chiefly urged against revealed religion, I chose to consider them in the second part. And the answer to them there, chap. vi. as urged against Christianity, being almost equally applicable to them as urged against the Religion of Nature; to avoid repetition, the reader is referred to that chapter.

to that degree of perfection which religion teaches us it shall; but which cannot appear, till much more of the Divine administration be seen, than can in the present life. And the design of this chapter is to inquire, how far this is the case: how far, over and above the moral nature[c] which God has given us, and our natural notion of him as righteous governor of those his creatures, to whom he has given this nature[d]; I say how far besides this, the principles and beginnings of a moral government over the world may be discerned, notwithstanding and amidst all the confusion and disorder of it.

Now one might mention here, what has been often urged with great force, that in general, less uneasiness and more satisfaction, are the natural consequences[e] of a virtuous than of a vicious course of life, in the present state, as an instance of a moral government established in nature; an instance of it, collected from experience and present matter of fact. But it must be owned a thing of difficulty to weigh and balance pleasures and uneasinesses, each amongst themselves, and also against each other, so as to make an estimate with any exactness, of the overplus of happiness on the side of virtue. And it is not impossible, that, amidst the infinite disorders of the world, there may be exceptions to the happiness of virtue; even with regard to those persons, whose course of life from their youth up has been blameless; and more with regard to those, who have gone on for some time in the ways of vice, and have afterwards reformed. For suppose an instance of the latter case; a person with his passions inflamed, his natural faculty of self-government impaired by habits

[c] Dissertation II.   [d] Chap. vi.
[e] See Lord Shaftesbury's Inquiry concerning Virtue, part II.

of indulgence, and with all his vices about him, like so many harpies, craving for their accustomed gratification: who can say how long it might be, before such a person would find more satisfaction in the reasonableness and present good consequences of virtue, than difficulties and self-denial in the restraints of it? Experience also shews, that men can, to a great degree, get over their sense of shame, so as that by professing themselves to be without principle, and avowing even direct villainy, they can support themselves against the infamy of it. But as the ill actions of any one will probably be more talked of, and oftener thrown in his way, upon his reformation; so the infamy of them will be much more felt, after the natural sense of virtue and of honour is recovered. Uneasinesses of this kind ought indeed to be put to the account of former vices: yet it will be said, they are in part the consequences of reformation. Still I am far from allowing it doubtful, whether virtue, upon the whole, be happier than vice in the present world. But if it were, yet the beginnings of a righteous administration may beyond all question be found in nature, if we will attentively inquire after them. And,

I. In whatever manner the notion of God's moral government over the world might be treated, if it did not appear, whether he were in a proper sense our governor at all: yet when it is certain matter of experience, that he does manifest himself to us under the character of a governor, in the sense explained [f]; it must deserve to be considered, whether there be not reason to apprehend, that he may be a righteous or moral governor. Since it appears to be fact, that God does govern mankind by the method

[f] Chap. ii.

of rewards and punishments, according to some settled rules of distribution; it is surely a question to be asked, What presumption is there against his finally rewarding and punishing them according to this particular rule, namely, as they act reasonably or unreasonably, virtuously or viciously? since rendering men happy or miserable by this rule, certainly falls in, much more falls in, with our natural apprehensions and sense of things, than doing so by any other rule whatever: since rewarding and punishing actions by any other rule, would appear much harder to be accounted for, by minds formed as he has formed ours. Be the evidence of religion then more or less clear, the expectation which it raises in us, that the righteous shall, upon the whole, be happy, and the wicked miserable, cannot however possibly be considered as absurd or chimerical; because it is no more than an expectation, that a method of government already begun, shall be carried on, the method of rewarding and punishing actions; and shall be carried on by a particular rule, which unavoidably appears to us at first sight more natural than any other, the rule which we call distributive justice. Nor,

II. Ought it to be entirely passed over, that tranquillity, satisfaction, and external advantages, being the natural consequences of prudent management of ourselves, and our affairs; and rashness, profligate negligence, and wilful folly, bringing after them many inconveniences and sufferings; these afford instances of a right constitution of nature: as the correction of children, for their own sakes, and by way of example, when they run into danger or hurt themselves, is a part of right education. And thus, that God governs the world by general fixed laws, that he has endued us with capacities of reflecting upon this constitution of things, and foreseeing the good and bad consequences of our behaviour; plainly implies some sort of moral government: since from such a constitution of things it cannot but follow, that prudence and imprudence, which are of the nature of virtue and vice g, must be, as they are, respectively rewarded and punished.

III. From the natural course of things, vicious actions are, to a great degree, actually punished as mischievous to society; and besides punishment actually inflicted upon this account, there is also the fear and apprehension of it in those persons, whose crimes have rendered them obnoxious to it, in case of a discovery; this state of fear being itself often a very considerable punishment. The natural fear and apprehension of it too, which restrains from such crimes, is a declaration of nature against them. It is necessary to the very being of society, that vices destructive of it, should be punished *as being so;* the vices of falsehood, injustice, cruelty: which punishment therefore is as natural as society; and so is an instance of a kind of moral government, naturally established, and actually taking place. And, since the certain natural course of things is the conduct of Providence or the government of God, though carried on by the instrumentality of men; the observation here made amounts to this, that mankind find themselves placed by him in such circumstances, as that they are unavoidably accountable for their behaviour, and are often punished, and sometimes rewarded under his government, in the view of their being mischievous, or eminently beneficial to society.

If it be objected that good actions, and such as are beneficial to society, are often punished, as in

g See Dissert. II.

the case of persecution and in other cases; and that ill and mischievous actions are often rewarded: it may be answered distinctly; first, that this is in no sort necessary, and consequently not natural, in the sense in which it is necessary, and therefore natural, that ill or mischievous actions should be punished: and in the next place, that good actions are never punished, considered as beneficial to society, nor ill actions rewarded, under the view of their being hurtful to it. So that it stands good, without any thing on the side of vice to be set over against it, that the Author of Nature has as truly directed, that vicious actions, considered as mischievous to society, should be punished, and put mankind under a necessity of thus punishing them; as he has directed and necessitated us to preserve our lives by food.

IV. In the natural course of things, virtue *as such* is actually rewarded, and vice *as such* punished: which seems to afford an instance or example, not only of government, but of moral government, begun and established; moral in the strictest sense; though not in that perfection of degree, which religion teaches us to expect. In order to see this more clearly, we must distinguish between actions themselves, and that quality ascribed to them, which we call virtuous or vicious. The gratification itself of every natural passion must be attended with delight: and acquisitions of fortune, however made, are acquisitions of the means or materials of enjoyment. An action then, by which any natural passion is gratified or fortune acquired, procures delight or advantage; abstracted from all consideration of the morality of such action. Consequently, the pleasure or advantage in this case, is gained by the action itself, not by the morality, the virtuousness or viciousness of it; though it be, perhaps, virtuous or vicious. Thus, to say such an action or course of behaviour, procured such pleasure or advantage, or brought on such inconvenience and pain, is quite a different thing from saying, that such good or bad effect was owing to the virtue or vice of such action or behaviour. In one case, an action abstracted from all moral consideration, produced its effect: in the other case, for it will appear that there are such cases, the morality of the action, the action under a moral consideration, i.e. the virtuousness or viciousness of it, produced the effect. Now I say virtue as such, naturally procures considerable advantages to the virtuous, and vice as such, naturally occasions great inconvenience and even misery to the vicious, in very many instances. The immediate effects of virtue and vice upon the mind and temper, are to be mentioned as instances of it. Vice as such is naturally attended with some sort of uneasiness, and, not uncommonly, with great disturbance and apprehension. That inward feeling, which, respecting lesser matters, and in familiar speech, we call being vexed with oneself, and in matters of importance and in more serious language, remorse; is an uneasiness naturally arising from an action of a man's own, reflected upon by himself as wrong, unreasonable, faulty, i.e. vicious in greater or less degrees: and this manifestly is a different feeling from that uneasiness, which arises from a sense of mere loss or harm. What is more common, than to hear a man lamenting an accident or event, and adding——but however he has the satisfaction that he cannot blame himself for it; or on the contrary, that he has the uneasiness of being sensible it was his own doing? Thus also the disturbance and fear, which often follow upon a man's having done an injury, arise from a sense of his being blameworthy; otherwise there would, in many cases, be no ground of disturbance, nor any reason to fear resentment or shame. On the other hand, inward security and peace, and a mind open to the several gratifications of life, are the natural attendants of innocence and virtue. To which must be added the complacency, satisfaction, and even joy of heart, which accompany the exercise, the real exercise, of gratitude, friendship, benevolence.

And here, I think, ought to be mentioned, the fears of future punishment, and peaceful hopes of a better life, in those who fully believe, or have any serious apprehension of religion: because these hopes and fears are present uneasiness and satisfaction to the mind, and cannot be got rid of by great part of the world, even by men who have thought most thoroughly upon that subject of religion. And no one can say, how considerable this uneasiness and satisfaction may be, or what upon the whole it may amount to.

In the next place comes in the consideration, that all honest and good men are disposed to befriend honest good men as such, and to discountenance the vicious as such, and do so in some degree; indeed in a considerable degree: from which favour and discouragement cannot but arise considerable advantage and inconvenience. And though the generality of the world have little regard to the morality of their own actions, and may be supposed to have less to that of others, when they themselves are not concerned; yet let any one be known to be a man of virtue, some how or other he will be favoured, and good offices will be done him, from regard to his character, without remote views, occasionally, and in some low degree, I think, by the generality of the world, as it happens to come in their way. Public honours too and advantages are the natural consequences, are sometimes at least the consequences in fact, of virtuous actions; of eminent justice, fidelity, charity, love to our country, considered in the view of being virtuous. And sometimes even death itself, often infamy and external inconveniences, are the public consequences of vice as vice. For instance, the sense which mankind have of tyranny, injustice, oppression, additional to the mere feeling or fear of misery, has doubtless been instrumental in bringing about revolutions, which make a figure even in the history of the world. For it is plain, men resent injuries as implying faultiness, and retaliate, not merely under the notion of having received harm, but of having received wrong; and they have this resentment in behalf of others, as well as of themselves. So likewise even the generality are, in some degree, grateful and disposed to return good offices, not merely because such an one has been the occasion of good to them, but under the view, that such good offices implied kind intention and good desert in the doer. To all this may be added two or three particular things, which many persons will think frivolous; but to me nothing appears so, which at all comes in towards determining a question of such importance, as, whether there be, or be not, a moral institution of government, in the strictest sense moral, *visibly* established and begun in nature. The particular things are these: That in domestic government, which is doubtless natural, children and others also are very generally punished for falsehood and injustice and ill-behaviour, as such, and rewarded for the contrary; which are instances where veracity, and justice, and right behaviour as such, are naturally enforced by rewards and punishments, whether more or less considerable in degree: That, though civil government be supposed to take cognizance of actions in no other view than as prejudicial to society, without respect to the immorality of them; yet as such actions are immoral, so the sense which men have of the immorality of them, very greatly contributes, in different ways, to bring offenders to justice: and that entire absence of all crime and guilt in the moral sense, when plainly appearing, will almost of course procure, and circumstances of aggravated guilt prevent, a remission of the penalties annexed to civil crimes, in many cases, though by no means in all.

Upon the whole then, besides the good and bad effects of virtue and vice upon men's own minds, the course of the world does, in some measure, turn upon the approbation and disapprobation of them as such, in others. The sense of well and ill doing, the presages of conscience, the love of good characters and dislike of bad ones, honour, shame, resentment, gratitude; all these, considered in themselves, and in their effects, do afford manifest real instances of virtue as such naturally favoured, and of vice as such discountenanced, more or less, in the daily course of human life; in every age, in every relation, in every general circumstance of it. That God has given us a moral nature[h], may most justly be urged as a proof of our being under his moral government: but that he has placed us in a condition, which gives this nature, as one may speak, scope to operate, and in which it does unavoidably

[h] See Dissert. II.

operate ; i. e. influence mankind to act, so as thus to favour and reward virtue, and discountenance and punish vice; this is not the same, but a further, additional proof of his moral government: for it is an instance of it. The first is a proof, that he will finally favour and support virtue effectually: the second is an example of his favouring and supporting it at present, in some degree.

If a more distinct inquiry be made, whence it arises, that virtue as such is often rewarded, and vice as such is punished, and this rule never inverted : it will be found to proceed, in part, immediately from the moral nature itself, which God has given us; and also in part, from his having given us, together with this nature, so great a power over each other's happiness and misery. For *first*, it is certain, that peace and delight, in some degree and upon some occasions, is the necessary and present effect of virtuous practice ; an effect arising immediately from that constitution of our nature. We are so made, that well-doing as such gives us satisfaction, at least, in some instances ; ill-doing as such, in none. And *secondly*, from our moral nature, joined with God's having put our happiness and misery in many respects in each other's power, it cannot but be, that vice as such, some kinds and instances of it at least, will be infamous, and men will be disposed to punish it as in itself detestable ; and the villain will by no means be able always to avoid feeling that infamy, any more than he will be able to escape this further punishment, which mankind will be disposed to inflict upon him, under the notion of his deserving it. But there can be nothing on the side of vice, to answer this ; because there is nothing in the human mind contradictory, as the logicians speak, to virtue. For virtue consists in a regard to what is right and reasonable, as being so; in a regard to veracity, justice, charity, in themselves: and there is surely no such thing, as a like natural regard to falsehood, injustice, cruelty. If it be thought, that there are instances of an approbation of vice, as such, in itself, and for its own sake, (though it does not appear to me, that there is any such thing at all; but supposing there be,) it is evidently monstrous: as much so, as the most acknowledged perversion of any passion whatever. Such instances of perversion then being left out, as merely imaginary, or, however, unnatural; it must follow, from the frame of our nature, and from our condition, in the respects now described, that vice cannot at all be, and virtue cannot but be, favoured as such by others, upon some occasions, and happy in itself, in some degree. For what is here insisted upon, is not the degree in which virtue and vice are thus distinguished, but only the thing itself, that they are so in some degree; though the whole good and bad effect of virtue and vice as such, is not inconsiderable in degree. But that they must be thus distinguished in some degree, is in a manner necessary: it is matter of fact of daily experience, even in the greatest confusion of human affairs.

It is not pretended but that in the natural course of things, happiness and misery appear to be distributed by other rules, than only the personal merit and demerit of characters. They may sometimes be distributed by way of mere discipline. There may be the wisest and best reasons, why the world should be governed by general laws, from whence such promiscuous distribution perhaps must follow; and also why our happiness and misery should be put in each other's power, in the degree which they are. And these things, as in general they contribute to the rewarding virtue and punishing vice, as such: so they often contribute also, not to the inversion of this, which is impossible; but to the rendering persons prosperous, though wicked; afflicted, though righteous; and, which is worse, to the *rewarding some actions*, though vicious, and *punishing other actions*, though virtuous. But all this cannot drown the voice of Nature in the conduct of Providence, plainly declaring itself for virtue, by way of distinction from vice, and preference to it. For our being so constituted as that virtue and vice are thus naturally favoured and discountenanced, rewarded and punished respectively as such, is an intuitive proof of the intent of Nature, that it should be so: otherwise the constitution of our mind, from which it thus immediately and directly proceeds, would be absurd. But it cannot be said, because virtuous actions are sometimes punished, and vicious actions rewarded, that Nature intended it. For, though this great disorder is brought about, as all actions are done, by means of some natural passion; yet *this may be*, as it undoubtedly is, brought about by the perversion of such passion, implanted in us for other, and those very good purposes. And indeed these other and good purposes, even of every passion, may be clearly seen.

We have then a declaration, in some degree of present effect, from Him who is supreme in Nature, which side He is of, or what part He takes: a declaration for virtue, and against vice. So far therefore as a man is true to virtue, to veracity and justice, to equity and charity, and the right of the case, in whatever he is concerned; so far he is on the side of the Divine administration, and cooperates with it: and from hence, to such a man, arises naturally a secret satisfaction and sense of security, and implicit hope of somewhat further. And,

V. This hope is confirmed by the necessary tendencies of virtue, which, though not of present effect, yet are at present discernible in nature; and so afford an instance of somewhat moral in the essential constitution of it. There is, in the nature of things, a tendency in virtue and vice to produce the good and bad effects now mentioned, in a greater degree than they do in fact produce them. For instance; good and bad men would be much more rewarded and punished as such, were it not, that justice is often artificially eluded, that characters are not known, and many, who would thus favour virtue and discourage vice, are hindered from doing so by accidental causes. These tendencies of virtue and vice are obvious with regard to *individuals*. But it may require more particularly to be considered, that power in a *society*, by being under the direction of virtue, naturally increases, and has a necessary tendency to prevail over opposite power, not under the direction of it; in like manner as power, by being under the direction of reason, increases, and has a tendency to prevail over brute force. There are several brute creatures of equal, and several of superior strength, to that of men; and possibly the sum of the whole strength of brutes may be greater than that of mankind: but reason gives us the advantage and superiority over them; and thus man is the acknowledged governing animal upon the earth. Nor is this superiority considered by any as accidental; but as what reason has a tendency, in the nature of the thing, to obtain. And yet perhaps difficulties may be raised about the meaning, as well as the truth, of the assertion, that virtue has the like tendency.

To obviate these difficulties, let us see more distinctly, how the case stands with regard to reason; which is so readily acknowledged to have this advantageous tendency. Suppose then two or three men, of the best and most improved understanding, in a desolate open plain, attacked by ten times the number of beasts of prey; would their reason secure them the victory in this unequal combat? Power then, though joined with reason, and under its direction, cannot be expected to prevail over opposite power, though merely brutal, unless the one bears some proportion to the other. Again: put the imaginary case, that rational and irrational creatures were of like external shape and manner: it is certain, before there were opportunities for the first to distinguish each other, to separate from their adversaries, and to form an union among themselves, they might be upon a level, or in several respects upon great disadvantage; though united they might be vastly superior: since union is of such efficacy, that ten men united, might be able to accomplish, what ten thousand of the same natural strength and understanding wholly ununited, could not. In this case then, brute force might more than maintain its ground against reason, for want of union among the rational creatures. Or suppose a number of men to land upon an island inhabited only by wild beasts; a number of men who, by the regulations of civil government, the inventions of art, and the experience of some years, could they be preserved so long, would be really sufficient to subdue the wild beasts, and to preserve themselves in security from them: yet a conjuncture of accidents might give such advantage to the irrational animals, as that they might at once overpower, and even extirpate, the whole species of rational ones. Length of time then, proper scope and opportunities, for reason to exert itself, may be absolutely necessary to its prevailing over brute force. Further still: there are many instances of brutes succeeding in attempts, which they could not have undertaken, had not their irrational nature rendered them incapable of foreseeing the danger of such attempts, or the fury of passion hindered their attending to it; and there are instances of reason and real prudence preventing men's undertaking what, it hath appeared afterwards, they might have succeeded in by a lucky rashness. And in certain conjunctures, ignorance and folly, weakness and discord, may have their advantages. So that rational animals have not necessarily the superiority over irrational ones: but, how improbable soever it may be, it is evidently possible, that in some globes the latter may be superior. And were the former wholly at variance and disunited, by false self-interest and envy, by treachery and injustice, and consequent rage and malice against each other, whilst the latter were firmly united among themselves by instinct; this might greatly contribute to the introducing such an inverted order of things. For every one would consider it as inverted: since reason has, in the nature of it, a tendency to prevail over brute force; notwithstanding the possibility it may not prevail, and the necessity, which there is, of many concurring circumstances to render it prevalent.

Now I say, virtue in a society has a like tendency to procure superiority and additional power: whether this power be considered as the means of security from opposite power, or of obtaining other advantages. And it has this tendency, by rendering public good, an object and end, to every member of the society; by putting every one upon consideration and diligence, recollection and self-government, both in order to see what is the most effectual method, and also in order to perform their proper part, for obtaining and preserving it; by uniting a society within itself, and so increasing its strength; and, which is particularly to be mentioned, uniting it by means of veracity and justice. For as these last are principal bonds of union, so benevolence or public spirit, undirected, unrestrained by them, is, nobody knows what.

And suppose the invisible world, and the invisible dispensations of Providence, to be, in any sort, analogous to what appears: or that both together make up one uniform scheme, the two parts of which, the part which we see, and that which is beyond our observation, are analogous to each other: then, there must be a like natural tendency in the derived power, throughout the universe, under the direction of virtue, to prevail in general over that, which is not under its direction; as there is in reason, derived reason in the universe, to prevail over brute force. But then, in order to the prevalence of virtue, or that it may actually produce, what it has a tendency to produce; the like concurrences are necessary, as are, to the prevalence of reason. There must be some proportion, between the natural power or force which is, and that which is not, under the direction of virtue: there must be sufficient length of time; for the complete success of virtue, as of reason, cannot, from the nature of the thing, be otherwise than gradual: there must be, as one may speak, a fair field of trial, a stage large and extensive enough, proper occasions and opportunities, for the virtuous to join together, to exert themselves against lawless force, and to reap the fruit of their united labours. Now indeed it is to be hoped, that the disproportion between the good and bad, even here on earth, is not so great, but that the former have natural power sufficient to their prevailing to a considerable degree, if circumstances would permit this power to be united. For, much less, very much less, power under the direction of virtue, would prevail over much greater not under the direction of it. However, good men over the face of the earth cannot unite; as for other reasons, so because they cannot be sufficiently ascertained of each other's characters. And the known course of human things, the scene we are now passing through, particularly the shortness of life, denies to virtue its full scope in several other respects. The natural tendency which we have been considering, though real, is *hindered* from being carried into effect in the present state: but these hinderances may be removed in a future one. Virtue, to borrow the Christian allusion, is militant here; and various untoward accidents contribute to its being often overborne: but it may combat with greater advantage hereafter, and prevail completely, and enjoy its consequent rewards, in some future states. Neglected as it is, perhaps unknown, perhaps despised and oppressed, here; there may be scenes in eternity, lasting enough, and in every other way adapted, to afford it a sufficient sphere of action; and a sufficient sphere for the natural consequences of it to follow in fact. If the soul be naturally immortal, and this state be a progress towards a future one, as childhood is towards mature age; good men may naturally unite, not only amongst themselves, but also with other orders of virtuous creatures, in that future state. For virtue, from the very nature of it, is a principle and bond of union, in some degree, amongst all who are endued with it, and known to each other; so as that by it, a good man cannot but recommend himself to the favour and protection of all virtuous beings, throughout the whole universe, who can be acquainted with his character, and can any way interpose in his behalf in any part of his duration. And one might add, that suppose all this advantageous tendency of virtue to become effect, amongst one or more orders of creatures, in any distant scenes and periods, and to be seen by any orders of vicious creatures, throughout the universal kingdom of God; this happy effect of virtue would have a tendency, by way of example, and possibly in other ways, to amend those of them, who are capable of amendment, and being recovered to a just sense of virtue. If our notions of the plan of Providence were enlarged in any sort proportionable to what late discoveries have enlarged our views with respect to the material world; representations of this kind would not appear absurd or extravagant. However, they are not to be taken as intended for a literal delineation of what is in fact the particular scheme of the universe, which cannot be known without revelation: for suppositions are not to be looked on as true, because not incredible: but they are mentioned to shew, that our finding virtue to be hindered from procuring to itself such superiority and advantages, is no objection against its having, in the essential nature of the thing, a tendency to procure them. And the suppositions now mentioned do plainly shew this: for they shew, that these hinderances are so far from being necessary, that we ourselves can easily conceive, how they may be removed in future states, and full scope be granted to virtue. And all these advantageous tendencies of it are to be considered as declarations of God in its favour. This however is taking a pretty large compass: though it is certain, that, as the material world appears to be, in a manner, boundless and immense; there must be *some* scheme of Providence vast in proportion to it.

But let us return to the earth our habitation; and we shall see this happy tendency of virtue, by imagining an instance not so vast and remote: by supposing a kingdom or society of men upon it, perfectly virtuous, for a succession of many ages; to which, if you please, may be given a situation advantageous for universal monarchy. In such a state, there would be no such thing as faction: but men of the greatest capacity would of course, all along, have the chief direction of affairs willingly yielded to them; and they would share it among themselves without envy. Each of these would have the part assigned him, to which his genius was peculiarly adapted: and others, who had not any distinguished genius, would be safe, and think themselves very happy, by being under the protection and guidance of those who had. Public determinations would really be the result of the united wisdom of the community: and they would faithfully be executed, by the united strength of it. Some would in a higher way contribute, but all would in some way contribute, to the public prosperity: and in it, each would enjoy the fruits of his own virtue. And as injustice, whether by fraud or force, would be unknown among themselves; so they would be sufficiently secured from it in their neighbours. For cunning and false self-interest, confederacies in injustice, ever slight, and accompanied with faction and intestine treachery; these on one hand would be found mere childish folly and weakness, when set in opposition against wisdom, public spirit, union inviolable, and fidelity on the other: allowing both a sufficient length of years to try their force. Add the general influence, which such a kingdom would have over the face of the earth, by way of example particularly, and the reverence which would be paid it. It would plainly be superior to all others, and the world must gradually come under its empire; not by means of lawless violence; but partly by what must be allowed to be just conquest; and partly by other kingdoms submitting themselves voluntarily to it, throughout a course of ages, and claiming its protection, one after another, in successive exigencies. The head of it would be an universal monarch, in another sense than any mortal has yet been; and the eastern style would be literally applicable to him, that *all people, nations, and languages should serve him.* And though indeed our knowledge of human nature, and the whole history of mankind, shew the impossibility, without some miraculous interposition, that a number of men, here on earth, should unite in one society or government, in the fear of God and universal practice of virtue; and that such a government should continue so united for a succession of ages: yet admitting or supposing this, the effect would be as now drawn out. And thus, for instance, the wonderful power and prosperity promised to the Jewish nation in the Scripture, would be, in a great measure, the consequence of what is predicted of them; that the *people should be all righteous, and inherit the land for ever*[i]; were we to understand the latter phrase of a long continuance only, sufficient to give things time to work. The predictions of this kind, for there are many of them, cannot come to pass, in the present known course of nature; but suppose them come to pass, and then, the dominion and preeminence promised must naturally follow, to a very considerable degree.

Consider now the general system of religion: that the government of the world is uniform, and one, and moral; that virtue and right shall finally have the advantage, and prevail over fraud and lawless force, over the deceits, as well as the violence of wickedness, under the conduct of one supreme governor: and from the observations above made, it will appear, that God has, by our reason, given us to see a peculiar connexion in the several parts of this scheme, and a tendency towards the completion of it, arising out of the very nature of virtue: which tendency is to be considered as somewhat moral in the essential constitution of things. If any one should think all this to be of little importance; I desire him to consider, what he would think, if vice had, essentially and in its nature, these advantageous tendencies; or if virtue had essentially the direct contrary ones.

But it may be objected, that, notwithstanding all these natural effects and these natural tendencies of virtue; yet things may be now going on throughout the universe, and may go on hereafter, in the same mixed way as here at present upon earth: virtue sometimes prosperous, sometimes depressed; vice sometimes punished, sometimes successful. The answer to which is, that it is not the purpose of this

[i] Isai. lx. 21.

chapter, nor of this treatise, properly to prove God's perfect moral government over the world, or the truth of Religion; but to observe what there is in the constitution and course of nature, to confirm the proper proof of it, supposed to be known: and that the weight of the foregoing observations to this purpose may be thus distinctly proved. Pleasure and pain are indeed to a certain degree, say to a very high degree, distributed amongst us without any apparent regard to the merit or demerit of characters. And were there nothing else concerning this matter discernible in the constitution and course of nature; there would be no ground from the constitution and course of nature to hope or to fear, that men would be rewarded or punished hereafter according to their deserts: which, however, it is to be remarked, implies, that even then there would be no ground from appearances to think, that vice upon the whole would have the advantage, rather than that virtue would. And thus the proof of a future state of retribution would rest upon the usual known arguments for it: which are I think plainly unanswerable; and would be so, though there were no additional confirmation of them from the things above insisted on. But these things are a very strong confirmation of them. For,

First, They shew, that the Author of Nature is not indifferent to virtue and vice. They amount to a declaration from him, determinate and not to be evaded, in favour of one, and against the other; such a declaration, as there is nothing to be set over against or answer, on the part of vice. So that were a man, laying aside the proper proof of Religion, to determine from the course of nature only, whether it were most probable, that the righteous or the wicked would have the advantage in a future life; there can be no doubt, but that he would determine the probability to be, that the former would. The course of nature then, in the view of it now given, furnishes us with a real practical proof of the obligations of Religion.

Secondly, When, conformably to what Religion teaches us, God shall reward and punish virtue and vice as such, so as that every one shall, upon the whole, have his deserts; this distributive justice will not be a thing different in *kind*, but only in *degree*, from what we experience in his present government. It will be that in *effect*, toward which we now see a *tendency*. It will be no more than the *completion* of that moral government, the *principles and beginning* of which have been shewn, beyond all dispute, discernible in the present constitution and course of nature. And from hence it follows,

Thirdly, That, as under the natural government of God, our experience of those kinds and degrees of happiness and misery, which we do experience at present gives just ground to hope for, and to fear, higher degrees and other kinds of both in a future state, supposing a future state admitted: so under his moral government, our experience, that virtue and vice are, in the manners above mentioned, actually rewarded and punished at present, in a certain degree, gives just ground to hope and to fear, that they *may be* rewarded and punished in an higher degree hereafter. It is acknowledged indeed that this alone is not sufficient ground to think, that they *actually will be* rewarded and punished in a higher degree, rather than in a lower: but then,

Lastly, There is sufficient ground to think so, from the good and bad tendencies of virtue and vice. For these tendencies are essential, and founded in the nature of things: whereas the hinderances to their becoming effect are, in numberless cases, not necessary, but artificial only. Now it may be much more strongly argued, that these tendencies, as well as the actual rewards and punishments, of virtue and vice, which arise directly out of the nature of things, will remain hereafter, than that the accidental hinderances of them will. And if these hinderances do not remain; those rewards and punishments cannot but be carried on much farther towards the perfection of moral government: i. e. the tendencies of virtue and vice will become effect: but when, or where, or in what particular way, cannot be known at all, but by revelation.

Upon the whole: there is a kind of moral government implied in God's natural government [k]: virtue and vice are naturally rewarded and punished as beneficial and mischievous to society [l]: and rewarded and punished directly as virtue and vice [m]. The notion then of a moral scheme of government is not fictitious, but natural: for it is suggested to our thoughts by the constitution and course of nature: and the execution of this scheme is actually begun, in the instances here mentioned. And these things are to be considered as a declaration of the Author of Nature, for virtue, and against vice: they give a credibility to the supposition of their being rewarded and punished hereafter; and also ground to hope and to fear, that they may be rewarded and punished in higher degrees than they are here. And as all this is confirmed, so the argument for Religion, from the constitution and course of nature, is carried on farther, by observing, that there are natural tendencies, and, in innumerable cases, only artificial hinderances, to this moral

[k] P. 51.   [l] P. 53.   [m] P. 54. &c.

scheme's being carried on much farther towards perfection, than it is at present[n]. The notion then of a moral scheme of government, much more perfect than what is seen, is not a fictitious, but a natural notion; for it is suggested to our thoughts, by the essential tendencies of virtue and vice. And these tendencies are to be considered as intimations, as implicit promises and threatenings, from the Author of Nature, of much greater rewards and punishments to follow virtue and vice, than do at present. And indeed, every *natural* tendency, which is to continue, but which is hindered from becoming effect by only *accidental* causes, affords a presumption, that such tendency will, some time or other, become effect: a presumption in degree proportionable to the length of the duration, through which such tendency will continue. And from these things together, arises a real presumption, that the moral scheme of government established in nature, shall be carried on much farther towards perfection hereafter; and, I think, a presumption that it will be absolutely completed. But from these things, joined with the moral nature which God has given us, considered as given us by him, arises a practical proof[o] that it will be completed: a proof from fact; and therefore a distinct one from that, which is deduced from the eternal and unalterable relations, the fitness and unfitness of actions.

[n] P. 62, &c.
[o] See this proof drawn out briefly, chap. vi.

CHAP. IV.

Of a state of probation, as implying trial, difficulties and danger.

THE general doctrine of Religion, that our present life is a state of probation for a future one, comprehends under it several particular things, distinct from each other. But the first and most common meaning of it seems to be, that our future interest is now depending, and depending upon ourselves; that we have scope and opportunities here, for that good and bad behaviour, which God will reward and punish hereafter; together with temptations to one, as well as inducements of reason to the other. And this is, in great measure, the same with saying, that we are under the moral government of God, and to give an account of our actions to him. For the notion of a future account and general righteous judgment, implies some sort of temptations to what is wrong: otherwise there would be no moral possibility of doing wrong, nor ground for judgment, or discrimination. But there is this difference, that the word *probation* is more distinctly and particularly expressive of allurements to wrong, or difficulties in adhering uniformly to what is right, and of the danger of miscarrying by such temptations, than the words *moral government*. A state of probation then, as thus particularly implying in it trial, difficulties and danger, may require to be considered distinctly by itself.

And as the moral government of God, which Religion teaches us, implies, that we are in a state of trial with regard to a future world: so also his natural government over us implies, that we are in a state of trial, in the like sense, with regard to the present world. Natural government by rewards and punishments, as much implies natural trial, as moral government does moral trial. The natural government of God here meant[a] consists in his annexing pleasure to some actions, and pain to others, which are in our power to do or forbear, and in giving us notice of such appointment beforehand. This necessarily implies, that he has made our happiness and misery, or our interest, to depend in part upon ourselves. And so far as men have temptations to any course of action which will probably occasion them greater temporal inconvenience and uneasiness, than satisfaction; so far their temporal interest is in danger from themselves, or they are in a state of trial with respect to it. Now people often blame others, and even themselves, for their misconduct in their temporal concerns. And we find many are greatly wanting to themselves, and miss of that natural happiness, which they might have obtained in the present life: perhaps every one does in some degree. But many run themselves into great inconvenience, and into extreme distress and misery: not through incapacity of knowing better, and doing better for themselves, which would be nothing to the present purpose; but through their own fault. And these things necessarily imply temptation, and danger of miscarrying, in a greater or less degree, with respect to our worldly interest or happiness. Every one too, without having Religion in his thoughts, speaks of the hazards which young people run, upon their setting out in the world: hazards from other causes, than merely their ignorance, and unavoidable accidents. And some courses of vice, at least, being contrary to men's worldly interest or good; temptations to these must

[a] Chap. ii.

at the same time be temptations to forego our present and our future interest. Thus in our natural or temporal capacity, we are in a state of trial, i. e. of difficulty and danger, analogous, or like to our moral and religious trial.

This will more distinctly appear to any one, who thinks it worth while, more distinctly, to consider, what it is which constitutes our trial in both capacities, and to observe, how mankind behave under it.

And that which constitutes this our trial, in both these capacities, must be somewhat either in our external circumstances or in our nature. For, on the one hand, persons may be betrayed into wrong behaviour upon surprise, or overcome upon any other very singular and extraordinary external occasions; who would, otherwise, have preserved their character of prudence and of virtue: in which cases, every one, in speaking of the wrong behaviour of these persons, would impute it to such particular external circumstances. And on the other hand, men who have contracted habits of vice and folly of any kind, or have some particular passions in excess, will seek opportunities, and, as it were, go out of their way, to gratify themselves in these respects, at the expense of their wisdom and their virtue; led to it, as every one would say, not by external temptations, but by such habits and passions. And the account of this last case is, that particular passions are no more coincident with prudence, or that reasonable self-love, the end of which is our worldly interest, than they are with the principle of virtue and religion; but often draw contrary ways to one, as well as to the other: and so such particular passions are as much temptations, to act imprudently with regard to our worldly interest, as to act viciously[b]. However, as when we say, men are misled by external circumstances of temptation; it cannot but be understood, that there is somewhat within themselves, to render those circumstances temptations, or to render them susceptible of impressions from them: so when we say, they are misled by passions; it is always supposed, that there are occasions, circumstances, and objects, exciting these passions, and affording means for gratifying them. And therefore, temptations from within, and from without, coincide, and mutually imply each other. Now the several external objects of the appetites, passions, and affections, being present to the senses, or offering themselves to the mind, and so exciting emotions suitable to their nature; not only in cases where they can be gratified consistently with innocence and prudence, but also in cases where they cannot, and yet can be gratified imprudently and viciously: this as really puts them in danger of voluntarily foregoing their present interest or good, as their future; and as really renders self-denial necessary to secure one, as the other: i. e. we are in a like state of trial with respect to both, by the very same passions, excited by the very same means. Thus mankind having a temporal interest depending upon themselves, and a prudent course of behaviour being necessary to secure it; passions inordinately excited, whether by means of example, or by any other external circumstance, towards such objects, at such times, or in such degrees, as that they cannot be gratified consistently with worldly prudence; are temptations, dangerous, and too often successful temptations, to forego a greater temporal

[b] See Sermons preached at the Rolls, 1726, 2nd ed. p. 205, &c. pref. p. 25, &c. Serm. p. 21, &c.

good for a less; i.e. to forego what is, upon the whole, our temporal interest, for the sake of a present gratification. This is a description of our state of trial in our temporal capacity. Substitute now the word *future* for *temporal*, and *virtue* for *prudence;* and it will be just as proper a description of our state of trial in our religious capacity; so analogous are they to each other.

If, from consideration of this our like state of trial in both capacities, we go on to observe farther, how mankind behave under it; we shall find there are some, who have so little sense of it, that they scarce look beyond the passing day: they are so taken up with present gratifications, as to have, in a manner, no feeling of consequences, no regard to their future ease or fortune in this life; any more than to their happiness in another. Some appear to be blinded and deceived by inordinate passion, in their worldly concerns, as much as in Religion. Others are, not deceived, but, as it were, forcibly carried away by the like passions, against their better judgment, and feeble resolutions too of acting better. And there are men, and truly they are not a few, who shamelessly avow, not their interest, but their mere will and pleasure, to be their law of life: and who, in open defiance of every thing that is reasonable, will go on in a course of vicious extravagance, foreseeing, with no remorse and little fear, that it will be their temporal ruin; and some of them, under the apprehension of the consequences of wickedness in another state. And to speak in the most moderate way, human creatures are not only continually liable to go wrong voluntarily, but we see likewise that they often actually do so, with respect to their temporal interests, as well as with respect to Religion.

Thus our difficulties and dangers, or our trials, in our temporal and our religious capacity, as they proceed from the same causes, and have the same effect upon men's behaviour, are evidently analogous, and of the same kind.

It may be added, that as the difficulties and dangers of miscarrying in our religious state of trial, are greatly increased, and one is ready to think, in a manner wholly *made*, by the ill behaviour of others; by a wrong education, wrong in a moral sense, sometimes positively vicious; by general bad example; by the dishonest artifices which are got into business of all kinds; and, in very many parts of the world, by religion's being corrupted into superstitions, which indulge men in their vices: so in like manner, the difficulties of conducting ourselves prudently in respect to our present interest, and our danger of being led aside from pursuing it, are greatly increased, by a foolish education; and, after we come to mature age, by the extravagance and carelessness of others, whom we have intercourse with; and by mistaken notions, very generally prevalent, and taken up for common opinion, concerning temporal happiness, and wherein it consists. And persons, by their own negligence and folly in their temporal affairs, no less than by a course of vice, bring themselves into new difficulties; and, by habits of indulgence, become less qualified to go through them: and one irregularity after another, embarrasses things to such a degree, that they know not whereabout they are; and often makes the path of conduct so intricate and perplexed, that it is difficult to trace it out; difficult even to determine what is the prudent or the moral part. Thus, for instance, wrong behaviour in one stage of life, youth; wrong, I mean, considering ourselves only in our temporal capacity, without taking in religion; this, in several ways, increases the difficulties of right behaviour in mature age; i. e. puts us into a more disadvantageous state of trial in our temporal capacity.

We are an inferior part of the creation of God. There are natural appearances of our being in a state of degradation[c]. And we certainly are in a condition which *does not seem*, by any means, the most advantageous we could imagine or desire, either in our natural or moral capacity, for securing either our present or future interest. However, this condition, low and careful and uncertain as it is, does not afford any just ground of complaint. For, as men may manage their temporal affairs with prudence, and so pass their days here on earth in tolerable ease and satisfaction, by a moderate degree of care: so likewise with regard to religion, there is no more required than what they are well able to do, and what they must be greatly wanting to themselves, if they neglect. And for persons to have that put upon them, which they are well able to go through, and no more, we naturally consider as an equitable thing; supposing it done by proper authority. Nor have we any more reason to complain of it, with regard to the Author of Nature, than of his not having given us other advantages, belonging to other orders of creatures.

But the thing here insisted upon is, that the state of trial, which Religion teaches us we are in, is rendered credible, by its being throughout uniform and of a piece with the general conduct of Providence towards us, in all other respects within the compass of our knowledge. Indeed if mankind, con-

[c] Part II. chap. v.

sidered in their natural capacity, as inhabitants of this world only, found themselves, from their birth to their death, in a settled state of security and happiness, without any solicitude or thought of their own: or if they were in no danger of being brought into inconveniences and distress, by carelessness, or the folly of passion, through bad example, the treachery of others, or the deceitful appearances of things: were this our natural condition, then it might seem strange, and be some presumption against the truth of Religion, that it represents our future and more general interest, as not secure of course, but as depending upon our behaviour, and requiring recollection and self-government to obtain it. For it might be alleged, "What you say is our condition in one respect, is not in any wise of a sort with what we find, by experience, our condition is in another. Our whole present interest is secured to our hands, without any solicitude of ours; and why should not our future interest, if we have any such, be so too?" But since, on the contrary, thought and consideration, the voluntary denying ourselves many things which we desire, and a course of behaviour, far from being always agreeable to us; are absolutely necessary to our acting even a common decent, and common prudent part, so as to pass with any satisfaction through the present world, and be received upon any tolerable good terms in it: since this is the case, all presumption against self-denial and attention being necessary to secure our higher interest, is removed. Had we not experience, it might, perhaps speciously, be urged, that it is improbable any thing of hazard and danger should be put upon us by an infinite Being; when every thing which is hazard and danger in our manner of conception, and will end in error, confusion, and misery, is now already certain in his foreknowledge. And indeed, why any thing of hazard and danger should be put upon such frail creatures as we are, may well be thought a difficulty in speculation; and cannot but be so, till we know the whole, or, however, much more of the case. But still the constitution of nature is as it is. Our happiness and misery are trusted to our conduct, and made to depend upon it. Somewhat, and, in many circumstances, a great deal too, is put upon us, either to do, or to suffer, as we choose. And all the various miseries of life, which people bring upon themselves by negligence and folly, and might have avoided by proper care, are instances of this: which miseries are beforehand just as contingent and undetermined as their conduct, and left to be determined by it.

These observations are an answer to the objections against the credibility of a state of trial, as implying temptations, and real danger of miscarrying with regard to our general interest, under the moral government of God: and they shew, that, if we are at all to be considered in such a capacity, and as having such an interest; the general analogy of Providence must lead us to apprehend ourselves in danger of miscarrying, in different degrees, as to this interest, by our neglecting to act the proper part belonging to us in that capacity. For we have a present interest, under the government of God, which we experience here upon earth. And this interest, as it is not forced upon us, so neither is it offered to our acceptance, but to our acquisition; in such sort, as that we are in danger of missing it, by means of temptations to neglect, or act contrary to it; and without attention and self-denial, must and do miss of it. It is then perfectly credible, that this may be our case, with respect to that chief and final good, which Religion proposes to us.

CHAP. V.

Of a state of probation, as intended for moral discipline and improvement.

From the consideration of our being in a probation-state, of so much difficulty and hazard, naturally arises the question, how we came to be placed in it? But such a general inquiry as this would be found involved in insuperable difficulties. For, though some of these difficulties would be lessened by observing, that all wickedness is voluntary, as is implied in its very notion; and that many of the miseries of life have apparent good effects: yet, when we consider other circumstances belonging to both, and what must be the consequence of the former in a life to come; it cannot but be acknowledged plain folly and presumption, to pretend to give an account of the whole reasons of this matter: the whole reasons of our being allotted a condition, out of which so much wickedness and misery, so circumstanced, would in fact arise. Whether it be not beyond our faculties, not only to find out, but even to understand, the whole account of this; or, though we should be supposed capable of understanding it, yet, whether it would be of service or prejudice to us to be informed of it; is impossible to say. But as our present condition can in no wise be shewn inconsistent with the perfect moral government of God: so Religion teaches us we were placed in it, that we might qualify ourselves, by the practice of virtue, for another state which is to follow it. And this, though but a partial answer, a very partial one indeed, to the inquiry now mentioned; yet, is a more satisfactory answer to another, which is of real, and of the utmost importance to us to have answered: the inquiry, What is our business here? The known end then, why we are placed in a state of so much affliction, hazard, and difficulty, is, our improvement in virtue and piety, as the requisite qualification for a future state of security and happiness.

Now the beginning of life, considered as an education for mature age in the present world, appears plainly, at first sight, analogous to this our trial for a future one: the former being in our temporal capacity, what the latter is in our religious capacity. But some observations common to both of them, and a more distinct consideration of each, will more distinctly shew the extent and force of the analogy between them; and the credibility, which arises from hence, as well as from the nature of the thing, that the present life was intended to be a state of discipline for a future one.

I. Every species of creatures is, we see, designed for a particular way of life; to which, the nature, the capacities, temper, and qualifications of each species, are as necessary, as their external circumstances. Both come into the notion of such state, or particular way of life, and are constituent parts of it. Change a man's capacities or character to the degree, in which it is conceivable they may be changed; and he would be altogether incapable of a human course of life, and human happiness; as incapable, as if, his nature continuing unchanged, he were placed in a world, where he had no sphere of action, nor any objects to answer his appetites, passions, and affections of any sort. One thing is set over against another, as an ancient writer expresses it. Our nature corresponds to our external condition. Without this correspondence, there would be no possibility of any such thing as human life and human happiness: which life and happiness are, therefore, a *result* from our nature and condition jointly: meaning by human life, not living in the literal sense, but the whole complex notion commonly understood by those words. So that, without determining what will be the employment and happiness, the particular life, of good men hereafter; there must be some determinate capacities, some necessary character and qualifications, without which persons cannot but be utterly incapable of it: in like manner, as there must be some, without which men would be incapable of their present state of life. Now,

II. The constitution of human creatures, and indeed of all creatures which come under our notice, is such, as that they are capable of naturally becoming qualified for states of life, for which they were once wholly unqualified. In imagination we may indeed conceive of creatures, as incapable of having any of their faculties naturally enlarged, or as being unable naturally to acquire any new qualifications: but the faculties of every species known to us are made for enlargement; for acquirements of experience and habits. We find ourselves in particular endued with capacities, not only of perceiving ideas, and of knowledge or perceiving truth, but also of storing up our ideas and knowledge by memory. We are capable, not only of acting, and of having different momentary impressions made upon us; but of getting a new facility in any kind of action, and of settled alterations in our temper or character. The power of the two last is the power of habits. But neither the perception of ideas, nor knowledge of any sort, are habits; though absolutely necessary to the forming of them. However, apprehension, reason, memory, which are the capacities of acquiring knowledge, are greatly improved by exercise. Whether the word *habit* is applicable to all these improvements, and in particular how far the powers of memory and of habits may be powers of the same nature, I shall not inquire. But that perceptions come into our minds readily and of course, by means of their having been there before, seems a thing of the same sort, as readiness in any particular kind of action, proceeding from being accustomed to it. And aptness to recollect practical observations of service in our conduct, is plainly habit in many cases. There are habits of perception, and habits of action. An instance of the former, is our constant and even involuntary readiness, in correcting the impressions of our sight concerning magnitudes and distances, so as to substitute judgment in the room of sensation imperceptibly to ourselves. And it seems as if all other associations of ideas not naturally connected might be called *passive habits*; as properly as our readiness in understanding languages upon sight, or hearing of words. And our readiness in speaking and writing them is an instance of the latter, of active habits. For distinctness, we may consider habits, as belonging to the body, or the mind: and the latter will be explained by the former. Under the former are comprehended all bodily activities or motions, whether graceful or unbecoming, which are owing to use: under the latter, general habits of life and conduct; such as those of obedience and submission to authority, or to any particular person; those of veracity, justice, and charity; those of attention, industry, self-government, envy, revenge. And habits of this latter kind seem produced by repeated acts, as well as the former. And in like manner as habits belonging to the body are produced by external acts: so habits of the mind are produced by the exertion of inward practical principles, i.e. by carrying them into act, or acting upon them; the principles of obedience, of veracity, justice, and charity. Nor can those habits be formed by any external course of action, otherwise than as it proceeds from these principles: because it is only these inward principles exerted, which are strictly acts of obedience, of veracity, of justice, and of charity. So likewise habits of attention, industry, self-government, are in the same manner acquired by exercise; and habits of envy and revenge by indulgence, whether in outward act, or in thought and intention, i.e. inward act: for such intention is an act. Resolutions also to do well are properly acts. And endeavouring to enforce upon our own minds a practical sense of virtue, or to beget in others that practical sense of it, which a man really has himself, is a virtuous act. All these, therefore, may and will contribute towards forming good habits. But going over the theory of virtue in one's thoughts, talking well, and drawing fine pictures, of it; this is so far from necessarily or certainly conducing to form an habit of it, in him who thus employs himself, that it may harden the mind in a contrary course, and render it gradually more insensible, i.e. form an habit of insensibility, to all moral considerations. For, from our very faculty of habits, passive impressions, by being repeated, grow weaker. Thoughts, by often passing through the mind, are felt less sensibly: being accustomed to danger, begets intrepidity, i. e. lessens fear; to distress, lessens the passion of pity; to instances of others' mortality, lessens the sensible apprehension of our own. And from these two observations together: that practical habits are formed and strengthened by repeated acts, and that passive impressions grow weaker by being repeated upon us; it must follow, that active habits may be gradually forming and strengthening, by a course of acting upon such and such motives and excitements, whilst these motives and excitements themselves are, by proportionable degrees, growing less sensible, i. e. are continually less and less sensibly felt, even as the active habits strengthen. And experience confirms this: for active principles, at the very time that they are less lively in perception than they were, are found to be, some how, wrought more thoroughly into the temper and character, and become more effectual in influencing our practice. The three things just mentioned may afford instances of it. Perception of danger is a natural excitement of passive fear, and active caution: and by being inured to danger, habits of the latter are gradually wrought, at the same time that the former gradually lessens. Perception of distress in others is a natural excitement, passively to pity, and actively to relieve it: but let a man set himself to attend to, inquire out, and relieve distressed persons, and he cannot but grow less and less sensibly affected with the various miseries of life, with which he must become acquainted: when yet, at the same time, benevolence, considered not as a passion, but as a practical principle of action, will strengthen: and whilst he passively compassionates the distressed less, he will acquire a greater aptitude actively to assist and befriend them. So also at the same time that the daily instances of men's dying around us give us daily a less sensible passive feeling or apprehension of our own mortality, such instances greatly contribute to the strengthening a practical regard to it in serious men; i. e. to forming an habit of acting with a constant view to it. And this seems again further to shew, that passive impressions made upon our minds by admonition, experience, example, though they may have a remote efficacy, and a very great one, towards forming active habits, yet can have this efficacy no otherwise than by inducing us to such a course of action: and that it is not being affected so and so, but acting, which forms those habits: only it must be always remembered, that real endeavours to enforce good impressions upon ourselves are a species of virtuous action. Nor do we know how far it is possible, in the nature of things, that effects should be wrought in us at once, equivalent to habits, i. e. what is wrought by use and exercise. However, the thing insisted upon is, not what may be possible, but what is in fact the appointment of nature: which is, that active habits are to be formed by exercise. Their progress may be so gradual, as to be imperceptible of its steps: it may be hard to explain the faculty, by which we are capable of habits, throughout its several parts; and to trace it up to its original, so as to distinguish it from all others in our mind: and it seems as if contrary effects were to be ascribed to it. But the thing in general, that our nature is formed to yield, in some such manner as this, to use and exercise, is matter of certain experience.

Thus, by accustoming ourselves to any course of action, we get an aptness to go on, a facility, readiness, and often pleasure, in it. The inclinations which rendered us averse to it grow weaker: the difficulties in it, not only the imaginary but the real ones, lessen: the reasons for it offer themselves of course to our thoughts upon all occasions: and the least glimpse of them is sufficient to make us go on, in a course of action, to which we have been accustomed. And practical principles appear to grow stronger, absolutely in themselves, by exercise; as well as relatively, with regard to contrary principles; which, by being accustomed to submit, do so habitually, and of course. And thus a new character, in several respects, may be formed; and many habitudes of life, not given by nature, but which nature directs us to acquire.

III. Indeed we may be assured, that we should never have had these capacities of improving by experience, acquired knowledge, and habits, had they not been necessary, and intended to be made use of. And accordingly we find them so necessary, and so much intended, that without them we should be utterly incapable of that, which was the end for which we were made, considered in our temporal capacity only: the employments and satisfactions of our mature state of life.

Nature does in no wise qualify us wholly, much less at once, for this mature state of life. Even maturity of understanding, and bodily strength, are not only arrived to gradually, but are also very much owing to the continued exercise of our powers of body and mind from infancy. But if we suppose a person brought into the world with both these in maturity, as far as this is conceivable; he would plainly at first be as unqualified for the human life of mature age, as an idiot. He would be in a manner distracted, with astonishment, and apprehension, and curiosity, and suspense: nor can one guess, how long it would be, before he would be familiarized to himself and the objects about him enough, even to set himself to any thing. It may be questioned too, whether the natural information of his sight and hearing would be of any manner of use at all to him in acting, before experience. And it seems, that men would be strangely headstrong and self-willed, and disposed to exert themselves with an impetuosity, which would render society insupportable, and the living in it impracticable; were it not for some acquired moderation and self-government, some aptitude and readiness in restraining themselves, and concealing their sense of things. What of every thing of this kind which is learnt would render a man as uncapable of society, as want of language would; or as his natural ignorance of any of the particular employments of life would render him uncapable of providing himself with the common conveniences, or supplying the necessary wants of it. In these respects, and probably in many more, of which we have no particular notion, mankind is left, by nature, an unformed, unfinished creature; utterly deficient and unqualified, before the acquirement of knowledge, experience, and habits, for that mature state of life, which was the end of his creation, considering him as related only to this world.

But then, as nature has endued us with a power of supplying those deficiencies, by acquired knowledge, experience, and habits: so likewise we are placed in a condition, in infancy, childhood, and youth, fitted for it; fitted for our acquiring those qualifications of all sorts, which we stand in need of in mature age. Hence children, from their very birth, are daily growing acquainted with the objects about them, with the scene in which they are placed, and to have a future part; and learning somewhat or other, necessary to the performance of it. The subordinations, to which they are accustomed in domestic life, teach them self-government in common behaviour abroad, and prepare them for subjection and obedience to civil authority. What passes before their eyes, and daily happens to them, gives them experience, caution against treachery and deceit, together with numberless little rules of action and conduct, which we could not live without; and which are learnt so insensibly and so perfectly, as to be mistaken perhaps for instinct: though they are the effect of long experience and exercise; as much so as language, or knowledge in particular business, or the qualifications and behaviour belonging to the several ranks and professions. Thus the beginning of our days is adapted to be, and is, a state of education in the theory and practice of mature life. We are much assisted in it by example, instruction, and the care of others; but a great deal is left to ourselves to do. And of this, as part is done easily and of course; so part requires diligence and care, the voluntary foregoing many things which we desire, and setting ourselves to what we should have no inclination to, but for the necessity or expedience of it. For, that labour and industry, which the station of so many absolutely requires, they would be greatly unqualified for, in maturity; as those in other stations would be, for any other sorts of application; if both were not accustomed to them in their youth. And according as persons behave themselves, in the general education which all go through, and in the particular ones adapted to particular employments; their character is formed, and made appear; they recommend themselves more or less; and are capable of, and placed in, different stations in the society of mankind.

The former part of life then is to be considered as an important opportunity, which nature puts into our hands; and which, when lost, is not to be recovered. And our being placed in a state of discipline throughout this life, for another world, is a providential disposition of things, exactly of the same kind, as our being placed in a state of discipline during childhood, for mature age. Our condition in both respects is uniform and of a piece, and comprehended under one and the same general law of nature.

And if we were not able at all to discern, how or in what way the present life could be our preparation for another; this would be no objection against the credibility of its being so. For we do not discern, how food and sleep contribute to the growth of the body; nor could have any thought that they would, before we had experience. Nor do children at all think, on the one hand, that the sports and exercises, to which they are so much addicted, contribute to their health and growth; nor, on the other, of the necessity which there is for their being restrained in them: nor are they capable of understanding the use of many parts of discipline, which nevertheless they must be made to go through, in order to qualify them for the business of mature age. Were we not able then to discover, in what respects the present life could form us for a future one; yet nothing would be more supposable than that it might, in some respects or other, from the general analogy of Providence. And this, for ought I see, might reasonably be said, even though we should not take in the consideration of God's moral government over the world. But,

IV. Take in this consideration, and consequently, that the character of virtue and piety is a necessary qualification for the future state; and then we may distinctly see, how, and in what respects, the present life may be a preparation for it: since we *want, and are capable of, improvement in that character, by moral and religious habits;* and *the present life is fit to be a state of discipline for such improvement:* in like manner as we have already observed, how, and in what respects, infancy, childhood, and youth are a necessary preparation, and a natural state of discipline, for mature age.

Nothing which we at present see would lead us to the thought of a solitary unactive state hereafter: but, if we judge at all from the analogy of nature, we must suppose, according to the Scripture account of it, that it will be a community. And there is no shadow of any thing unreasonable in conceiving, though there be no analogy for it, that this community will be, as the Scripture represents it, under the more immediate, or, if such an expression may be used, the more sensible government of God. Nor is our ignorance, what will be the employments of this happy community, nor our consequent ignorance, what particular scope or occasion there will be for the exercise of veracity, justice, and charity, amongst the members of it with regard to each other; any proof, that there will be no sphere of exercise for those virtues. Much less, if that were possible, is our ignorance any proof, that there will be no occasion for that frame of mind, or character, which is formed by the daily practice of those particular virtues here, and which is a result from it. This at least must be owned in general, that, as the government established in the universe is moral, the character of virtue and piety must, in some way or other, be the condition of our happiness, or the qualification for it.

Now from what is above observed, concerning our natural power of habits, it is easy to see, that we are *capable* of moral improvement by discipline. And how greatly we *want* it, need not be proved to any one who is acquainted with the great wickedness of mankind; or even with those imperfections, which the best are conscious of. But it is not perhaps distinctly attended to by every one, that the occasion which human creatures have for discipline, to improve in them this character of virtue and piety, is to be traced up higher than to excess in the passions, by indulgence and habits of vice. Mankind, and perhaps all finite creatures, from the very constitution of their nature, before habits of virtue, are deficient, and in danger of deviating from what is right; and therefore stand in need of virtuous habits, for a security against this danger. For, together with the general principle of moral understanding, we have in our inward frame various affections towards particular external objects. These affections are naturally, and of right, subject to the government of the moral principle, as to the occasions upon which they may be gratified; as to the times, degrees, and manner in which the objects of them may be pursued; but then the principle of virtue can neither excite them, nor prevent their being excited. On the contrary, they are naturally felt, when the objects of them are present to the mind, not only before all consideration, whether they can be obtained by lawful means, but after it is found they cannot. For the natural objects of affection continue so; the necessaries, conveniences, and pleasures of life, remain naturally desirable; though they cannot be obtained innocently: nay, though they cannot possibly be obtained at all. And when the objects of any affection whatever cannot be obtained without unlawful means; but may be obtained by them: such affection, though its being excited, and its continuing some time in the mind, be as innocent as it is natural and necessary; yet cannot but be conceived to have a tendency to incline persons to venture upon such unlawful means: and therefore must be conceived as putting them in some danger of it. Now what is the general security against this danger, against their actually deviating from right? As the danger is, so also must the security be, from within: from the practical principle of virtue [a]. And the strengthening or improving

[a] It may be thought, that sense of interest would as effectually restrain creatures from doing wrong. But if by a *sense of interest* is meant a speculative conviction or belief, that such and such indulgence would occasion them greater uneasiness, upon the whole, than satisfaction; it is contrary to present experience to say, that this sense of interest is sufficient to restrain them from thus indulging themselves. And if by a *sense of interest* is meant a practical regard to what is upon the whole our happiness; this is not only coincident with the principle of virtue or moral rectitude, but is a part of the idea itself. And it is evident this reasonable self-love wants to be improved, as really as any principle in our nature. For we daily see it overmatched, not only by the more boisterous passions, but by curiosity, shame, love of imitation, by any thing, even indolence: especially if the interest, the temporal interest, suppose, which is the end of such self-love, be at a distance. So greatly are profligate men

this principle, considered as practical, or as a principle of action, will lessen the danger, or increase the security against it. And this moral principle is capable of improvement, by proper discipline and exercise: by recollecting the practical impressions which example and experience have made upon us: and, instead of following humour and mere inclination, by continually attending to the equity and right of the case, in whatever we are engaged, be it in greater or less matters; and accustoming ourselves always to act upon it; as being itself the just and natural motive of action; and as this moral course of behaviour must necessarily, under Divine government, be our final interest. *Thus the principle of virtue, improved into an habit, of which improvement we are thus capable, will plainly be, in proportion to the strength of it, a security against the danger which finite creatures are in, from the very nature of propension, or particular affections.* This way of putting the matter, supposes particular affections to remain in a future state; which it is scarce possible to avoid supposing. And if they do; we clearly see, that acquired habits of virtue and self-government may be necessary for the regulation of them. However, though we were not distinctly to take in this supposition, but to speak only in general; the thing really comes to the same. For habits of virtue, thus acquired by discipline, are improvement in virtue: and improvement in virtue must be advancement in happiness, if the government of the universe be moral.

From these things we may observe, and it will

mistaken, when they affirm they are wholly governed by interestedness and self-love. And so little cause is there for moralists to disclaim this principle. See p. 77, 78.

farther shew this our natural and original need of being improved by discipline, how it comes to pass, that creatures made upright fall; and that those who preserve their uprightness, by so doing, raise themselves to a more secure state of virtue. To say that the former is accounted for by the nature of liberty, is to say no more than that an event's actually happening is accounted for by a mere possibility of its happening. But it seems distinctly conceivable from the very nature of particular affections or propensions. For, suppose creatures intended for such a particular state of life, for which such propensions were necessary: suppose them endued with such propensions, together with moral understanding, as well including a practical sense of virtue, as a speculative perception of it: and that all these several principles, both natural and moral, forming an inward constitution of mind, were in the most exact proportion possible: i.e. in a proportion the most exactly adapted to their intended state of life; such creatures would be made upright, or finitely perfect. Now particular propensions, from their very nature, must be felt, the objects of them being present; though they cannot be gratified at all, or not with the allowance of the moral principle. But if they can be gratified without its allowance, or by contradicting it; then they must be conceived to have some tendency, in how low a degree soever, yet some tendency, to induce persons to such forbidden gratification. This tendency, in some one particular propension, may be increased, by the greater frequency of occasions naturally exciting it, than of occasions exciting others. The least voluntary indulgence in forbidden circumstances, though but in thought, will increase this wrong tendency: and may increase it further, till, peculiar conjunctures perhaps conspiring, it becomes effect; and danger of deviating from right, ends in actual deviation from it: a danger necessarily arising from the very nature of propension; and which therefore could not have been prevented, though it might have been escaped, or got innocently through. The case would be, as if we were to suppose a straight path marked out for a person, in which such a degree of attention would keep him steady: but if he would not attend in this degree, any one of a thousand objects, catching his eye, might lead him out of it. Now it is impossible to say, how much even the first full overt act of irregularity might disorder the inward constitution; unsettle the adjustments, and alter the proportions, which formed it, and in which the uprightness of its make consisted: but repetition of irregularities would produce habits. And thus the constitution would be spoiled; and creatures made upright, become corrupt and depraved in their settled character, proportionably to their repeated irregularities in occasional acts. But, on the contrary, these creatures might have improved and raised themselves, to an higher and more secure state of virtue, by the contrary behaviour: by steadily following the moral principle, supposed to be one part of their nature: and thus withstanding that unavoidable danger of defection, which necessarily arose from propension, the other part of it. For, by thus preserving their integrity for some time, their danger would lessen; since propensions, by being inured to submit, would do it more easily and of course: and their security against this lessening danger would increase; since the moral principle would gain additional strength by exercise:

both which things are implied in the notion of virtuous habits. Thus then vicious indulgence is not only criminal in itself, but also depraves the inward constitution and character. And virtuous self-government is not only right in itself, but also improves the inward constitution or character: and may improve it to such a degree, that though we should suppose it impossible, for particular affections to be absolutely coincident with the moral principle; and consequently should allow, that such creatures as have been above supposed, would for ever remain defectible; yet their danger of actually deviating from right may be almost infinitely lessened, and they fully fortified against what remains of it; if that may be called danger, against which there is an adequate effectual security. But still, this their higher perfection may continue to consist in habits of virtue formed in a state of discipline, and this their more complete security remain to proceed from them. And thus it is plainly conceivable, that creatures without blemish, as they came out of the hands of God, may be in danger of going wrong; and so may stand in need of the security of virtuous habits, additional to the moral principle wrought into their natures by him. That which is the ground of their danger, or their want of security, may be considered as a deficiency in them, to which virtuous habits are the natural supply. And as they are naturally capable of being raised and improved by discipline, it may be a thing fit and requisite that they should be placed in circumstances with an eye to it: in circumstances peculiarly fitted to be, to them, a state of discipline for their improvement in virtue.

But how much more strongly must this hold with respect to those, who have corrupted their natures, are fallen from their original rectitude, and whose passions are become excessive by repeated violations of their inward constitution? Upright creatures may want to be improved: depraved creatures want to be renewed. Education and discipline, which may be in all degrees and sorts of gentleness and of severity, is expedient for those: but must be absolutely necessary for these. For these, discipline of the severer sort too, and in the higher degrees of it, must be necessary, in order to wear out vicious habits; to recover their primitive strength of self-government, which indulgence must have weakened; to repair, as well as raise into an habit, the moral principle, in order to their arriving at a secure state of virtuous happiness.

Now whoever will consider the thing, may clearly see, that the present world is *peculiarly fit* to be a state of discipline for this purpose, to such as will set themselves to mend and improve. For, the various temptations with which we are surrounded; our experience of the deceits of wickedness; having been in many instances led wrong ourselves; the great viciousness of the world; the infinite disorders consequent upon it; our being made acquainted with pain and sorrow, either from our own feeling of it, or from the sight of it in others; these things, though some of them may indeed produce wrong effects upon our minds, yet when duly reflected upon, have, all of them, a direct tendency to bring us to a settled moderation and reasonableness of temper: the contrary both to thoughtless levity, and also to that unrestrained self-will, and violent bent to follow present inclination, which may be observed in undisciplined minds. Such experience, as the present state affords, of the frailty of our nature; of the boundless extravagance of ungoverned passion; of the power which an infinite Being has over us, by the various capacities of misery which he has given us; in short, that kind and degree of experience, which the present state affords us, that the constitution of nature is such as to admit the possibility, the danger, and the actual event, of creatures losing their innocence and happiness, and becoming vicious and wretched; hath a tendency to give us a practical sense of things, very different from a mere speculative knowledge, that we are liable to vice, and capable of misery. And who knows, whether the security of creatures in the highest and most settled state of perfection, may not in part arise, from their having had such a sense of things as this, formed, and habitually fixed within them, in some state of probation. And passing through the present world with that moral attention, which is necessary to the acting a right part in it, may leave everlasting impressions of this sort upon our minds. But to be a little more distinct: allurements to what is wrong; difficulties in the discharge of our duty; our not being able to act an uniform right part without some thought and care; and the opportunities which we have, or imagine we have, of avoiding what we dislike, or obtaining what we desire, by unlawful means, when we either cannot do it at all, or at least not so easily, by lawful ones; these things, i.e. the snares and temptations of vice, are what render the present world peculiarly fit to be a state of discipline, to those who will preserve their integrity: because they render being upon our guard, resolution, and the denial of our passions, necessary in order to that end. And the exercise of such particular recollection, intention of mind, and self-government, in the practice of virtue, has, from the make of our nature, a peculiar tendency to form habits of virtue; as implying, not only a real, but also a more continued, and a more intense exercise of the virtuous principle; or a more constant and a stronger effort of virtue exerted into act. Thus suppose a person to know himself to be in particular danger, for some time, of doing any thing wrong, which yet he fully resolves not to do: continued recollection, and keeping upon his guard, in order to make good his resolution, is a *continued* exerting of that act of virtue in a *high degree,* which need have been, and perhaps would have been, only *instantaneous* and *weak,* had the temptation been so. It is indeed ridiculous to assert, that self-denial is essential to virtue and piety: but it would have been nearer the truth, though not strictly the truth itself, to have said, that it is essential to discipline and improvement. For though actions materially virtuous, which have no sort of difficulty, but are perfectly agreeable to our particular inclinations, may possibly be done only from these particular inclinations, and so may not be any exercise of the principle of virtue, i.e. not be virtuous actions at all; yet, on the contrary, they may be an exercise of that principle: and when they are, they have a tendency to form and fix the habit of virtue. But when the exercise of the virtuous principle is more continued, oftener repeated, and more intense; as it must be in circumstances of danger, temptation, and difficulty, of any kind and in any degree; this tendency is increased proportionably, and a more confirmed habit is the consequence.

This undoubtedly holds to a certain length: but how far it may hold, I know not. Neither our intellectual powers nor our bodily strength can be improved beyond such a degree : and both may be over-wrought. Possibly there may be somewhat analogous to this, with respect to the moral character; which is scarce worth considering. And I mention it only, lest it should come into some persons' thoughts, not as an exception to the foregoing observations, which perhaps it is; but as a confutation of them, which it is not. And there may be several other exceptions. Observations of this kind cannot be supposed to hold minutely, and in every case. It is enough that they hold in general. And these plainly hold so far, as that from them may be seen distinctly, which is all that is intended by them, that *the present world is peculiarly fit to be a state of discipline, for our improvement in virtue and piety:* in the same sense as some sciences, by requiring and engaging the attention, not to be sure of such persons as will not, but of such as will, set themselves to them; are fit to form the mind to habits of attention.

Indeed the present state is so far from proving, in event, a discipline of virtue to the generality of men, that, on the contrary, they seem to make it a discipline of vice. And the viciousness of the world is, in different ways, the great temptation, which renders it a state of virtuous discipline, in the degree it is, to good men. The whole end, and the whole occasion, of mankind's being placed in such a state as the present, is not pretended to be accounted for. That which appears amidst the general corruption is, that there are some persons, who, having within them the principle of amendment and recovery, attend to and follow the notices of virtue and religion, be they more clear or more obscure, which are afforded them; and that the present world is, not only an exercise of virtue in these persons, but an exercise of it in ways and degrees, peculiarly apt to improve it: apt to improve it, in some respects, even beyond what would be, by the exercise of it required in a perfectly virtuous society, or in a society of equally imperfect virtue with themselves. But that the present world does not actually become a state of moral discipline to many, even to the generality, i. e. that they do not improve or grow better in it, cannot be urged as a proof, that it was not intended for moral discipline, by any who at all observe the analogy of nature. For, of the numerous seeds of vegetables and bodies of animals, which are adapted and put in the way, to improve to such a point or state of natural maturity and perfection, we do not see perhaps that one in a million actually does. Far the greatest part of them decay before they are improved to it; and appear to be absolutely destroyed. Yet no one, who does not deny all final causes, will deny, that those seeds and bodies, which do attain to that point of maturity and perfection, answer the end for which they were really designed by nature; and therefore that nature designed them for such perfection. And I cannot forbear adding, though it is not to the present purpose, that the *appearance* of such an amazing *waste* in nature, with respect to these seeds and bodies, by foreign causes, is to us as unaccountable, as, what is much more terrible, the present and future ruin of so many moral agents by themselves, i. e. by vice.

Against this whole notion of moral discipline, it may be objected, in another way; that so far as a course of behaviour, materially virtuous, proceeds from hope and fear, so far it is only a discipline and strengthening of self-love. But doing what God commands, because he commands it, is obedience, though it proceeds from hope or fear. And a course of such obedience will form habits of it. And a constant regard to veracity, justice, and charity, may form distinct habits of these particular virtues; and will certainly form habits of self-government, and of denying our inclinations, whenever veracity, justice, or charity requires it. Nor is there any foundation for this great nicety, with which some affect to distinguish in this case, in order to depreciate all Religion proceeding from hope or fear. For, veracity, justice, and charity, regard to God's authority, and to our own chief interest, are not only all three coincident; but each of them is, in itself, a just and natural motive or principle of action. And he who begins a good life from any one of them, and perseveres in it, as he is already in some degree, so he cannot fail of becoming more and more, of that character, which is correspondent to the constitution of nature as moral; and to the relation, which God stands in to us as moral Governor of it: nor consequently can he fail of obtaining that happiness, which this constitution and relation necessarily suppose connected with that character.

These several observations, concerning the active principle of virtue and obedience to God's commands, are applicable to passive submission or resignation to his will: which is another essential part of a right character, connected with the former, and very much in our power to form ourselves to. It may be imagined, that nothing but afflictions can give occasion for, or require this virtue; that it can have no respect to, nor be any way necessary to qualify for, a state of perfect happiness: but it is not experience which can make us think thus. Prosperity itself, whilst any thing supposed desirable is not ours, begets extravagant and unbounded thoughts. Imagination is altogether as much a source of discontent, as any thing in our external condition. It is indeed true, that there can be no scope for patience, when sorrow shall be no more: but there may be need of a temper of mind, which shall have been formed by patience. For, though self-love, considered merely as an active principle leading us to pursue our chief interest, cannot but be uniformly coincident with the principle of obedience to God's commands, our interest being rightly understood; because this obedience, and the pursuit of our own chief interest, must be in every case one and the same thing: yet it may be questioned, whether self-love, considered merely as the desire of our own interest or happiness, can, from its nature, be thus absolutely and uniformly coincident with the will of God; any more than particular affections can[b]: coincident in such sort, as not to be liable to be excited upon occasions and in degrees, impossible to be gratified consistently with the constitution of things, or the Divine appointments. So that *habits* of resignation may, upon this account, be requisite for all creatures: habits, I say; which signify what is formed by use. However, in general it is obvious that both self-love and particular affections in human creatures, considered only as passive feelings, distort and rend the mind; and therefore stand in need of discipline. Now denial of those particular affections, in a cours of active virtue and obedience to God's will, has a tendency to moderate them; and seems also to have a tendency to habituate the mind, to

[b] P. 82.

be easy and satisfied with that degree of happiness which is allotted us, i. e. to moderate self-love. But the proper discipline for resignation is affliction. For a right behaviour under that trial; recollecting ourselves so as to consider it in the view, in which Religion teaches us to consider it, as from the hand of God; receiving it as what he appoints, or thinks proper to permit, in his world and under his government; this will habituate the mind to a dutiful submission. And such submission, together with the active principle of obedience, make up the temper and character in us, which answers to his sovereignty; and which absolutely belongs to the condition of our being, as dependent creatures. Nor can it be said, that this is only breaking the mind to a submission to mere power; for mere power may be accidental and precarious and usurped: but it is forming within ourselves the temper of resignation to his rightful authority, who is, by nature, supreme over all.

Upon the whole: such a character, and such qualifications, are necessary for a mature state of life in the present world, as nature alone does in no wise bestow; but has put it upon us, in great part, to acquire, in our progress from one stage of life to another, from childhood to mature age; put it upon us to acquire them, by giving us capacities of doing it, and by placing us, in the beginning of life, in a condition fit for it. And this is a general analogy to our condition in the present world, as in a state of moral discipline for another. It is in vain then to object against the credibility of the present life's being intended for this purpose, that all the trouble and the danger, unavoidably accompanying such discipline, might have been saved us, by our being made at once the creatures and the characters, *which we were to be.* For we experience, that *what we were to be,* was to be the effect of *what we would do:* and that the general conduct of nature is, not to save us trouble or danger, but to make us capable of going through them, and to put it upon us to do so. Acquirements of our own, experience and habits, are the *natural* supply to our deficiencies, and security against our dangers: since it is as plainly natural to set ourselves to acquire the qualifications, as the external things, which we stand in need of. In particular, it is as plainly a general law of nature, that we should, with regard to our temporal interest, form and cultivate practical principles within us, by attention, use, and discipline, as anything whatever is a natural law; chiefly in the beginning of life, but also throughout the whole course of it. And the alternative is left to our choice: either to improve ourselves, and better our condition; or, in default of such improvement, to remain deficient and wretched. It is therefore perfectly credible, from the analogy of nature, that the same may be our case, with respect to the happiness of a future state, and the qualifications necessary for it.

There is a third thing, which may seem implied in the present world's being a state of probation; that it is a theatre of action, for the manifestation of persons' characters, with respect to a future one: not to be sure to an all-knowing Being, but to his creation or part of it. This may, perhaps, be only a consequence of our being in a state of probation in the other senses. However, it is not impossible, that men's shewing and making manifest what is in their heart, what their real character is, may have respect to a future life, in ways and manners which we are not acquainted with: particularly it may be a means, for the Author of Nature does not appear to do any thing without means, of their being disposed of suitably to their characters; and of its being known to the creation, by way of example, that they are thus disposed of. But not to enter upon any conjectural account of this; one may just mention, that the manifestation of persons' characters contributes very much, in various ways, to the carrying on a great part of that general course of nature, respecting mankind, which comes under our observation at present. I shall only add, that probation, in both these senses, as well as in that treated of in the foregoing chapter, is implied in moral government; since by persons' behaviour under it, their characters cannot but be manifested, and, if they behave well, improved.

CHAP. VI.

Of the opinion of necessity, considered as influencing practice.

THROUGHOUT the foregoing Treatise it appears, that the condition of mankind, considered as inhabitants of this world only, and under the government of God which we experience, is greatly analogous to our condition, as designed for another world, or under that farther government, which Religion teaches us. If therefore any assert, as a Fatalist must, that the opinion of universal Necessity is reconcilable with the former; there immediately arises a question in the way of analogy, whether he must not also own it to be reconcilable with the latter, i. e. with the system of Religion itself, and the proof of it. The reader then will observe, that the question now before us is not absolute, Whether the opinion of Fate be reconcilable with Religion; but hypothetical, Whether, upon supposition of its being reconcilable with the constitution of Nature, it be not reconcilable with Religion also: or, what pretence a Fatalist, not other persons, but a Fatalist, has to conclude from his opinion, that there can be no such thing as Religion. And as the puzzle and obscurity, which must unavoidably arise from arguing upon so absurd a supposition as that of universal Necessity, will, I fear, easily be seen; it will, I hope, as easily be excused.

But since it has been all along taken for granted, as a thing proved, that there is an intelligent Author of Nature, or natural Governor of the world; and since an objection may be made against the proof of this, from the opinion of universal Necessity, as it may be supposed, that such Necessity will itself account for the origin and preservation of all things: it is requisite, that this objection be distinctly answered; or that it be shewn, that a Fatality, supposed consistent with what we certainly experience, does not destroy the proof of an intelligent Author and Governor of Nature; before we proceed to consider, whether it destroys the proof of a moral Governor of it, or of our being in a state of Religion.

Now, when it is said by a Fatalist, that the whole constitution of Nature, and the actions of men, that every thing, and every mode and circumstance of every thing, is necessary, and could not possibly have been otherwise; it is to be observed, that this Necessity does not exclude deliberation, choice, preference, and acting from certain principles, and to certain ends: because all this is matter of undoubted experience, acknowledged by all, and what every man may, every moment, be conscious of. And from hence it follows, that Necessity, alone and of itself, is in no sort an account of the constitution of Nature, and how things came *to be* and *to continue* as they are; but only an account of this *circumstance* relating to their origin and continuance, that they could not have been otherwise than they are and have been. The assertion, that every thing is by Necessity of Nature, is not an answer to the question; Whether the world came into being as it is, by an intelligent Agent forming it thus, or not: but to quite another question; Whether it came into being as it is, in that way and manner which we call *necessarily*, or in that way and manner which we call *freely*. For suppose farther, that one who was a Fatalist, and one who kept to his natural sense of things, and believed himself a Free Agent, were disputing together, and vindicating their respective opinions; and they should happen to instance in a house: they would agree that it was built by an architect. Their difference concerning Necessity and Freedom would occasion no difference of judgment concerning this; but only concerning another matter; whether the architect built it necessarily or freely. Suppose then they should proceed to inquire concerning the constitution of Nature: in a lax way of speaking, one of them might say, it was by Necessity; and the other, by Freedom: but if they had any meaning to their words, as the latter must mean a Free Agent, so the former must at length be reduced to mean an Agent, whether he would say one or more, acting by Necessity: for abstract notions can do nothing. Indeed we ascribe to God a necessary existence, uncaused by any agent. For we find within ourselves the idea of infinity, i. e. immensity and eternity, impossible, even in imagination, to be removed out of being. We seem to discern intuitively, that there must, and cannot but be, somewhat, external to ourselves, answering this idea, or the archetype of it. And from hence (for *this abstract*, as much as any other, implies a *concrete*) we conclude, that there is, and cannot but be, an infinite and immense eternal Being existing, prior to all design contributing to his existence, and exclusive of it. And from the scantiness of language, a manner of speaking has been introduced; that Necessity is the foundation, the reason, the account of the existence of God. But it is not alleged, nor can it be at all intended, that *every thing* exists as it does, by this kind of Necessity; a Necessity antecedent in nature to design: it cannot, I say, be meant that every thing exists as it does, by this kind of Necessity, upon several accounts; and particularly because it is admitted, that design, in the actions of men, contributes to many alterations in nature. For if any deny this, I shall not pretend to reason with them.

From these things it follows; first, That when a Fatalist asserts, that every thing is *by Necessity*, he must mean, *by an Agent acting necessarily*; he must I say mean this, for I am very sensible he would not choose to mean it: and secondly, That the Necessity, by which such an Agent is supposed to act, does not exclude intelligence and design. So that, were the system of Fatality admitted, it would just as much account for the formation of the world, as for the structure of an house, and no more. Necessity as much requires and supposes a Necessary Agent, as Freedom requires and supposes a Free Agent, to be the former of the world. And the appearances of *design* and of *final causes* in the constitution of nature as really prove this acting Agent to be an *intelligent designer*, or to act from choice; upon the scheme of Necessity, supposed possible, as upon that of Freedom.

It appearing thus, that the notion of Necessity does not destroy the proof, that there is an intelligent Author of Nature and natural Governor of the world; the present question, which the analogy before mentioned[a] suggests, and which, I think, it will answer, is this: Whether the opinion of Necessity, supposed consistent with possibility, with the constitution of the world, and the natural government which we experience exercised over it, destroys all reasonable ground of belief, that we are in a state of Religion: or whether that opinion be reconcilable with Religion; with the system, and the proof of it.

Suppose then a Fatalist to educate any one, from his youth up, in his own principles; that the child should reason upon them, and conclude, that since he cannot possibly behave otherwise than he does, he is not a subject of blame or commendation, nor can deserve to be rewarded or punished: imagine him to eradicate the very perceptions of blame and commendation out of his mind, by means of this system; to form his temper and character and behaviour to it; and from it to judge of the treatment he was to expect, say, from reasonable men, upon his coming abroad into the world: as the Fatalist judges from this system, what he is to expect from the Author of Nature, and with regard to a future state. I cannot forbear stopping here to ask, whether any one of common sense would think fit, that a child should be put upon these speculations, and be left to apply them to practice. And a man has little pretence to

[a] P. 111.

reason, who is not sensible, that we are all children in speculations of this kind. However, the child would doubtless be highly delighted to find himself freed from the restraints of fear and shame, with which his playfellows were fettered and embarrassed; and highly conceited in his superior knowledge, so far beyond his years. But conceit and vanity would be the least bad part of the influence, which these principles must have, when thus reasoned and acted upon, during the course of his education. He must either be allowed to go on, and be the plague of all about him, and himself too, even to his own destruction: or else correction must be continually made use of, to supply the want of those natural perceptions of blame and commendation, which we have supposed to be removed; and to give him a practical impression, of what he had reasoned himself out of the belief of, that he was in fact an accountable child, and to be punished for doing what he was forbid. It is therefore in reality impossible, but that the correction which he must meet with, in the course of his education, must convince him, that if the scheme he was instructed in were not false; yet that he reasoned inconclusively upon it, and somehow or other misapplied it to practice and common life; as what the Fatalist experiences of the conduct of Providence at present, ought in all reason to convince him, that this scheme is misapplied when applied to the subject of Religion[b]. But supposing the child's temper could remain still formed to the system, and his expectation of the treatment he was to have in the world be regulated by it; so as to expect that no reasonable man would blame or punish him, for any thing which he should

[b] P. 126.

do, because he could not help doing it: upon this supposition it is manifest he would, upon his coming abroad into the world, be insupportable to society, and the treatment which he would receive from it would render it so to him; and he could not fail of doing somewhat, very soon, for which he would be delivered over into the hands of civil justice. And thus, in the end, he would be convinced of the obligations he was under to his wise instructor. Or suppose this scheme of Fatality, in any other way, applied to practice, such practical application of it will be found equally absurd; equally fallacious in a practical sense: for instance, that if a man be destined to live such a time, he shall live to it, though he take no care of his own preservation; or if he be destined to die before that time, no care can prevent it: therefore all care about preserving one's life is to be neglected: which is the fallacy instanced in by the ancients. But now on the contrary, none of these practical absurdities can be drawn, from reasoning upon the supposition, that we are free; but all such reasoning with regard to the common affairs of life is justified by experience. And therefore, though it were admitted that this opinion of Necessity were speculatively true; yet, with regard to practice, it is as if it were false, so far as our experience reaches; that is, to the whole of our present life. For, the constitution of the present world, and the condition in which we are actually placed, is, as if we were free. And it may perhaps justly be concluded, that since the whole process of action, through every step of it, suspense, deliberation, inclining one way, determining, and at last doing as we determine, is as if we were free, therefore we are so. But the thing here insisted upon is, that under the present natural government of the world, we find we are treated and dealt with, as if we were free, prior to all consideration whether we are or not. Were this opinion therefore of Necessity admitted to be ever so true; yet such is in fact our condition and the natural course of things, that whenever we apply it to life and practice, this application of it always misleads us, and cannot but mislead us, in a most dreadful manner, with regard to our present interest. And how can people think themselves so very secure then, that the same application of the same opinion may not mislead them also, in some analogous manner, with respect to a future, a more general, and more important interest? For, Religion being a practical subject; and the analogy of nature shewing us, that we have not faculties to apply this opinion, were it a true one, to practical subjects; whenever we do apply it to the subject of Religion, and thence conclude, that we are free from its obligations, it is plain this conclusion cannot be depended upon. There will still remain just reason to think, whatever appearances are, that we deceive ourselves; in somewhat of a like manner, as when people fancy they can draw contradictory conclusions from the idea of infinity.

From these things together, the attentive reader will see it follows, that if upon supposition of Freedom the evidence of Religion be conclusive, it remains so, upon supposition of Necessity, because the notion of Necessity is not applicable to practical subjects: i. e. with respect to them, is as if it were not true. Nor does this contain any reflection upon reason; but only upon what is unreasonable. For to pretend to act upon reason, in opposition to practical principles, which the Author of our Nature gave us to act upon; and to pretend to apply our reason to subjects, with regard to which, our own short views, and even our experience, will shew us, it cannot be depended upon; and such, at best, the subject of Necessity must be; this is vanity, conceit, and unreasonableness.

But this is not all. For we find within ourselves a will, and are conscious of a character. Now if this, in us, be reconcilable with Fate, it is reconcilable with it, in the Author of Nature. And besides, natural government and final causes imply a character and a will in the Governor and Designer[c]; a will concerning the creatures whom he governs. The Author of Nature then being certainly by some character or other, notwithstanding Necessity; it is evident this Necessity is as reconcilable with the particular character of benevolence, veracity, and justice in him, which attributes are the foundation of Religion, as with any other character; since we find this Necessity no more hinders *men* from being benevolent, than cruel; true, than faithless; just, than unjust; or if the Fatalist pleases, what we call unjust. For it is said indeed, that what, upon supposition of Freedom, would be just punishment; upon supposition of Necessity, becomes manifestly unjust: because it is punishment inflicted for doing that which persons could not avoid doing. As if the Necessity, which is supposed to destroy the injustice of murder, for instance, would not also destroy the injustice of punishing it. However, as little to the purpose as

[c] By *will* and *character* is meant that, which, in speaking of men, we should express, not only by these words, but also by the words *temper, taste, dispositions, practical principles: that whole frame of mind, from whence we act in one manner rather than another.*

this objection is in itself, it is very much to the purpose to observe from it, how the notions of justice and injustice remain, even whilst we endeavour to suppose them removed; how they force themselves upon the mind, even whilst we are making suppositions destructive of them: for there is not, perhaps, a man in the world, but would be ready to make this objection at first thought.

But though it is most evident, that universal Necessity, if it be reconcilable with any thing, is reconcilable with that character in the Author of Nature, which is the foundation of Religion; " Yet, does it not plainly destroy the proof, that he is of that character, and consequently the proof of Religion?" By no means. For we find, that happiness and misery are not our fate, in any such sense as not to be the consequences of our behaviour; but that they are the consequences of it [d]. We find God exercises the same kind of government over us, with that, which a father exercises over his children, and a civil magistrate over his subjects. Now, whatever becomes of abstract questions concerning Liberty and Necessity, it evidently appears to us, that veracity and justice must be the natural rule and measure of exercising this authority or government, to a Being who can have no competitions or interfering of interests, with his creatures and his subjects.

But as the doctrine of Liberty, though we experience its truth, may be perplexed with difficulties, which run up into the most abstruse of all speculations; and as the opinion of Necessity seems to be the very basis, upon which infidelity grounds itself; it may be of some use to offer a more particular proof of the obligations of Religion, which may distinctly be shewn not to be destroyed by this opinion.

[d] Chap. ii.

The proof from final causes of an intelligent Author of Nature is not affected by the opinion of Necessity; supposing necessity a thing possible in itself, and reconcilable with the constitution of things[e]. And it is a matter of fact, independent on this or any other speculation, that he governs the world by the method of rewards and punishments[f]: and also that he hath given us a moral faculty, by which we distinguish between actions, and approve some as virtuous and of good desert, and disapprove others as vicious and of ill desert[g]. Now this moral discernment implies, in the notion of it, a rule of action, and a rule of a very peculiar kind: for it carries in it authority and a right of direction; authority in such a sense, as that we cannot depart from it without being self-condemned[h]. And that the dictates of this moral faculty, which are by nature a rule to us, are moreover the laws of God, laws in a sense including sanctions; may be thus proved. Consciousness of a rule or guide of action, in creatures who are capable of considering it as given them by their Maker, not only raises immediately a sense of duty, but also a sense of security in following it, and of danger in deviating from it. A direction of the Author of Nature, given to creatures capable of looking upon it as such, is plainly a command from him: and a command from him necessarily includes in it, at least, an implicit promise in case of obedience, or threatening in case of disobedience. But then the sense or perception of good and ill desert[i], which is contained in the moral discernment, renders the sanction explicit, and makes it appear, as one may say expressed. For since his method of government is to

[e] P. 112, &c.   [f] Chap. ii.   [g] Dissert. II.
[h] Serm. II. at the Rolls.   [i] Dissert. II.

reward and punish actions, his having annexed to some actions an inseparable sense of good desert, and to others of ill, this surely amounts to declaring, upon whom his punishments shall be inflicted, and his rewards be bestowed. For he must have given us this discernment and sense of things, as a presentiment of what is to be hereafter : that is, by way of information beforehand, what we are finally to expect in his world. There is then most evident ground to think, that the government of God, upon the whole, will be found to correspond to the nature which he has given us : and that in the upshot and issue of things, happiness and misery shall, in fact and event, be made to follow virtue and vice respectively; as he has already, in so peculiar a manner, associated the ideas of them in our minds. And from hence might easily be deduced the obligations of religious worship, were it only to be considered as a means of preserving upon our minds a sense of this moral government of God, and securing our obedience to it : which yet is an extremely imperfect view of that most important duty.

Now I say, no objection from Necessity can lie against this general proof of religion. None against the proposition reasoned upon, that we have such a moral faculty and discernment; because this is a mere matter of fact, a thing of experience, that human kind is thus constituted: none against the conclusion; because it is immediate and wholly from this fact. For the conclusion, that God will finally reward the righteous and punish the wicked, is not here drawn, from its appearing to us fit[k]

---

[k] However, I am far from intending to deny, that the will of God is determined, by what is fit, by the right and reason of the case ; though one chooses to decline matters of such abstract speculation,

that *he should;* but from its appearing, that he has to us, *he will.* And this he hath certainly told us, in the promise and threatening, which it hath been observed the notion of a command implies, and the sense of good and ill desert which he has given us, more distinctly expresses. And this reasoning from fact is confirmed, and in some degree even verified, by other facts; by the natural tendencies of virtue and of vice[l]; and by this, that God, in the natural course of his providence, punishes vicious actions as mischievous to society; and also vicious actions as such in the strictest sense[m]. So that the general proof of Religion is unanswerably real, even upon the wild supposition which we are arguing upon.

It must likewise be observed farther, that natural Religion hath, besides this, an external evidence; which the doctrine of Necessity, if it could be true, would not affect. For suppose a person, by the observations and reasoning above, or by any other, convinced of the truth of Religion; that there is a God, who made the world, who is the moral Governor

and to speak with caution when one does speak of them. But if it be intelligible to say, that *it is fit and reasonable for every one to consult his own happiness,* then *fitness of action, or the right and reason of the case,* is an intelligible manner of speaking. And it seems as inconceivable, to suppose God to approve one course of action, or one end, preferably to another, which yet his acting at all from design implies that he does, without supposing somewhat prior in that end, to be the ground of the preference; as to suppose him to discern an abstract proposition to be true, without supposing somewhat prior in it, to be the ground of the discernment. It doth not therefore appear, that moral right is any more relative to perception, than abstract truth is; or that it is any more improper, to speak of the fitness and rightness of actions and ends, as founded in the nature of things, than to speak of abstract truth, as thus founded.

[l] P. 62, 63.   [m] P. 53, &c.

and Judge of mankind, and will upon the whole deal with every one according to his works : I say, suppose a person convinced of this by reason ; but to know nothing at all of antiquity, or the present state of mankind : it would be natural for such an one to be inquisitive, what was the history of this system of doctrine ; at what time, and in what manner, it came first into the world ; and whether it were believed by any considerable part of it. And were he upon inquiry to find, that a particular person, in a late age, first of all proposed it, as a deduction of reason, and that mankind were before wholly ignorant of it ; then, though its evidence from reason would remain, there would be no additional probability of its truth, from the account of its discovery. But instead of this being the fact of the case, on the contrary, he would find, what could not but afford him a very strong confirmation of its truth : First, That somewhat of this system, with more or fewer additions and alterations, hath been professed in all ages and countries, of which we have any certain information relating to this matter. Secondly, That it is certain historical fact, so far as we can trace things up, that this whole system of belief, that there is one God, the Creator and moral Governor of the world, and that mankind is in a state of Religion, was received in the first ages. And Thirdly, That as there is no hint or intimation in history, that this system was first reasoned out ; so there is express historical or traditional evidence, as ancient as history, that it was taught first by revelation. Now these things must be allowed to be of great weight. The first of them, general consent, shews this system to be conformable to the common sense of mankind. The second, namely, that Religion was believed in the first ages of the world, especially as it does not appear that there were then any superstitious or false additions to it, cannot but be a farther confirmation of its truth. For it is a proof of this alternative: either that it came into the world by revelation; or that it is natural, obvious, and forces itself upon the mind. The former of these is the conclusion of learned men. And whoever will consider, how unapt for speculation rude and uncultivated minds are, will, perhaps from hence alone, be strongly inclined to believe it the truth. And as it is shewn in the Second Part[u] of this Treatise, that there is nothing of such peculiar presumption against a revelation in the beginning of the world, as there is supposed to be against subsequent ones: a sceptic could not, I think, give any account, which would appear more probable even to himself, of the early pretences to revelation; than by supposing some real original one, from whence they were copied. And the third thing above mentioned, that there is express historical or traditional evidence as ancient as history, of the system of Religion being taught mankind by revelation; this must be admitted as some degree of real proof, that it was so taught. For why should not the most ancient tradition be admitted, as some additional proof of a fact, against which there is no presumption? And this proof is mentioned here, because it has its weight to shew, that Religion came into the world by revelation, prior to all consideration of the proper authority of any book supposed to contain it; and even prior to all consideration, whether the revelation itself be uncorruptly handed down, and related, or mixed and darkened with fables. Thus the his-

[u] Chap. ii.

torical account, which we have, of the origin of Religion, taking in all circumstances, is a real confirmation of its truth, no way affected by the opinion of Necessity. And the *external* evidence, even of natural Religion, is by no means inconsiderable.

But it is carefully to be observed, and ought to be recollected after all proofs of virtue and religion, which are only general; that as speculative reason may be neglected, prejudiced, and deceived, so also may our moral understanding be impaired and perverted, and the dictates of it not impartially attended to. This indeed proves nothing against the reality of our speculative or practical faculties of perception; against their being intended by nature, to inform us in the theory of things, and instruct us how we are to behave, and what we are to expect in consequence of our behaviour. Yet our liableness, in the degree we are liable, to prejudice and perversion, is a most serious admonition to us to be upon our guard, with respect to what is of such consequence, as our determinations concerning virtue and religion; and particularly not to take custom and fashion and slight notions of honour, or imaginations of present ease, use, and convenience to mankind, for the only moral rule[o].

The foregoing observations, drawn from the nature of the thing, and the history of Religion, amount, when taken together, to a real practical proof of it, not to be confuted: such a proof as, considering the infinite importance of the thing, I apprehend, would be admitted fully sufficient, in reason, to influence the actions of men, who act upon thought and reflection; if it were admitted that there is no proof of the contrary. But it may be said: "There are

[o] Dissert. II.

many probabilities, which cannot indeed be confuted, i. e. shewn to be no probabilities, and yet may be overbalanced by greater probabilities on the other side; much more by demonstration. And there is no occasion to object against particular arguments alleged for an opinion, when the opinion itself may be clearly shewn to be false, without meddling with such arguments at all, but leaving them just as they are[p]. Now the method of government by rewards and punishments, and especially rewarding and punishing good and ill desert as such respectively, must go upon supposition, that we are Free and not Necessary Agents. And it is incredible, that the Author of Nature should govern us upon a supposition as true, which he knows to be false; and therefore absurd to think, he will reward or punish us for our actions hereafter; especially that he will do it under the notion, that they are of good or ill desert." Here then the matter is brought to a point. And the answer to all this is full, and not to be evaded: that the whole constitution and course of things, the whole analogy of Providence, shews beyond possibility of doubt, that the conclusion from this reasoning is false; wherever the fallacy lies. The doctrine of freedom indeed clearly shews where: in supposing ourselves Necessary, when in truth we are Free Agents. But upon the supposition of Necessity, the fallacy lies in taking for granted, that it is incredible Necessary Agents should be rewarded and punished. But that, some how or other, the conclusion now mentioned is false, is most certain. For it is fact, that God does govern even brute creatures by the method of rewards and punishments, in the natural course of things. And men are rewarded and

[p] Page 1, 9.

punished for their actions, punished for actions mischievous to society as being so, punished for vicious actions as such; by the natural instrumentality of each other, under the present conduct of Providence. Nay even the affection of gratitude, and the passion of resentment, and the rewards and punishments following from them, which in general are to be considered as natural, i. e. from the Author of Nature; these rewards and punishments, being naturally[q] annexed to actions considered as implying good intention and good desert, ill intention and ill desert; these natural rewards and punishments, I say, are as much a contradiction to the conclusion above, and shew its falsehood, as a more exact and complete rewarding and punishing of good and ill desert as such. So that if it be incredible, that Necessary Agents should be thus rewarded and punished; then, men are not necessary but free; since it is matter of fact, that they are thus rewarded and punished. But if, on the contrary, which is the supposition we have been arguing upon, it be insisted, that men are Necessary Agents; then, there is nothing incredible in the farther supposition of Necessary Agents being thus rewarded and punished: since we ourselves are thus dealt with.

From the whole therefore it must follow, that a Necessity supposed possible, and reconcilable with the constitution of things, does in no sort prove that the Author of Nature will not, nor destroy the proof that he will, finally and upon the whole, in his eternal government, render his creatures happy or miserable, by some means or other, as they behave well or ill. Or, to express this conclusion in words conformable to the title of the chapter, the analogy

[q] Serm. VIIIth, at the Rolls.

of nature shews us, that the opinion of Necessity, considered as practical, is false. And if Necessity, upon the supposition above mentioned, doth not destroy the proof of natural Religion, it evidently makes no alteration in the proof of revealed.

From these things likewise we may learn, in what sense to understand that general assertion, that the opinion of Necessity is essentially destructive of all religion. First, in a practical sense; that by this notion, atheistical men pretend to satisfy and encourage themselves in vice, and justify to others their disregard to all religion. And secondly, in the strictest sense; that it is a contradiction to the whole constitution of nature, and to what we may every moment experience in ourselves, and so overturns every thing. But by no means is this assertion to be understood, as if Necessity, supposing it could possibly be reconciled with the constitution of things and with what we experience, were not also reconcilable with Religion: for upon this supposition, it demonstrably is so.

CHAP. VII.

Of the government of God, considered as a scheme or constitution, imperfectly comprehended.

THOUGH it be, as it cannot but be, acknowledged, that the analogy of nature gives a strong credibility to the general doctrine of Religion, and to the several particular things contained in it, considered as so many matters of fact; and likewise that it shews this credibility not to be destroyed by any notions of Necessity: yet still, objections may be insisted upon, against the wisdom, equity, and goodness of the Divine government implied in the notion of Religion, and against the method by which this government is conducted; to which objections analogy can be no direct answer. For the credibility, or the certain truth, of a matter of fact, does not immediately prove any thing concerning the wisdom or goodness of it: and analogy can do no more, immediately or directly, than shew such and such things to be true or credible, considered only as matters of fact. But still, if, upon supposition of a moral constitution of nature and a moral government over it, analogy suggests and makes it credible, that this government must be a scheme, system, or constitution of government, as distinguished from a number of single unconnected acts of distributive justice and goodness; and likewise, that it must be a scheme, so imperfectly comprehended, and of such a sort in other respects, as to afford a direct general answer to all objections against the justice and goodness of it: then analogy is, remotely, of great service in answering those objections; both by suggesting the answer, and shewing it to be a credible one.

Now this, upon inquiry, will be found to be the case. For, first, Upon supposition that God exercises a moral government over the world, the analogy of his natural government suggests and makes it credible, that his moral government must be a scheme, quite beyond our comprehension: and this affords a general answer to all objections against the justice and goodness of it. And, secondly, A more distinct observation of some particular things contained in God's scheme of natural government, the like things being supposed, by analogy, to be contained in his moral government, will farther shew, how little weight is to be laid upon these objections.

I. Upon supposition that God exercises a moral government over the world, the analogy of his natural government suggests and makes it credible, that his moral government must be a scheme, quite beyond our comprehension; and this affords a general answer to all objections against the justice and goodness of it. It is most obvious, analogy renders it highly credible, that, upon supposition of a moral government, it must be a scheme: for the world, and the whole natural government of it, appears to be so: to be a scheme, system, or constitution, whose parts correspond to each other, and to a whole; as really as any work of art, or as any particular model of a civil constitution and government. In this great scheme of the natural world, individuals have various peculiar relations to other individuals of their own species. And whole species are, we find, variously related to other species, upon this earth. Nor do we know, how much farther these kinds of relations may extend. And, as there is not any action or natural event, which we are acquainted with, so single and unconnected, as not to have a respect to some other actions and events: so possibly each of them, when it has not an immediate, may yet have a remote, natural relation to other actions and events, much beyond the compass of this present world. There seems indeed nothing, from whence we can so much as make a conjecture, whether all creatures, actions, and events, throughout the whole of nature, have relations to each other. But, as it is obvious, that all events have future unknown consequences; so if we trace any, as far as we can go, into what is connected with it, we shall find, that if such event were not connected with somewhat farther in nature unknown to us, somewhat both past and present, such event could not possibly have been at all. Nor can we give the whole account of any one thing whatever; of all its causes, ends, and necessary adjuncts; those adjuncts, I mean, without which it could not have been. By this most astonishing connection, these reciprocal correspondencies and mutual relations, every thing which we see in the course of nature is actually brought about. And things seemingly the most insignificant imaginable are perpetually observed to be necessary conditions to other things of the greatest importance: so that any one thing whatever may, for ought we know to the contrary, be a necessary condition to any other. The natural world then, and natural government of it, being such an incomprehensible scheme; so incomprehensible, that a man must, really in the literal sense, know nothing at all, who is not sensible of his ignorance in it; this immediately suggests, and strongly shews the credibility, that the moral world and government of it may be so too. Indeed the natural and moral constitution and government of the world are so connected, as to make up together but one scheme: and it is highly probable, that the first is formed and carried on merely in subserviency to the latter; as the vegetable world is for the animal, and organized bodies for minds. But the thing intended here is, without inquiring how far the administration of the natural world is subordinate to that of the moral, only to observe the credibility, that one should be analogous or similar to the other: that therefore every act of Divine justice and goodness may be supposed to look much beyond itself, and its immediate object; may have some reference to other parts of God's moral administration, and to a general moral plan; and that every circumstance of this his moral government may be adjusted beforehand with a view to the whole of it. Thus for example: the determined length of time, and the degrees and ways, in which virtue is to remain in a state of warfare and discipline, and in which wickedness is permitted to have its progress; the times appointed for the execution of justice; the appointed instruments of it; the kinds of rewards and punishments, and the manners of their distribution; all particular instances of Divine justice and goodness, and every circumstance of them, may have such respects to each other, as to make up altogether a whole, connected and related in all its parts; a scheme or system, which is as properly one as the natural world is, and of the like kind. And supposing this to be the case; it is most evident, that we are not competent judges of this scheme, from the small parts of it which come within our view in the present life: and therefore no objections against any of these parts can be insisted upon by reasonable men.

This our ignorance, and the consequence here drawn from it, are universally acknowledged upon other occasions; and though scarce denied, yet are universally forgot, when persons come to argue against Religion. And it is not perhaps easy, even for the most reasonable men, always to bear in mind the degree of our ignorance, and make due allowances for it. Upon these accounts, it may not be useless to go on a little farther, in order to shew more distinctly, how just an answer our ignorance is, to objections against the scheme of Providence. Suppose then a person boldly to assert, that the things complained of, the origin and continuance of evil, might easily have been prevented by repeated interpositions[a]; interpositions so guarded and circumstanced, as would preclude all mischief arising from them; or, if this were impracticable, that a *scheme* of government is itself an imperfection; since more good might have been produced, without any scheme, system, or constitution at all, by continued single unrelated acts of distributive justice and goodness; because these would have occasioned no irregularities. And farther than this, it is presumed, the objections will not be carried. Yet the answer is obvious: that were these assertions true, still the observations above, concerning our ignorance in the scheme of Divine government, and the consequence drawn from it, would hold, in great measure; enough to vindicate Religion, against all objections from the disorders of the present state. Were these assertions true, yet the government of the world might be just and good notwithstanding; for, at the most, they would infer nothing more than that it might have been better. But indeed they are mere arbitrary assertions; no man being sufficiently acquainted with the possibilities of things, to bring any proof of them to the lowest degree of probability. For however possible what is asserted may seem; yet many instances may be alleged, in things much less out of our reach, of suppositions absolutely impossible, and reducible to the most palpable self-contradictions, which, not every one by any means would perceive to be such, nor perhaps any one at first sight suspect. From these things, it is easy to see distinctly, how our ignorance, as it is the common, is really a satisfactory answer

[a] P. 138, 139.

to all objections against the justice and goodness of Providence. If a man, contemplating any one providential dispensation, which had no relation to any others, should object, that he discerned in it a disregard to justice, or a deficiency of goodness; nothing would be less an answer to such objection, than our ignorance in other parts of Providence, or in the possibilities of things, no way related to what he was contemplating. But when we know not but the parts objected against may be relative to other parts unknown to us; and when we are unacquainted with what is, in the nature of the thing, practicable in the case before us; then our ignorance is a satisfactory answer; because, some unknown relation, or some unknown impossibility, may render what is objected against, just and good; nay good in the highest practicable degree.

II. And how little weight is to be laid upon such objections, will farther appear, by a more distinct observation of some particular things contained in the natural government of God, the like to which may be supposed, from analogy, to be contained in his moral government.

First, As in the scheme of the natural world, no ends appear to be accomplished without means; so we find that means very undesirable, often conduce to bring about ends in such a measure desirable, as greatly to overbalance the disagreeableness of the means. And in cases where such means are conducive to such ends, it is not reason, but experience, which shews us, that they are thus conducive. Experience also shews many means to be conducive and necessary to accomplish ends, which means, before experience, we should have thought, would have had even a contrary tendency. Now from these observations relating to the natural scheme of the world, the moral being supposed analogous to it, arises a great credibility, that the putting our misery in each other's power to the degree it is, and making men liable to vice to the degree we are; and in general, that those things which are objected against the moral scheme of Providence, may be, upon the whole, friendly and assistant to virtue, and productive of an overbalance of happiness: i. e. the things objected against may be means, by which an overbalance of good will, in the end, be found produced. And from the same observations, it appears to be no presumption against this, that we do not, if indeed we do not, see those means to have any such tendency; or that they seem to us to have a contrary one. Thus those things, which we call irregularities, may not be so at all: because they may be means of accomplishing wise and good ends more considerable. And it may be added, as above [b], that they may also be the only means, by which these wise and good ends are capable of being accomplished.

After these observations it may be proper to add, in order to obviate an absurd and wicked conclusion from any of them, that though the constitution of our nature, from whence we are capable of vice and misery, may, as it undoubtedly does, contribute to the perfection and happiness of the world; and though the actual permission of evil may be beneficial to it: (i. e. it would have been more mischievous, not that a wicked person had himself abstained from his own wickedness, but that any one had forcibly prevented it, than that it was permitted:) yet notwithstanding, it might have been

[b] P. 135.

much better for the world, if this very evil had never been done. Nay it is most clearly conceivable, that the very commission of wickedness may be beneficial to the world, and yet, that it would be infinitely more beneficial for men to refrain from it. For thus, in the wise and good constitution of the natural world, there are disorders which bring their own cures; diseases, which are themselves remedies. Many a man would have died, had it not been for the gout or a fever; yet it would be thought madness to assert, that sickness is a better or more perfect state than health; though the like, with regard to the moral world, has been asserted. But,

Secondly, The natural government of the world is carried on by general laws. For this there may be wise and good reasons: the wisest and best, for ought we know to the contrary. And that there are such reasons, is suggested to our thoughts by the analogy of nature: by our being made to experience good ends to be accomplished, as indeed all the good which we enjoy is accomplished, by this means, that the laws, by which the world is governed, are general. For we have scarce any kind of enjoyments, but what we are, in some way or other, instrumental in procuring ourselves, by acting in a manner which we foresee likely to procure them: now this foresight could not be at all, were not the government of the world carried on by general laws. And though, for ought we know to the contrary, every single case may be, at length, found to have been provided for even by these: yet to prevent all irregularities, or remedy them as they arise, by the wisest and best general laws, may be impossible in the nature of things; as we see it is absolutely impossible in civil government. But then we are ready to think, that, the constitution of nature remaining as it is, and the course of things being permitted to go on, in other respects, as it does, there might be interpositions to prevent irregularities; though they could not have been prevented or remedied by any general laws. And there would indeed be reason to wish, which, by the way, is very different from a right to claim, that all irregularities were prevented or remedied by present interpositions, if these interpositions would have no other effect than this. But it is plain they would have some visible and immediate bad effects: for instance, they would encourage idleness and negligence; and they would render doubtful the natural rule of life, which is ascertained by this very thing, that the course of the world is carried on by general laws. And farther, it is certain they would have distant effects, and very great ones too; by means of the wonderful connections before mentioned[c]. So that we cannot as much as guess, what would be the whole result of the interpositions desired. It may be said, any bad result might be prevented by farther interpositions, whenever there was occasion for them: but this again is talking quite at random, and in the dark[d]. Upon the whole then, we see wise reasons, why the course of the world should be carried on by general laws, and good ends accomplished by this means: and, for ought we know, there may be the wisest reasons for it, and the best ends accomplished by it. We have no ground to believe, that all irregularities could be remedied as they arise, or could have been precluded, by general laws. We find that interpositions would produce evil, and prevent good: and, for ought we know, they would

[c] P. 131, &c.   [d] P. 134.

produce greater evil than they would prevent; and prevent greater good than they would produce. And if this be the case, then the not interposing is so far from being a ground of complaint, that it is an instance of goodness. This is intelligible and sufficient: and going farther, seems beyond the utmost reach of our faculties.

But it may be said, that 'after all, these supposed impossibilities and relations are what we are unacquainted with; and we must judge of Religion, as of other things, by what we do know, and look upon the rest as nothing: or however, that the answers here given to what is objected against Religion, may equally be made use of to invalidate the proof of it; since their stress lies so very much upon our ignorance.' But,

First, though total ignorance in any matter does indeed equally destroy, or rather preclude, all proof concerning it, and objections against it; yet partial ignorance does not. For we may in any degree be convinced, that a person is of such a character, and consequently will presume such ends; though we are greatly ignorant, what is the proper way of acting, in order the most effectually to obtain those ends: and in this case, objections against his manner of acting, as seemingly not conducive to obtain them, might be answered by our ignorance; though the proof that such ends were intended, might not at all be invalidated by it. Thus, the proof of Religion is a proof of the moral character of God, and consequently that his government is moral, and that every one upon the whole shall receive according to his deserts; a proof that this is the designed end of his government. But we are not competent judges, what is the proper way of acting, in order the most effectually to accomplish this end [c]. Therefore our ignorance is an answer to objections against the conduct of Providence, in permitting irregularities, as seeming contradictory to this end. Now, since it is so obvious, that our ignorance may be a satisfactory answer to objections against a thing, and yet not affect the proof of it; till it can be shewn, it is frivolous to assert, that our ignorance invalidates the proof of Religion, as it does the objections against it.

Secondly, Suppose unknown impossibilities, and unknown relations, might justly be urged to invalidate the proof of Religion, as well as to answer objections against it: and that, in consequence of this, the proof of it were doubtful. Yet still, let the assertion be despised, or let it be ridiculed, it is undeniably true, that moral obligations would remain certain, though it were not certain what would, upon the whole, be the consequences of observing or violating them. For, these obligations arise immediately and necessarily from the judgment of our own mind, unless perverted, which we cannot violate without being self-condemned. And they would be certain too, from considerations of interest. For though it were doubtful, what will be the future consequences of virtue and vice; yet it is, however, credible, that they may have those consequences, which Religion teaches us they will: and this credibility is a certain [f] obligation in point of prudence, to abstain from all wickedness, and to live in the conscientious practice of all that is good. But,

Thirdly, The answers above given to the objections against Religion cannot equally be made use of to

[c] P. 8, 9.   [f] Page 3; and part II. chap. vi.

invalidate the proof of it. For, upon supposition that God exercises a moral government over the world, analogy does most strongly lead us to conclude, that this moral government must be a scheme, or constitution, beyond our comprehension. And a thousand particular analogies shew us, that parts of such a scheme, from their relation to other parts, may conduce to accomplish ends, which we should have thought they had no tendency at all to accomplish: nay ends, which, before experience, we should have thought such parts were contradictory to, and had a tendency to prevent. And therefore all these analogies shew, that the way of arguing made use of in objecting against Religion is delusive: because they shew it is not at all incredible, that, could we comprehend the whole, we should find the permission of the disorders objected against to be consistent with justice and goodness; and even to be instances of them. Now this is not applicable to the proof of Religion, as it is to the objections against it [g]; and therefore cannot invalidate that proof, as it does these objections.

Lastly, From the observation now made, it is easy to see, that the answers above given to the objections against Providence, though, in a general way of speaking, they may be said to be taken from our ignorance; yet are by no means taken merely from that, but from somewhat which analogy shews us concerning it. For analogy shews us positively, that our ignorance in the possibilities of things, and the various relations in nature, renders us incompetent judges, and leads us to false conclusions, in cases similar to this, in which we pretend to judge and to object. So that the things above insisted

[g] Serm. at the Rolls. p. 312, 2d ed.

upon are not mere suppositions of unknown impossibilities and relations: but they are suggested to our thoughts, and even forced upon the observation of serious men, and rendered credible too, by the analogy of nature. And therefore, to take these things into the account, is to judge by experience and what we do know: and it is not judging so, to take no notice of them.

CONCLUSION.

THE observations of the last chapter lead us to consider this little scene of human life, in which we are so busily engaged, as having a reference, of sort or other, to a much larger plan of things. Whether we are, any way, related to the more distant parts of the boundless universe, into which we are brought, is altogether uncertain. But it is evident, that the course of things, which comes within our view, is connected with somewhat, past, present, and future, beyond it [h]. So that we are placed, as one may speak, in the middle of a scheme, not a fixt but a progressive one, every way incomprehensible: incomprehensible, in a manner equally, with respect to what has been, what now is, and what shall be hereafter. And this scheme cannot but contain in it somewhat as wonderful, and as much beyond our thought and conception [i], as any thing in that of Religion. For, will any man in his senses say, that it is less difficult to conceive, how the world came to be and to continue as it is, without, than with, an intelligent Author and Governor of it? or, admitting an intelligent Governor of it, that there is

[h] P. 131, &c.   [i] See part II. chap. ii.

some other rule of government more natural, and of easier conception, than that which we call moral? Indeed, without an intelligent Author and Governor of Nature, no account at all can be given, how this universe, or the part of it particularly in which we are concerned, came to be, and the course of it to be carried on, as it is: nor any, of its general end and design, without a moral Governor of it. That there is an intelligent Author of Nature, and natural Governor of the world, is a principle gone upon in the foregoing treatise, as proved, and generally known and confessed to be proved. And the very notion of an intelligent Author of Nature, proved by particular final causes, implies a will and a character [k]. Now, as our whole nature, the nature which he has given us, leads us to conclude his will and character to be moral, just, and good: so we can scarce in imagination conceive, what it can be otherwise. However, in consequence of this his will and character, whatever it be, he formed the universe as it is, and carries on the course of it as he does, rather than in any other manner; and has assigned to us, and to all living creatures, a part and a lot in it. Irrational creatures act this their part, and enjoy and undergo the pleasures and the pains allotted them, without any reflection. But one would think it impossible, that creatures endued with reason could avoid reflecting sometimes upon all this; reflecting, if not from whence we came, yet, at least, whither we are going; and what the mysterious scheme, in the midst of which we find ourselves, will at length come out and produce: a scheme in which it is certain we are highly interested, and in which we may be interested even beyond concep-

[k] P. 119.

tion. For many things prove it palpably absurd to conclude, that we shall cease to be, at death. Particular analogies do most sensibly shew us, that there is nothing to be thought strange, in our being to exist in another state of life. And that we are now living beings, affords a strong probability that we shall *continue* so; unless there be some positive ground, and there is none from reason or analogy, to think death will destroy us. Were a persuasion of this kind ever so well grounded, there would, surely, be little reason to take pleasure in it. But indeed it can have no other ground, than some such imagination, as that of our gross bodies being ourselves; which is contrary to experience. Experience too most clearly shews us the folly of concluding, from the body and the living agent affecting each other mutually, that the dissolution of the former is the destruction of the latter. And there are remarkable instances of their not affecting each other, which lead us to a contrary conclusion. The supposition then, which in all reason we are to go upon, is, that our living nature will *continue* after death. And it is infinitely unreasonable to form an institution of life, or to act, upon any other supposition. Now all expectation of immortality, whether more or less certain, opens an unbounded prospect to our hopes and our fears: since we see the constitution of nature is such, as to admit of misery, as well as to be productive of happiness, and experience ourselves to partake of both in some degree; and since we cannot but know, what higher degrees of both we are capable of. And there is no presumption against believing farther, that our future interest depends upon our present behaviour: for we see our present interest doth; and that the happiness and misery, which are naturally annexed to our actions, very frequently do not follow, till long after the actions are done, to which they are respectively annexed. So that were speculation to leave us uncertain, whether it were likely, that the Author of Nature, in giving happiness and misery to his creatures, hath regard to their actions or not: yet, since we find by experience that he hath such regard, the whole sense of things which he has given us, plainly leads us, at once and without any elaborate inquiries, to think, that it may, indeed must, be to good actions chiefly that he hath annexed happiness, and to bad actions misery; or that he will, upon the whole, reward those who do well, and punish those who do evil. To confirm this from the constitution of the world, it has been observed, that some sort of moral government is necessarily implied in that natural government of God, which we experience ourselves under: that good and bad actions, at present, are naturally rewarded and punished, not only as beneficial and mischievous to society, but also as virtuous and vicious: and that there is, in the very nature of the thing, a tendency to their being rewarded and punished in a much higher degree than they are at present. And though this higher degree of distributive justice, which nature thus points out and leads towards, is prevented for a time from taking place; it is by obstacles, which the state of this world unhappily throws in its way, and which therefore are in their nature temporary. Now, as these things in the natural conduct of Providence are observable on the side of virtue; so there is nothing to be set against them on the side of vice. A moral scheme of government then is visibly established, and, in some degree, carried into execution: and this, together with the essential tendencies of virtue and vice duly considered, naturally raise in us an apprehension, that it will be carried on farther towards perfection in a future state, and that every one shall there receive according to his deserts. And if this be so, then our future and general interest, under the moral government of God, is appointed to depend upon our behaviour; notwithstanding the difficulty, which this may occasion, of securing it, and the danger of losing it: just in the same manner as our temporal interest, under his natural government, is appointed to depend upon our behaviour; notwithstanding the like difficulty and danger. For, from our original constitution, and that of the world which we inhabit, we are naturally trusted with ourselves; with our own conduct and our own interest. And from the same constitution of nature, especially joined with that course of things which is owing to men, we have temptations to be unfaithful in this trust; to forfeit this interest, to neglect it, and run ourselves into misery and ruin. From these temptations arise the difficulties of behaving so as to secure our temporal interest, and the hazard of behaving so as to miscarry in it. There is therefore nothing incredible in supposing there may be the like difficulty and hazard with regard to that chief and final good, which Religion lays before us. Indeed the whole account, how it came to pass that we were placed in such a condition as this, must be beyond our comprehension. But it is in part accounted for by what Religion teaches us, that the character of virtue and piety must be a necessary qualification for a future state of security and happiness, under the moral government of God; in like manner, as some certain qualifications or other are necessary for every particular condition of life, under his natural government: and that the present state was intended to be a school of discipline, for improving in ourselves that character. Now this intention of nature is rendered highly credible by observing; that we are plainly made for improvement of all kinds: that it is a general appointment of Providence, that we cultivate practical principles, and form within ourselves habits of action, in order to become fit for what we were wholly unfit for before: that in particular, childhood and youth is naturally appointed to be a state of discipline for mature age: and that the present world is peculiarly fitted for a state of moral discipline. And, whereas objections are urged against the whole notion of moral government and a probation-state, from the opinion of Necessity; it has been shown, that God has given us the evidence, as it were, of experience, that all objections against Religion, on this head, are vain and delusive. He has also, in his natural government, suggested an answer to all our shortsighted objections, against the equity and goodness of his moral government; and in general he has exemplified to us the latter by the former.

These things, which, it is to be remembered, are matters of fact, ought, in all common sense, to awaken mankind; to induce them to consider in earnest their condition, and what they have to do. It is absurd, absurd to the degree of being ridiculous, if the subject were not of so serious a kind, for men to think themselves secure in a vicious life; or even in that immoral thoughtlessness, which far the greatest part of them are fallen into. And the credibility of Religion, arising from experience and facts here considered, is fully sufficient, in reason, to engage them to live in the general practice of all virtue and piety;

under the serious apprehension, though it should be mixed with some doubt[1], of a righteous administration established in nature, and a future judgment in consequence of it: especially when we consider, how very questionable it is, whether any thing at all can be gained by vice[m]; how unquestionably little, as well as precarious, the pleasures and profits of it are at the best; and how soon they must be parted with at the longest. For, in the deliberations of reason, concerning what we are to pursue and what to avoid, as temptations to any thing from mere passion are supposed out of the case: so inducements to vice, from cool expectations of pleasure and interest so small and uncertain and short, are really so insignificant, as, in the view of reason, to be almost nothing in themselves; and in comparison with the importance of Religion, they quite disappear and are lost. Mere passion indeed may be alleged, though not as a reason, yet as an excuse, for a vicious course of life. And how sorry an excuse it is, will be manifest by observing, that we are placed in a condition, in which we are unavoidably inured to govern our passions, by being necessitated to govern them: and to lay ourselves under the same kind of restraints, and as great ones too, from temporal regards, as virtue and piety, in the ordinary course of things, require. The plea of ungovernable passion then, on the side of vice, is the poorest of all things; for it is no reason, and but a poor excuse. But the proper motives to Religion are the proper proofs of it, from our moral nature, from the presages of conscience, and our natural apprehension of God under the character of a righteous Governor and Judge; a nature and

[1] Part II. ch. vi.   [m] P. 50.

conscience and apprehension given us by him; and from the confirmation of the dictates of reason, by *life and immortality brought to light by the Gospel; and the wrath of God revealed from heaven against all ungodliness and unrighteousness of men.*

THE END OF THE FIRST PART.

THE

ANALOGY OF RELIGION

TO THE

CONSTITUTION AND COURSE OF NATURE.

PART II.

OF REVEALED RELIGION.

CHAP. I.

Of the importance of Christianity.

SOME persons, upon pretence of the sufficiency of the light of nature, avowedly reject all revelation as, in its very notion, incredible, and what must be fictitious. And indeed it is certain, no revelation would have been given, had the light of nature been sufficient in such a sense, as to render one not wanting and useless. But no man, in seriousness and simplicity of mind, can possibly think it so, who considers the state of Religion in the heathen world before revelation, and its present state in those places which have borrowed no light from it: particularly, the doubtfulness of some of the greatest men, concerning things of the utmost importance, as well as the natural inattention and ignorance of mankind in general. It is impossible to say, who would have been able to have reasoned out that whole system, which we call natural Religion, in its genuine simplicity, clear of superstition: but there is certainly no ground to affirm that the generality could. If they could, there is no sort of probability that they would. Admitting there were, they would highly want a standing admonition to remind them of it, and inculcate it upon them. And farther still, were they as much disposed to attend to Religion, as the better sort of men are; yet even upon this supposition, there would be various occasions for supernatural instruction and assistance, and the greatest advantages might be afforded by them. So that to say revelation is a thing superfluous, what there was no need of, and what can be of no service, is, I think, to talk quite wildly and at random. Nor would it be more extravagant to affirm, that mankind is so entirely at ease in the present state, and life so completely happy, that it is a contradiction to suppose our condition capable of being, in any respect, better.

There are other persons, not to be ranked with these, who seem to be getting into a way of neglecting, and, as it were, overlooking revelation, as of small importance, provided natural Religion be kept to. With little regard either to the evidence of the former, or to the objections against it, and even upon supposition of its truth; "the only design of it," say they, "must be, to establish a belief of the moral system of nature, and to enforce the practice of natural piety and virtue. The belief and practice of these things were, perhaps, much promoted by the first publication of Christianity: but whether they are believed and practised, upon the evidence and motives of nature or of revelation, is no great matter[a]." This way of considering revelation, though

[a] Invenis multos—propterea nolle fieri Christianos, quia quasi sufficiunt sibi de bona vita sua. Bene vivere opus est, ait. Quid

it is not the same with the former, yet borders nearly upon it, and very much, at length, runs up into it: and requires to be particularly considered, with regard to the persons who seem to be getting into this way. The consideration of it will likewise farther shew the extravagance of the former opinion, and the truth of the observations in answer to it, just mentioned. And an inquiry into the Importance of Christianity, cannot be an improper introduction to a treatise concerning the credibility of it.

Now if God has given a revelation to mankind, and commanded those things which are commanded in Christianity; it is evident, at first sight, that it cannot in any wise be an indifferent matter, whether we obey or disobey those commands: unless we are certainly assured, that we know all the reasons for them, and that all those reasons are now ceased, with regard to mankind in general, or to ourselves in particular. And it is absolutely impossible we can be assured of this. For our ignorance of these reasons proves nothing in the case: since the whole analogy of nature shews, what is indeed in itself evident, that there may be infinite reasons for things, with which we are not acquainted.

But the importance of Christianity will more distinctly appear, by considering it more distinctly: first, as a republication, and external institution, of natural or essential Religion, adapted to the present circumstances of mankind, and intended to promote natural piety and virtue: and secondly, as containing

mihi præcepturus est Christus? Ut bene vivam? Jam bene vivo. Quid mihi necessarius est Christus? Nullum homicidium, nullum furtum, nullam rapinam facio, res alienas non concupisco, nullo adulterio contaminor. Nam inveniatur in vita mea aliquid quod reprehendatur, et qui reprehenderit faciat Christianum. *Aug. in Psal.* xxxi.

an account of a dispensation of things not discoverable by reason, in consequence of which, several distinct precepts are enjoined us. For though natural Religion is the foundation and principal part of Christianity, it is not in any sense the whole of it.

I. Christianity is a republication of natural Religion. It instructs mankind in the moral system of the world: that it is the work of an infinitely perfect Being, and under his government; that virtue is his law; and that he will finally judge mankind in righteousness, and render to all according to their works, in a future state. And, which is very material, it teaches natural Religion in its genuine simplicity; free from those superstitions, with which it was totally corrupted, and under which it was in a manner lost.

Revelation is farther, an authoritative publication of natural Religion, and so affords the evidence of testimony for the truth of it. Indeed the miracles and prophecies recorded in Scripture, were intended to prove a particular dispensation of Providence, the redemption of the world by the Messiah: but this does not hinder, but that they may also prove God's general providence over the world, as our moral Governor and Judge. And they evidently do prove it; because this character of the Author of Nature, is necessarily connected with and implied in that particular revealed dispensation of things: it is likewise continually taught expressly, and insisted upon, by those persons who wrought the miracles and delivered the prophecies. So that indeed natural Religion seems as much proved by the Scripture revelation, as it would have been, had the design of revelation been nothing else than to prove it.

But it may possibly be disputed, how far miracles can prove natural Religion; and notable objections may be urged against this proof of it, considered as a matter of speculation: but considered as a practical thing, there can be none. For suppose a person to teach natural Religion to a nation, who had lived in total ignorance or forgetfulness of it; and to declare he was commissioned by God so to do: suppose him, in proof of his commission, to foretell things future, which no human foresight could have guessed at; to divide the sea with a word; feed great multitudes with bread from heaven; cure all manner of diseases; and raise the dead, even himself, to life: would not this give additional credibility to his teaching, a credibility beyond what that of a common man would have; and be an authoritative publication of the law of nature, i.e. a new proof of it? It would be a practical one, of the strongest kind, perhaps, which human creatures are capable of having given them. The Law of Moses then, and the Gospel of Christ, are authoritative publications of the religion of nature; they afford a proof of God's general providence, as moral Governor of the world, as well as of his particular dispensations of providence towards sinful creatures, revealed in the Law and the Gospel. As they are the only evidence of the latter, so they are an additional evidence of the former.

To shew this further, let us suppose a man of the greatest and most improved capacity, who had never heard of revelation, convinced upon the whole, notwithstanding the disorders of the world, that it was under the direction and moral government of an infinitely perfect Being; but ready to question, whether he were not got beyond the reach of his faculties: suppose him brought, by this suspicion, into great danger of being carried away by the universal bad example of almost every one around him, who appeared to have no sense, no practical sense at least, of these things: and this, perhaps, would be as advantageous a situation with regard to Religion, as nature alone ever placed any man in. What a confirmation now must it be to such a person, all at once, to find, that this moral system of things was revealed to mankind, in the name of that infinite Being, whom he had from principles of reason believed in: and that the publishers of the revelation proved their commission from him, by making it appear, that he had intrusted them with a power of suspending and changing the general laws of nature.

Nor must it by any means be omitted, for it is a thing of the utmost importance, that life and immortality are eminently brought to light by the Gospel. The great doctrines of a future state, the danger of a course of wickedness, and the efficacy of repentance, are not only confirmed in the Gospel, but are taught, especially the last is, with a degree of light, to which that of nature is but darkness.

Farther: As Christianity served these ends and purposes, when it was first published, by the miraculous publication itself; so it was intended to serve the same purposes in future ages, by means of the settlement of a visible church: of a society, distinguished from common ones, and from the rest of the world, by peculiar religious institutions; by an instituted method of instruction, and an instituted form of external Religion. Miraculous powers were given to the first preachers of Christianity, in order to their introducing it into the world: a visible church was established, in order to continue it, and

carry it on successively throughout all ages. Had
Moses and the Prophets, Christ and his Apostles,
only taught, and by miracles proved, Religion to
their contemporaries; the benefits of their instructions would have reached but to a small part of mankind. Christianity must have been, in a great degree, sunk and forgot in a very few ages. To prevent
this, appears to have been one reason why a visible
church was instituted: to be, like a city upon a hill,
a standing memorial to the world of the duty which
we owe our Maker: to call men continually, both by
example and instruction, to attend to it, and, by the
form of Religion, ever before their eyes, remind them
of the reality: to be the repository of the oracles of
God: to hold up the light of revelation in aid to
that of nature, and propagate it throughout all
generations to the end of the world—the light of
revelation, considered here in no other view, than as
designed to enforce natural Religion. And in proportion as Christianity is professed and taught in the
world, Religion, natural or essential Religion, is thus
distinctly and advantageously laid before mankind,
and brought again and again to their thoughts, as a
matter of infinite importance. A visible church has
also a farther tendency to promote natural Religion,
as being an instituted method of education, originally
intended to be of more peculiar advantage to those
who would conform to it. For one end of the institution was, that by admonition and reproof, as well as
instruction; by a general regular discipline, and
public exercises of Religion; *the body of Christ*, as
the Scripture speaks, should be *edified*; i. e. trained
up in piety and virtue for a higher and better state.
This settlement then appearing thus beneficial; tending in the nature of the thing to answer, and in some

degree actually answering, those ends; it is to be remembered, that the very notion of it implies positive institutions; for the visibility of the church consists in them. Take away every thing of this kind, and you lose the very notion itself. So that if the things now mentioned are advantages, the reason and importance of positive institutions in general is most obvious; since without them these advantages could not be secured to the world. And it is mere idle wantonness, to insist upon knowing the reasons, why such particular ones were fixed upon rather than others.

The benefit arising from this supernatural assistance, which Christianity affords to natural Religion, is what some persons are very slow in apprehending. And yet it is a thing distinct in itself, and a very plain obvious one. For will any in good earnest really say, that the bulk of mankind in the heathen world were in as advantageous a situation with regard to natural Religion, as they are now amongst us: that it was laid before them, and enforced upon them, in a manner as distinct, and as much tending to influence their practice?

The objections against all this, from the perversion of Christianity, and from the supposition of its having had but little good influence, however innocently they may be proposed, yet cannot be insisted upon as conclusive, upon any principles, but such as lead to downright Atheism: because the manifestation of the law of nature by reason, which, upon all principles of Theism, must have been from God, has been perverted and rendered ineffectual in the same manner. It may indeed, I think, truly be said, that the good effects of Christianity have not been small; nor its supposed ill effects, any effects at all of it, properly speaking. Perhaps too the things themselves done have been aggravated; and if not, Christianity hath been often only a pretence ; and the same evils in the main would have been done upon some other pretence. However, great and shocking as the corruptions and abuses of it have really been, they cannot be insisted upon as arguments against it, upon principles of Theism. For one cannot proceed one step in reasoning upon natural Religion, any more than upon Christianity, without laying it down as a first principle, that the dispensations of Providence are not to be judged of by their perversions, but by their genuine tendencies : not by what they do actually seem to effect, but by what they would effect, if mankind did their part ; that part which is justly put and left upon them.¹ It is altogether as much the language of one as of the other ; *He that is unjust, let him be unjust still : and he that is holy, let him be holy still*[b]. The light of reason does not, any more than that of revelation, force men to submit to its authority; both admonish them of what they ought to do and avoid, together with the consequences of each; and after this, leave them at full liberty to act just as they please, till the appointed time of judgment. Every moment's experience shews, that this is God's general rule of government.

To return then : Christianity being a promulgation of the law of nature; being moreover an authoritative promulgation of it ; with new light, and other circumstances of peculiar advantage, adapted to the wants of mankind; these things fully shew its importance. And it is to be observed farther, that as the nature of the case requires, so all Christians are commanded to contribute, by their profession of Christi-

[b] Rev. xxii. 11.

anity, to preserve it in the world, and render it such a promulgation and enforcement of Religion. For it is the very scheme of the Gospel, that each Christian should, in his degree, contribute towards continuing and carrying it on : all by uniting in the public profession and external practice of Christianity; some by instructing, by having the oversight and taking care of this religious community, the Church of God. Now this farther shews the importance of Christianity; and, which is what I chiefly intend, its importance in a practical sense: or the high obligations we are under, to take it into our most serious consideration; and the danger there must necessarily be, not only in treating it despitefully, which I am not now speaking of, but in disregarding and neglecting it. For this is neglecting to do what is expressly enjoined us, for continuing those benefits to the world, and transmitting them down to future times. And all this holds, even though the only thing to be considered in Christianity were its subserviency to natural Religion. But,

II. Christianity is to be considered in a further view; as containing an account of a dispensation of things, not at all discoverable by reason, in consequence of which several distinct precepts are enjoined us. Christianity is not only an external institution of natural Religion, and a new promulgation of God's general providence, as righteous Governor and Judge of the world; but it contains also a revelation of a particular dispensation of Providence, carrying on by his Son and Spirit, for the recovery and salvation of mankind, who are represented in Scripture to be in a state of ruin. And in consequence of this revelation being made, we are commanded *to be baptized*, not only *in the name of the*

Father, but also, *of the Son, and of the Holy Ghost:* and other obligations of duty, unknown before, to the Son and the Holy Ghost, are revealed. Now the importance of these duties may be judged of, by observing that they arise, not from positive command merely, but also from the offices, which appear, from Scripture, to belong to those divine persons in the Gospel dispensation; or from the relations, which, we are there informed, they stand in to us. By reason is revealed the relation which God the Father stands in to us. Hence arises the obligation of duty which we are under to him. In Scripture are revealed the relations which the Son and Holy Spirit stand in to us. Hence arise the obligations of duty which we are under to them. The truth of the case, as one may speak, in each of these three respects being admitted: that God is the governor of the world, upon the evidence of reason; that Christ is the mediator between God and man, and the Holy Ghost our guide and sanctifier, upon the evidence of revelation: the truth of the case, I say, in each of these respects being admitted; it is no more a question, why it should be commanded, that we be baptized in the name of the Son and of the Holy Ghost, than that we be baptized in the name of the Father. This matter seems to require to be more fully stated [c].

Let it be remembered then, that Religion comes under the twofold consideration of internal and external: for the latter is as real a part of Religion, of true Religion, as the former. Now when Religion is considered under the first notion, as an inward principle, to be exerted in such and such inward acts of the mind and heart; the essence of natural Religion

[c] See the Nature, Obligation, and Efficacy of the Christian Sacraments, &c., and Colliber of revealed Religion, as there quoted.

may be said to consist in religious regards to *God the Father Almighty*: and the essence of revealed Religion, as distinguished from natural, to consist in religious regards to *the Son* and to *the Holy Ghost*. And the obligation we are under, of paying these religious regards to each of these Divine persons respectively, arises from the respective relations which they each stand in to us. How these relations are made known, whether by reason or revelation, makes no alteration in the case: because the duties arise out of the relations themselves, not out of the manner in which we are informed of them. The Son and Spirit have each his proper office in that great dispensation of Providence, the redemption of the world; the one our mediator, the other our sanctifier. Does not then the duty of religious regards to both these Divine persons, as immediately arise, to the view of reason, out of the very nature of these offices and relations; as the inward good-will and kind intention, which we owe to our fellow-creatures, arises out of the common relations between us and them? But it will be asked, "What are the inward religious regards, appearing thus obviously due to the Son and Holy Spirit; as arising, not merely from command in Scripture, but from the very nature of the revealed relations, which they stand in to us?" I answer, the religious regards of reverence, honour, love, trust, gratitude, fear, hope. In what external manner this inward worship is to be expressed, is a matter of pure revealed command; as perhaps the external manner, in which God the Father is to be worshipped, may be more so, than we are ready to think: but the worship, the internal worship itself, to the Son and Holy Ghost, is no farther matter of pure revealed command, than as the relations they stand in to us are matter of pure revelation : for the relations being known, the obligations to such internal worship are obligations of reason, arising out of those relations themselves. In short, the history of the Gospel as immediately shews us the reason of these obligations, as it shews us the meaning of the words, Son and Holy Ghost.

If this account of the Christian Religion be just; those persons who can speak lightly of it, as of little consequence, provided natural religion be kept to, plainly forget, that Christianity, even what is peculiarly so called, as distinguished from natural Religion, has yet somewhat very important, even of a moral nature. For the office of our Lord being made known, and the relation he stands in to us, the obligation of religious regards to him is plainly moral, as much as charity to mankind is; since this obligation arises, before external command, immediately out of that his office and relation itself. Those persons appear to forget, that revelation is to be considered, as informing us of somewhat new, in the state of mankind, and in the government of the world: as acquainting us with some relations we stand in, which could not otherwise have been known. And these relations being real, (though before revelation we could be under no obligations from them, yet upon their being revealed,) there is no reason to think, but that neglect of behaving suitably to them will be attended with the same kind of consequences under God's government, as neglecting to behave suitably to any other relations made known to us by reason. And ignorance, whether unavoidable or voluntary, so far as we can possibly see, will, just as much, and just as little, excuse in one case as in the other: the ignorance being supposed equally unavoidable, or equally voluntary, in both cases.

If therefore Christ be indeed the mediator between God and man, i.e. if Christianity be true; if he be indeed our Lord, our Saviour, and our God; no one can say, what may follow, not only the obstinate, but the careless disregard to him, in those high relations. Nay no one can say, what may follow such disregard, even in the way of natural consequence[d]. For, as the natural consequences of vice in this life are doubtless to be considered as judicial punishments inflicted by God; so likewise, for ought we know, the judicial punishments of the future life may be, in a like way or a like sense, the natural consequence of vice[e]: of men's violating or disregarding the relations which God has placed them in here, and made known to them.

Again: If mankind are corrupted and depraved in their moral character, and so are unfit for that state, which Christ is gone to prepare for his disciples; and if the assistance of God's Spirit be necessary to renew their nature, in the degree requisite to their being qualified for that state; all which is implied in the express, though figurative declaration, *Except a man be born of the Spirit, he cannot enter into the kingdom of God*[f]: supposing this, is it possible any serious person can think it a slight matter, whether or no he makes use of the means, expressly commanded by God, for obtaining this Divine assistance? especially since the whole analogy of nature shews, that we are not to expect any benefits without making use of the appointed means for obtaining or enjoying them. Now reason shews us nothing, of the particular immediate means of obtaining either

[d] P. 32, 33.   [e] Chap. v.   [f] John iii. 5.

temporal or spiritual benefits. This therefore we must learn, either from experience or revelation. And experience, the present case does not admit of.

The conclusion from all this evidently is, that, Christianity being supposed either true or credible, it is unspeakable irreverence, and really the most presumptuous rashness, to treat it as a light matter. It can never justly be esteemed of little consequence, till it be positively supposed false. Nor do I know a higher and more important obligation which we are under, than that of examining most seriously into the evidence of it, supposing its credibility; and of embracing it, upon supposition of its truth.

The two following deductions may be proper to be added, in order to illustrate the foregoing observations, and to prevent their being mistaken.

First, Hence we may clearly see, where lies the distinction between what is positive and what is moral in Religion. Moral *precepts* are precepts, the reasons of which we see: positive *precepts* are precepts, the reasons of which we do not see [g]. Moral *duties* arise out of the nature of the case itself, prior to external command. Positive *duties* do not arise out of the nature of the case, but from external command; nor would they be duties at all, were it not for such command, received from him whose creatures and subjects we are. But the manner in which the nature of the case, or the fact of the

---

[g] This is the distinction between moral and positive precepts considered respectively as such. But yet, since the latter have somewhat of a moral nature, we may see the reason of them, considered in this view. Moral and positive precepts are in some respects alike, in other respects different. So far as they are alike, we discern the reasons of both; so far as they are different, we discern the reasons of the former, but not of the latter. See p. 156, &c., and 166.

relation, is made known, this doth not denominate any duty either positive or moral. That we be baptized in the name of the Father, is as much a positive duty, as that we be baptized in the name of the Son; because both arise equally from revealed command; though the relation which we stand in to God the Father is made known to us by reason; the relation we stand in to Christ, by revelation only. On the other hand, the dispensation of the Gospel admitted, gratitude as immediately becomes due to Christ, from his being the voluntary minister of this dispensation, as it is due to God the Father, from his being the fountain of all good; though the first is made known to us by revelation only, the second by reason. Hence also we may see, and, for distinctness sake, it may be worth mentioning, that positive institutions come under a twofold consideration. They are either institutions founded on natural Religion, as Baptism in the name of the Father; though this has also a particular reference to the Gospel dispensation, for it is in the name of God, as the Father of our Lord Jesus Christ: or they are external institutions founded on revealed Religion; as Baptism in the name of the Son and of the Holy Ghost.

Secondly, From the distinction between what is moral and what is positive in Religion, appears the ground of that peculiar reference, which the Scripture teaches us to be due to the former.

The reason of positive institutions in general is very obvious; though we should not see the reason, why such particular ones are pitched upon rather than others. Whoever therefore, instead of cavilling at words, will attend to the thing itself, may clearly see, that positive institutions in general, as distinguished from this or that particular one, have the nature of moral commands; since the reasons of them appear. Thus, for instance, the *external* worship of God is a moral duty, though no particular mode of it be so. Care then is to be taken, when a comparison is made between positive and moral duties, that they be compared no farther than as they are different; no farther than as the former are positive, or arise out of mere external command, the reasons of which we are not acquainted with; and as the latter are moral, or arise out of the apparent reason of the case, without such external command. Unless this caution be observed, we shall run into endless confusion.

Now this being premised, suppose two standing precepts enjoined by the same authority; that, in certain conjunctures, it is impossible to obey both; that the former is moral, i. e. a precept of which we see the reasons, and that they hold in the particular case before us; but that the latter is positive, i. e. a precept of which we do not see the reasons: it is indisputable that our obligations are to obey the former; because there is an apparent reason for this preference, and none against it. Farther, positive institutions, I suppose all those which Christianity enjoins, are means to a moral end: and the end must be acknowledged more excellent than the means. Nor is observance of these institutions any religious obedience at all, or of any value, otherwise than as it proceeds from a moral principle. This seems to be the strict logical way of stating and determining this matter; but will, perhaps, be found less applicable to practice, than may be thought at first sight.

And therefore, in a more practical, though more lax way of consideration, and taking the words, *moral law* and *positive institutions*, in the popular sense; I add, that the whole moral law is as much matter of revealed command, as positive institutions are: for the Scripture enjoins every moral virtue. In this respect then they are both upon a level. But the moral law is, moreover, written upon our hearts; interwoven into our very nature. And this is a plain intimation of the Author of it, which is to be preferred, when they interfere.

But there is not altogether so much necessity for the determination of this question, as some persons seem to think. Nor are we left to reason alone to determine it. For, first, Though mankind have, in all ages, been greatly prone to place their religion in peculiar positive rites, by way of equivalent for obedience to moral precepts; yet, without making any comparison at all between them, and consequently without determining which is to have the preference, the nature of the thing abundantly shews all notions of that kind to be utterly subversive of true Religion: as they are, moreover, contrary to the whole general tenor of Scripture; and likewise to the most express particular declarations of it, that nothing can render us accepted of God, without moral virtue. Secondly, Upon the occasion of mentioning together positive and moral duties, the Scripture always puts the stress of Religion upon the latter, and never upon the former: which, though no sort of allowance to neglect the former, when they do not interfere with the latter, yet is a plain intimation, that when they do, the latter are to be preferred. And farther, as mankind are for placing the stress of their religion any where, rather than upon virtue;

lest both the reason of the thing, and the general spirit of Christianity, appearing in the intimation now mentioned, should be ineffectual against this prevalent folly: our Lord himself, from whose command alone the obligation of positive institutions arises, has taken occasion to make the comparison between them and moral precepts; when the Pharisees censured him, for *eating with publicans and sinners;* and also when they censured his disciples, for *plucking the ears of corn on the Sabbath-day.* Upon this comparison, he has determined expressly, and in form, which shall have the preference when they interfere. And by delivering his authoritative determination in a proverbial manner of expression, he has made it general: I *will have mercy, and not sacrifice* [h]. The propriety of the word *proverbial* is not the thing insisted upon: though I think the manner of speaking is to be called so. But that the manner of speaking very remarkably renders the determination general, is surely indisputable. For, had it, in the latter case, been said only, that God preferred mercy to the rigid observance of the Sabbath; even then, by parity of reason, most justly might we have argued, that he preferred mercy likewise, to the observance of other ritual institutions; and in general, moral duties, to positive ones. And thus the determination would have been general; though its being so were inferred and not expressed. But as the passage really stands in the Gospel, it is much stronger. For the sense and the very literal words of our Lord's answer are as applicable to any other instance of a comparison, between positive and moral duties, as to this upon which they were spoken. And if, in case of competition,

[h] Matt. ix. 13, and xii. 7.

mercy is to be preferred to positive institutions, it will scarce be thought, that justice is to give place to them. It is remarkable too, that, as the words are a quotation from the Old Testament, they are introduced, on both the forementioned occasions, with a declaration, that the Pharisees did not understand the meaning of them. This, I say, is very remarkable. For, since it is scarce possible, for the most ignorant person, not to understand the literal sense of the passage, in the Prophet [i]; and since understanding the literal sense would not have prevented their *condemning the guiltless* [k]; it can hardly be doubted, that the thing which our Lord really intended in that declaration was, that the Pharisees had not learnt from it, as they might, wherein the *general* spirit of Religion consists: that it consists in moral piety and virtue, as distinguished from forms, and ritual observances. However, it is certain we may learn this from his Divine application of the passage, in the Gospel.

But, as it is one of the peculiar weaknesses of human nature, when, upon a comparison of two things, one is found to be of greater importance than the other, to consider this other as of scarce any importance at all: it is highly necessary that we remind ourselves, how great presumption it is, to make light of any institutions of Divine appointment; that our obligations to obey all God's commands whatever are absolute and indispensable; and that commands merely positive, admitted to be from him, lay us under a moral obligation to obey them: an obligation moral in the strictest and most proper sense.

To these things I cannot forbear adding, that the

[i] Hosea vi. [k] See Matth. xii. 7.

account now given of Christianity most strongly shews and enforces upon us the obligation of searching the Scriptures, in order to see, what the scheme of revelation really is; instead of determining beforehand, from reason, what the scheme of it must be[y]. Indeed if in revelation there be found any passages, the seeming meaning of which is contrary to natural Religion; we may most certainly conclude, such seeming meaning not to be the real one. But it is not any degree of a presumption against an interpretation of Scripture, that such interpretation contains a doctrine, which the light of nature cannot discover[z]; or a precept, which the law of nature does not oblige to.

CHAP. II.

Of the supposed presumption against a revelation, considered as miraculous.

HAVING shewn the importance of the Christian revelation, and the obligations which we are under seriously to attend to it, upon supposition of its truth, or its credibility: the next thing in order, is to consider the supposed presumptions against revelation in general; which shall be the subject of this chapter: and the objections against the Christian in particular; which shall be the subject of some following ones[a]. For it seems the most natural method, to remove these prejudices against Christianity, before we proceed to the consideration of the positive evidence for it, and the objections against that evidence[b].

[y] See chap. iii.   [z] P. 172, 173.   [a] Ch. iii, iv, v, vi.   [b] Ch. vii.

It is, I think, commonly supposed, that there is some peculiar presumption, from the analogy of nature, against the Christian scheme of things; at least against miracles; so as that stronger evidence is necessary to prove the truth and reality of them, than would be sufficient to convince us of other events, or matters of fact. Indeed the consideration of this supposed presumption cannot but be thought very insignificant, by many persons. Yet, as it belongs to the subject of this Treatise; so it may tend to open the mind, and remove some prejudices: however needless the consideration of it be, upon its own account.

I. I find no appearance of a presumption, from the analogy of nature, against the general scheme of Christianity, that God created and invisibly governs the world by Jesus Christ; and by him also will hereafter judge it in righteousness, i. e. render to every one according to his works; and that good men are under the secret influence of his Spirit. Whether these things are, or are not, to be called miraculous, is, perhaps, only a question about words; or however, is of no moment in the case. If the analogy of nature raises any presumption against this general scheme of Christianity, it must be, either because it is not discoverable by reason or experience; or else, because it is unlike that course of nature, which is. But analogy raises no presumption against the truth of this scheme, upon either of these accounts.

First, There is no presumption, from analogy, against the truth of it, upon account of its not being discoverable by reason or experience. For suppose one who never heard of revelation, of the most improved understanding, and acquainted with our whole system of natural philosophy and natural religion: such an one could not but be sensible, that it was but a very small part of the natural and moral system of the universe, which he was acquainted with. He could not but be sensible, that there must be innumerable things, in the dispensations of Providence past, in the invisible government over the world at present carrying on, and in what is to come; of which he was wholly ignorant[c], and which could not be discovered without revelation. Whether the scheme of nature be, in the strictest sense, infinite or not; it is evidently vast, even beyond all possible imagination. And doubtless that part of it, which is opened to our view, is but as a point, in comparison of the whole plan of Providence, reaching throughout eternity past and future; in comparison of what is even now going on in the remote parts of the boundless universe; nay in comparison of the whole scheme of this world. And therefore, that things lie beyond the natural reach of our faculties, is no sort of presumption against the truth and reality of them: because it is certain, there are innumerable things, in the constitution and government of the universe, which are thus beyond the natural reach of our faculties. Secondly, Analogy raises no presumption against any of the things contained in this general doctrine of Scripture now mentioned, upon account of their being unlike the known course of nature. For there is no presumption at all from analogy, that the *whole* course of things, or Divine government, naturally unknown to us, and *every thing* in it, is like to any thing in that which is known; and therefore no peculiar presumption against any thing in the former, upon account

[c] P. 131.

of its being unlike to any thing in the latter. And in the constitution and natural government of the world, as well as in the moral government of it, we see things, in a great degree, unlike one another: and therefore ought not to wonder at such unlikeness between things visible and invisible. However, the scheme of Christianity is by no means entirely unlike the scheme of nature; as will appear in the following part of this Treatise.

The notion of a miracle, considered as a proof of a Divine mission, has been stated with great exactness by divines; and is, I think, sufficiently understood by every one. There are also invisible miracles, the Incarnation of Christ, for instance, which, being secret, cannot be alleged as a proof of such a mission; but require themselves to be proved by visible miracles. Revelation itself too is miraculous; and miracles are the proof of it; and the supposed presumption against these shall presently be considered. All which I have been observing here is, that, whether we choose to call every thing in the dispensations of Providence, not discoverable without revelation, nor like the known course of things, miraculous; and whether the general Christian dispensation now mentioned is to be called so, or not; the foregoing observations seem certainly to shew, that there is no presumption against it from the analogy of nature.

II. There is no presumption, from analogy, against some operations, which we should now call miraculous; particularly none against a revelation at the beginning of the world: nothing of such presumption against it, as is supposed to be implied or expressed in the word *miraculous*. For a miracle, in its very notion, is relative to a course of nature; and implies somewhat different from it, considered as being so. Now, either there was no course of nature at the time which we are speaking of; or if there were, we are not acquainted what the course of nature is, upon the first peopling of worlds. And therefore the question, whether mankind had a revelation made to them at that time, is to be considered, not as a question concerning a miracle, but as a common question of fact. And we have the like reason, be it more or less, to admit the report of tradition, concerning this question, and concerning common matters of fact of the same antiquity; for instance, what part of the earth was first peopled.

Or thus: When mankind was first placed in this state, there was a power exerted, totally different from the present course of nature. Now, whether this power, thus wholly different from the present course of nature, for we cannot properly apply to it the word *miraculous;* whether this power stopped immediately after it had made man, or went on, and exerted itself farther in giving him a revelation, is a question of the same kind, as whether an ordinary power exerted itself in such a particular degree and manner, or not.

Or suppose the power exerted in the formation of the world be considered as miraculous, or rather, be called by that name; the case will not be different: since it must be acknowledged, that such a power was exerted. For supposing it acknowledged, that our Saviour spent some years in a course of working miracles: there is no more presumption, worth mentioning, against his having exerted this miraculous power, in a certain degree greater, than in a certain degree less; in one or two more instances, than in one or two fewer; in this, than in another manner.

It is evident then, that there can be no peculiar presumption, from the analogy of nature, against supposing a revelation, when man was first placed upon the earth.

Add, that there does not appear the least intimation in history or tradition, that Religion was first reasoned out: but the whole of history and tradition makes for the other side, that it came into the world by revelation. Indeed the state of Religion in the first ages, of which we have any account, seems to suppose and imply, that this was the original of it amongst mankind. And these reflections together, without taking in the peculiar authority of Scripture, amount to real and a very material degree of evidence, that there was a revelation at the beginning of the world. Now this, as it is a confirmation of natural Religion, and therefore mentioned in the former part of this Treatise[d] : so likewise it has a tendency to remove any prejudices against a subsequent revelation.

III. But still it may be objected, that there is some peculiar presumption, from analogy, against miracles; particularly against revelation, after the settlement and during the continuance of a course of nature.

Now with regard to this supposed presumption, it is to be observed in general, that before we can have ground for raising what can, with any propriety, be called an *argument* from analogy, for or against revelation considered as somewhat miraculous, we must be acquainted with a similar or parallel case. But the history of some other world, seemingly in like circumstances with our own, is no more than a parallel case : and therefore nothing short of this can

[d] Page 123, &c.

be so. Yet, could we come at a presumptive proof, for or against a revelation, from being informed, whether such world had one, or not; such a proof, being drawn from one single instance only, must be infinitely precarious. More particularly: First of all; There is a very strong presumption against common speculative truths, and against the most ordinary facts, before the proof of them; which yet is overcome by almost any proof. There is a presumption of millions to one, against the story of Cæsar, or of any other man. For suppose a number of common facts so and so circumstanced, of which one had no kind of proof, should happen to come into one's thoughts; every one would, without any possible doubt, conclude them to be false. And the like may be said of a single common fact. And from hence it appears, that the question of importance, as to the matter before us, is, concerning the degree of the peculiar presumption supposed against miracles; not whether there be any peculiar presumption at all against them. For, if there be the presumption of millions to one, against the most common facts; what can a small presumption, additional to this, amount to, though it be peculiar? It cannot be estimated, and is as nothing. The only material question is, whether there be any such presumption against miracles, as to render them in any sort incredible. Secondly, If we leave out the consideration of Religion, we are in such total darkness, upon what causes, occasions, reasons, or circumstances, the present course of nature depends; that there does not appear any improbability for or against supposing, that five or six thousand years may have given scope for causes, occasions, reasons, or circumstances, from whence miraculous interpositions may have arisen. And from this, joined with the foregoing observation, it will follow, that there must be a presumption, beyond all comparison, greater, against the *particular* common facts just now instanced in, than against miracles *in general;* before any evidence of either. But, thirdly, Take in the consideration of Religion, or the moral system of the world, and then we see distinct particular reasons for miracles: to afford mankind instruction additional to that of nature, and to attest the truth of it. And this gives a real credibility to the supposition, that it might be part of the original plan of things, that there should be miraculous interpositions. Then, lastly, Miracles must not be compared to common natural events; or to events which, though uncommon, are similar to what we daily experience: but to the extraordinary phenomena of nature. And then the comparison will be between the presumption against miracles, and the presumption against such uncommon appearances, suppose, as comets, and against there being any such powers in nature as magnetism and electricity, so contrary to the properties of other bodies not endued with these powers. And before any one can determine, whether there be any peculiar presumption against miracles, more than against other extraordinary things; he must consider, what, upon first hearing, would be the presumption against the last-mentioned appearances and powers, to a person acquainted only with the daily, monthly, and annual course of nature respecting this earth, and with those common powers of matter which we every day see.

Upon all this I conclude; that there certainly is no such presumption against miracles, as to render them in any wise incredible: that on the contrary, our being able to discern reasons for them, gives a positive credibility to the history of them, in cases where those reasons hold: and that it is by no means certain, that there is any peculiar presumption at all, from analogy, even in the lowest degree, against miracles, as distinguished from other extraordinary phenomena: though it is not worth while to perplex the Reader with inquiries into the abstract nature of evidence, in order to determine a question, which, without such inquiries, we see[z] is of no importance.

CHAP. III.

Of our incapacity of judging, what were to be expected in a revelation; and the credibility, from analogy, that it must contain things appearing liable to objections.

BESIDES the objections against the evidence for Christianity, many are alleged against the scheme of it; against the whole manner in which it is put and left with the world; as well as against several particular relations in Scripture: objections drawn from the deficiencies of revelation; from things in it appearing to men *foolishness*[a]; from its containing matters of offence, which have led, and it must have been foreseen would lead, into strange enthusiasm and superstition, and be made to serve the purposes of tyranny and wickedness; from its not being universal; and, which is a thing of the same kind from its evidence not being so convincing and satisfactory as it might have been: for this last is sometimes turned into a positive argument against its truth[b]. It would be tedious, indeed impossible,

[z] P. 176.   [a] 1 Cor. i. 28.   [b] See chap. vi.

to enumerate the several particulars comprehended under the objections here referred to; they being so various, according to the different fancies of men. There are persons, who think it a strong objection against the authority of Scripture, that it is not composed by rules of art, agreed upon by critics, for polite and correct writing. And the scorn is inexpressible, with which some of the prophetic parts of Scripture are treated: partly through the rashness of interpreters; but very much also, on account of the hieroglyphical and figurative language, in which they are left us. Some of the principal things of this sort shall be particularly considered in following chapters. But my design at present is to observe in general, with respect to this whole way of arguing, that, upon supposition of a revelation, it is highly credible beforehand, we should be incompetent judges of it to a great degree: and that it would contain many things appearing to us liable to great objections; in case we judge of it otherwise, than by the analogy of nature. And therefore, though objections against the evidence of Christianity are most seriously to be considered; yet objections against Christianity itself are, in a great measure, frivolous: almost all objections against it, excepting those which are alleged against the particular proofs of its coming from God. I express myself with caution, lest I should be mistaken to vilify reason; which is indeed the only faculty we have wherewith to judge concerning any thing, even revelation itself: or be misunderstood to assert, that a supposed revelation cannot be proved false, from internal characters. For, it may contain clear immoralities or contradictions; and either of these would prove it false. Nor will I take upon me to affirm, that nothing else can possibly render any supposed revelation incredible. Yet still the observation above is, I think, true beyond doubt; that objections against Christianity, as distinguished from objections against its evidence, are frivolous. To make out this, is the general design of the present chapter. And with regard to the whole of it, I cannot but particularly wish, that the proofs might be attended to; rather than the assertions cavilled at, upon account of any unacceptable consequences, whether real or supposed, which may be drawn from them. For, after all, that which is true, must be admitted, though it should shew us the shortness of our faculties; and that we are in no wise judges of many things, of which we are apt to think ourselves very competent ones. Nor will this be any objection with reasonable men, at least upon second thought it will not be any objection with such, against the justness of the following observations:

As God governs the world, and instructs his creatures, according to certain laws or rules, in the known course of nature; known by reason together with experience: so the Scripture informs us of a scheme of Divine providence, additional to this. It relates, that God has, by revelation, instructed men in things concerning his government, which they could not otherwise have known; and reminded them of things, which they might otherwise know; and attested the truth of the whole by miracles. Now if the natural and the revealed dispensation of things are both from God, if they coincide with each other, and together make up one scheme of Providence; our being incompetent judges of one, must render it credible, that we may be incompetent judges also of the other. Since, upon experience, the acknowledged constitution and course of nature is found to be greatly different from what, before experience, would have been expected; and such as, men fancy, there lie great objections against: this renders it beforehand highly credible, that they may find the revealed dispensation likewise, if they judge of it as they do of the constitution of nature, very different from expectations formed beforehand; and liable, in appearance, to great objections: objections against the scheme itself, and against the degrees and manners of the miraculous interpositions, by which it was attested and carried on. Thus suppose a prince to govern his dominions in the wisest manner possible, by common known laws; and that upon some exigencies he should suspend these laws; and govern, in several instances, in a different manner: if one of his subjects were not a competent judge beforehand, by what common rules the government should or would be carried on; it could not be expected, that the same person would be a competent judge, in what exigencies, or in what manner, or to what degree, those laws commonly observed would be suspended or deviated from. If he were not a judge of the wisdom of the ordinary administration, there is no reason to think he would be a judge of the wisdom of the extraordinary. If he thought he had objections against the former; doubtless, it is highly supposable, he might think also, that he had objections against the latter. And thus, as we fall into infinite follies and mistakes, whenever we pretend, otherwise than from experience and analogy, to judge of the constitution and course of nature; it is evidently supposable beforehand, that we should fall into as great, in pretending to judge, in like manner, concerning revelation. Nor is there any more ground to expect that this latter should appear to us clear of objections, than that the former should.

These observations, relating to the whole of Christianity, are applicable to inspiration in particular. As we are in no sort judges beforehand, by what laws or rules, in what degree, or by what means, it were to have been expected, that God would naturally instruct us; so upon supposition of his affording us light and instruction by revelation, additional to what he has afforded us by reason and experience, we are in no sort judges, by what methods, and in what proportion, it were to be expected, that this supernatural light and instruction would be afforded us. We know not beforehand, what degree or kind of natural information, it were to be expected God would afford men, each by his own reason and experience: nor how far he would enable and effectually dispose them to communicate it, whatever it should be, to each other; nor whether the evidence of it would be certain, highly probable, or doubtful; nor whether it would be given with equal clearness and conviction to all. Nor could we guess, upon any good ground I mean, whether natural knowledge, or even the faculty itself, by which we are capable of attaining it, reason, would be given us at once, or gradually. In like manner, we are wholly ignorant, what degree of new knowledge, it were to be expected, God would give mankind by revelation, upon supposition of his affording one: or how far, or in what way, he would interpose miraculously, to qualify them, to whom he should originally make the revelation, for communicating the knowledge given by it; and to secure their doing it to the age in which they should live; and to secure its being transmitted to posterity. We are equally ignorant, whether the evidence of it would be certain, or highly probable, or doubtful[c]: or whether all who should have any degree of instruction from it, and any degree of evidence of its truth, would have the same: or whether the scheme would be revealed at once, or unfolded gradually. Nay we are not in any sort able to judge, whether it were to have been expected, that the revelation should have been committed to writing; or left to be handed down, and consequently corrupted, by verbal tradition, and at length sunk under it, if mankind so pleased, and during such time as they are permitted, in the degree they evidently are, to act as they will.

But it may be said, " that a revelation in some of the above-mentioned circumstances, one, for instance, which was not committed to writing, and thus secured against danger of corruption, would not have answered its purpose." I ask, what purpose? It would not have answered all the purposes, which it has now answered, and in the same degree: but it would have answered others, or the same in different degrees. And which of these were the purposes of God, and best fell in with his general government, we could not at all have determined beforehand.

Now since it has been shewn, that we have no principles of reason, upon which to judge beforehand, how it were to be expected revelation should have been left, or what was most suitable to the Divine plan of government, in any of the forementioned respects; it must be quite frivolous to object afterwards as to any of them, against its being left in one way, rather than another: for this would be to object against things, upon account of their being different from expectations, which have been shewn

[c] See chap. vi.

to be without reason. And thus we see, that the only question concerning the truth of Christianity is, whether it be a real revelation; not whether it be attended with every circumstance which we should have looked for: and concerning the authority of Scripture, whether it be what it claims to be; not whether it be a book of such sort, and so promulged, as weak men are apt to fancy a book containing a Divine revelation should. And therefore, neither obscurity, nor seeming inaccuracy of style, nor various readings, nor early disputes about the authors of particular parts; nor any other things of the like kind, though they had been much more considerable in degree than they are, could overthrow the authority of the Scripture: unless the Prophets, Apostles, or our Lord, had promised, that the book containing the Divine revelation should be secure from those things. Nor indeed can any objections overthrow such a kind of revelation as the Christian claims to be, since there are no objections against the morality of it[d], but such as can shew, that there is no proof of miracles wrought originally in attestation of it; no appearance of any thing miraculous in its obtaining in the world; nor any of prophecy, that is, of events foretold, which human sagacity could not foresee. If it can be shewn, that the proof alleged for all these is absolutely none at all, then is revelation overturned. But were it allowed, that the proof of any one or all of them is lower than is allowed; yet, whilst any proof of them remains, revelation will stand upon much the same foot it does at present, as to all the purposes of life and practice, and ought to have the like influence upon our behaviour.

[d] Page 193.

From the foregoing observations too, it will follow, and those who will thoroughly examine into revelation will find it worth remarking; that there are several ways of arguing, which, though just with regard to other writings, are not applicable to Scripture: at least not to the prophetic parts of it. We cannot argue, for instance, that this cannot be the sense or intent of such a passage of Scripture; for, if it had, it would have been expressed more plainly, or have been represented under a more apt figure or hieroglyphic; yet we may justly argue thus, with respect to common books. And the reason of this difference is very evident; that in Scripture we are not competent judges, as we are in common books, how plainly it were to have been expected, what is the true sense, should have been expressed, or under how apt an image figured. The only question is, what appearance there is, that this is the sense; and scarce at all, how much more determinately or accurately it might have been expressed or figured.

"But is it not self-evident, that internal improbabilities of all kinds weaken external probable proof?" Doubtless. But to what practical purpose can this be alleged here, when it has been proved before [c], that real internal improbabilities, which rise even to moral certainty, are overcome by the most ordinary testimony; and when it now has been made appear, that we scarce know what are improbabilities, as to the matter we are here considering: as it will farther appear from what follows.

For though from the observations above made it is manifest, that we are not in any sort competent judges, what supernatural instruction were to have

[c] Page 177.

been expected; and though it is self-evident, that the objections of an incompetent judgment must be frivolous; yet it may be proper to go one step farther, and observe; that if men will be regardless of these things, and pretend to judge of the Scripture by preconceived expectations; the analogy of nature shews beforehand, not only that it is highly credible they may, but also probable that they will, imagine they have strong objections against it, however really unexceptionable: for so, prior to experience, they would think they had, against the circumstances, and degrees, and the whole manner of that instruction, which is afforded by the ordinary course of nature. Were the instruction which God affords to brute creatures by instincts and mere propensions, and to mankind by these together with reason, matter of probable proof, and not of certain observation; it would be rejected as incredible, in many instances of it, only upon account of the means by which this instruction is given, the seeming disproportions, the limitations, necessary conditions, and circumstances of it. For instance: would it not have been thought highly improbable, that men should have been so much more capable of discovering, even to certainty, the general laws of matter, and the magnitudes, paths, and revolutions of the heavenly bodies; than the occasions and cures of distempers, and many other things, in which human life seems so much more nearly concerned, than in astronomy? How capricious and irregular a way of information, would it be said, is that of *invention*, by means of which nature instructs us in matters of science, and in many things, upon which the affairs of the world greatly depend: that a man should, by this faculty, be made acquainted with a thing in an instant, when perhaps he is thinking of somewhat else, which he has in vain been searching after, it may be, for years. So likewise the imperfections attending the only method, by which nature enables and directs us to communicate our thoughts to each other, are innumerable. Language is, in its very nature, inadequate, ambiguous, liable to infinite abuse, even from negligence; and so liable to it from design, that every man can deceive and betray by it. And, to mention but one instance more; that brutes, without reason, should act, in many respects, with a sagacity and foresight vastly greater than what men have in those respects, would be thought impossible. Yet it is certain they do act with such superior foresight: whether it be their own indeed, is another question. From these things, it is highly credible beforehand, that upon supposition God should afford men some additional instruction by revelation, it would be with circumstances, in manners, degrees, and respects, which we should be apt to fancy we had great objections against the credibility of. Nor are the objections against the Scripture, nor against Christianity in general, at all more or greater, than the analogy of nature would beforehand—not perhaps give ground to expect; for this analogy may not be sufficient, in some cases, to ground an expectation upon; but no more nor greater, than analogy would shew it, beforehand, to be supposable and credible, that there might seem to lie against revelation.

By applying these general observations to a particular objection, it will be more distinctly seen, how they are applicable to others of the like kind: and indeed to almost all objections against Christianity, as distinguished from objections against its evidence.

It appears from Scripture, that, as it was not unusual in the apostolic age, for persons, upon their conversion to Christianity, to be endued with miraculous gifts; so, some of those persons exercised these gifts in a strangely irregular and disorderly manner; and this is made an objection against their being really miraculous. Now the foregoing observations quite remove this objection, how considerable soever it may appear at first sight. For, consider a person endued with any of these gifts; for instance, that of tongues: it is to be supposed, that he had the same power over this miraculous gift, as he would have had over it, had it been the effect of habit, of study and use, as it ordinarily is; or the same power over it, as he had over any other natural endowment. Consequently, he would use it in the same manner he did any other; either regularly, and upon proper occasions only, or irregularly, and upon improper ones: according to his sense of decency, and his character of prudence. Where then is the objection? Why, if this miraculous power was indeed given to the world to propagate Christianity, and attest the truth of it, we might, it seems, have expected, that other sort of persons should have been chosen to be invested with it; or that these should, at the same time, have been endued with prudence; or that they should have been continually restrained and directed in the exercise of it: i. e. that God should have miraculously interposed, if at all, in a different manner, or higher degree. But, from the observations made above, it is undeniably evident, that we are not judges in what degrees and manners it were to have been expected he should miraculously interpose; upon supposition of his doing it in some degree and manner. Nor, in the natural course of

Providence, are superior gifts of memory, eloquence, knowledge, and other talents of great influence, conferred only on persons of prudence and decency, or such as are disposed to make the properest use of them. Nor is the instruction and admonition naturally afforded us for the conduct of life, particularly in our education, commonly given in a manner the most suited to recommend it; but often with circumstances apt to prejudice us against such instruction.

One might go on to add, that there is a great resemblance between the light of nature and of revelation, in several other respects. Practical Christianity, or that faith and behaviour which renders a man a Christian, is a plain and obvious thing: like the common rules of conduct, with respect to our ordinary temporal affairs. The more distinct and particular knowledge of those things, the study of which the Apostle calls *going on unto perfection*[f], and of the prophetic parts of revelation, like many parts of natural and even civil knowledge, may require very exact thought, and careful consideration. The hinderances too, of natural, and of supernatural light and knowledge, have been of the same kind. And as it is owned the whole scheme of Scripture is not yet understood; so, if it ever comes to be understood, before the *restitution of all things*[g], and without miraculous interpositions; it must be in the same way as natural knowledge is come at: by the continuance and progress of learning and of liberty; and by particular persons attending to, comparing and pursuing, intimations scattered up and down it, which are overlooked and disregarded by the generality of the world. For this is the way, in which all improvements are made; by thoughtful men's

[f] Heb. vi. 1. [g] Acts iii. 21.

tracing on obscure hints, as it were, dropped us by nature accidentally, or which seem to come into our minds by chance. Nor is it at all incredible, that a book, which has been so long in the possession of mankind, should contain many truths as yet undiscovered. For, all the same phenomena, and the same faculties of investigation, from which such great discoveries in natural knowledge have been made in the present and last age, were equally in the possession of mankind several thousand years before. And possibly it might be intended, that events, as they come to pass, should open and ascertain the meaning of several parts of Scripture.

It may be objected, that this analogy fails in a material respect: for that natural knowledge is of little or no consequence. But I have been speaking of the general instruction which nature does or does not afford us. And besides, some parts of natural knowledge, in the more common restrained sense of the words, are of the greatest consequence to the ease and convenience of life. But suppose the analogy did, as it does not, fail in this respect; yet it might be abundantly supplied, from the whole constitution and course of nature: which shews, that God does not dispense his gifts according to our notions of the advantage and consequence they would be of to us. And this in general, with his method of dispensing knowledge in particular, would together make out an analogy full to the point before us.

But it may be objected still farther and more generally; "The Scripture represents the world as in a state of ruin, and Christianity as an expedient to recover it, to help in these respects where nature fails: in particular, to supply the deficiencies of natural light. Is it credible then, that so many ages should have been let pass, before a matter of such a sort, of so great and so general importance, was made known to mankind; and then that it should be made known to so small a part of them? Is it conceivable, that this supply should be so very deficient, should have the like obscurity and doubtfulness, be liable to the like perversions, in short, lie open to all the like objections, as the light of nature itself[h]?" Without determining how far this in fact is so, I answer; it is by no means incredible, that it might be so, if the light of nature and of revelation be from the same hand. Men are naturally liable to diseases: for which God, in his good providence, has provided natural remedies[i]. But remedies existing in nature have been unknown to mankind for many ages: are known but to few now; probably many valuable ones are not known yet. Great has been and is the obscurity and difficulty, in the nature and application of them. Circumstances seem often to make them very improper, where they are absolutely necessary. It is after long labour and study, and many unsuccessful endeavours, that they are brought to be as useful as they are; after high contempt and absolute rejection of the most useful we have; and after disputes and doubts, which have seemed to be endless. The best remedies too, when unskilfully, much more if dishonestly applied, may produce new diseases; and with the rightest application the success of them is often doubtful. In many cases they are not at all effectual: where they are, it is often very slowly: and the application of them, and the necessary regimen accompanying it, is, not uncommonly, so disagreeable, that some will not submit to them; and satisfy themselves with the excuse,

[h] Chap. vi.   [i] See chap. v.

that, if they would, it is not certain whether it would be successful. And many persons, who labour under diseases, for which there are known natural remedies, are not so happy as to be always, if ever, in the way of them. In a word, the remedies which nature has provided for diseases are neither certain, perfect, nor universal. And indeed the same principles of arguing, which would lead us to conclude, that they must be so, would lead us likewise to conclude, that there could be no occasion for them; i. e. that there could be no diseases at all. And therefore our experience that there are diseases shews, that it is credible beforehand, upon supposition nature has provided remedies for them, that these remedies may be, as by experience we find they are, not certain, nor perfect, nor universal; because it shews, that the principles upon which we should expect the contrary are fallacious.

And now, what is the just consequence from all these things? Not that reason is no judge of what is offered to us as being of Divine revelation. For this would be to infer, that we are unable to judge of any thing, because we are unable to judge of all things. Reason can, and it ought to judge, not only of the meaning, but also of the morality and the evidence of revelation. First, It is the province of reason to judge of the morality of the Scripture; i. e. not whether it contains things different from what we should have expected from a wise, just, and good Being; for objections from hence have been now obviated: but whether it contains things plainly contradictory to wisdom, justice, or goodness; to what the light of nature teaches us of God. And I know nothing of this sort objected against Scripture, excepting such objections as are formed upon suppositions, which would equally conclude, that the constitution of nature is contradictory to wisdom, justice, or goodness; which most certainly it is not. Indeed there are some particular precepts in Scripture, given to particular persons, requiring actions, which would be immoral and vicious, were it not for such precepts. But it is easy to see, that all these are of such a kind, as that the precept changes the whole nature of the case and of the action; and both constitutes and shews that not to be unjust or immoral, which, prior to the precept, must have appeared and really have been so: which may well be, since none of these precepts are contrary to immutable morality. If it were commanded, to cultivate the principles and act from the spirit of treachery, ingratitude, cruelty; the command would not alter the nature of the case or of the action, in any of these instances. But it is quite otherwise in precepts, which require only the doing an external action: for instance, taking away the property or life of any. For men have no right to either life or property, but what arises solely from the grant of God: when this grant is revoked, they cease to have any right at all in either: and when this revocation is made known, as surely it is possible it may be, it must cease to be unjust to deprive them of either. And though a course of external acts, which without command would be immoral, must make an immoral habit; yet a few detached commands have no such natural tendency. I thought proper to say thus much of the few Scripture precepts, which require, not vicious actions, but actions which would have been vicious had it not been for such precepts; because they are sometimes weakly urged as immoral, and great weight is laid upon objections drawn from them. But to me there seems no difficulty at all in these precepts, but what arises from their being offences: i. e. from their being liable to be perverted, as indeed they are, by wicked designing men, to serve the most horrid purposes; and, perhaps, to mislead the weak and enthusiastic. And objections from this head are not objections against revelation; but against the whole notion of religion, as a trial; and against the general constitution of nature. Secondly, Reason is able to judge, and must, of the evidence of revelation, and of the objections urged against that evidence: which shall be the subject of a following chapter [k].

But the consequence of the foregoing observations is, that the question upon which the truth of Christianity depends is scarce at all, what objections there are against its scheme, since there are none against the morality of it; but *what objections there are against its evidence; or, what proof there remains of it, after due allowances made for the objections against that proof:* because it has been shewn, that the *objections against Christianity, as distinguished from objections against its evidence, are frivolous.* For surely very little weight, if any at all, is to be laid upon a way of arguing and objecting, which, when applied to the general constitution of nature, experience shews not to be conclusive: and such, I think, is the whole way of objecting treated of throughout this chapter. It is resolvable into principles, and goes upon suppositions, which mislead us to think, that the Author of Nature would not act, as we experience he does; or would act, in such and such cases, as we experience he does not in like cases. But the unreasonableness of this way of ob-

[k] Chap. vii.

jecting will appear yet more evidently from hence, that the chief things thus objected against are justified, as shall be farther shewn[z], by distinct, particular, and full analogies, in the constitution and course of nature.

But it is to be remembered, that, as frivolous as objections of the foregoing sort against revelation are, yet, when a supposed revelation is more consistent with itself, and has a more general and uniform tendency to promote virtue, than, all circumstances considered, could have been expected from enthusiasm and political views; this is a presumptive proof of its not proceeding from them, and so of its truth: because we are competent judges, what might have been expected from enthusiasm and political views.

CHAP. IV.

Of Christianity, considered as a scheme or constitution, imperfectly comprehended.

It hath been now shewn[a], that the analogy of nature renders it highly credible beforehand, that supposing a revelation to be made, it must contain many things very different from what we should have expected, and such as appear open to great objections: and that this observation, in good measure, takes off the force of those objections, or rather precludes them. But it may be alleged, that this is a very partial answer to such objections, or a very unsatisfactory way of obviating them: because it

[z] Chap. iv. latter part, and v, vi.
[a] In the foregoing chapter.

doth not shew at all, that the things objected against can be wise, just, and good; much less, that it is credible they are so. It will therefore be proper to shew this distinctly; by applying to these objections against the wisdom, justice, and goodness of Christianity, the answer above[b] given to the like objections against the constitution of Nature: before we consider the particular analogies in the latter, to the particular things objected against in the former. Now that which affords a sufficient answer to objections against the wisdom, justice, and goodness of the constitution of Nature, is its being a constitution, a system, or scheme, imperfectly comprehended; a scheme in which means are made use of to accomplish ends; and which is carried on by general laws. For from these things it has been proved, not only to be possible, but also to be credible, that those things which are objected against may be consistent with wisdom, justice, and goodness; nay, may be instances of them: and even that the constitution and government of Nature may be perfect in the highest possible degree. If Christianity then be a scheme, and of the like kind; it is evident, the like objections against it must admit of the like answer. And,

I. Christianity is a scheme, quite beyond our comprehension. The moral government of God is exercised, by gradually conducting things so in the course of his providence, that every one, at length and upon the whole, shall receive according to his deserts; and neither fraud nor violence, but truth and right, shall finally prevail. Christianity is a particular scheme under this general plan of Providence, and a part of it, conducive to its completion, with regard to man-

[b] Part I. ch. vii. to which this all along refers.

kind: consisting itself also of various parts, and a mysterious economy, which has been carrying on from the time the world came into its present wretched state, and is still carrying on, for its recovery, by a Divine person, the Messiah; who is to *gather together in one the children of God that are scattered abroad*[c], and establish *an everlasting kingdom, wherein dwelleth righteousness*[d]. And in order to it; after various manifestations of things, relating to this great and general scheme of Providence, through a succession of many ages: (for *the Spirit of Christ which was in the prophets, testified beforehand his sufferings, and the glory that should follow: unto whom it was revealed, that not unto themselves, but unto us they did minister the things which are now reported unto us by them that have preached the Gospel; which things the angels desire to look into*[e]:)—after various dispensations, looking forward, and preparatory, to this final salvation: *in the fulness of time,* when infinite wisdom thought fit; He, *being in the form of God,—made himself of no reputation, and took upon him the form of a servant, and was made in the likeness of men: and being found in fashion as a man, he humbled himself, and became obedient to death, even the death of the cross: wherefore God also hath highly exalted him, and given him a name, which is above every name: that at the name of Jesus every knee should bow, of things in heaven, and things in the earth, and things under the earth: and that every tongue should confess, that Jesus Christ is Lord, to the glory of God the Father*[f]. Parts likewise of this economy are the miraculous mission of the Holy Ghost, and his ordinary assistances given to good

[c] John xi. 52.
[e] 1 Pet. i. 11, 12.
[d] 2 Pet. iii. 13.
[f] Phil. ii. 6–11.

men: the invisible government, which Christ at present exercises over his church: that which he himself refers to in these words; *In my Father's house are many mansions—I go to prepare a place for you*[g]*:* and his future return to *judge the world in righteousness,* and completely reestablish the kingdom of God. *For the Father judgeth no man; but hath committed all judgment unto the Son: that all men should honour the Son, even as they honour the Father*[h]. *All power is given unto him in heaven and in earth*[i]. *And he must reign, till he hath put all enemies under his feet. Then cometh the end, when he shall have delivered up the kingdom to God, even the Father; when he shall have put down all rule, and all authority and power. And when all things shall be subdued unto him, then shall the Son also himself be subject unto him that put all things under him, that God may be all in all*[k]. Now little, surely, need be said to shew, that this system, or scheme of things, is but imperfectly comprehended by us. The Scripture expressly asserts it to be so. And indeed one cannot read a passage relating to this *great mystery of godliness*[l], but what immediately runs up into something which shews us our ignorance in it; as every thing in nature shews us our ignorance in the constitution of nature. And whoever will seriously consider that part of the Christian scheme, which is revealed in Scripture, will find so much more unrevealed, as will convince him, that, to all the purposes of judging and objecting, we know as little of it, as of the constitution of nature. Our ignorance, therefore, is as much an

[g] John xiv. 2. [h] John v. 22, 23. [i] Matt. xxviii. 18.
[k] 1 Cor. xv. 25-28.   [l] 1 Tim. iii. 16.

answer to our objections against the perfection of one, as against the perfection of the other [m].

II. It is obvious too, that in the Christian dispensation, as much as in the natural scheme of things, means are made use of to accomplish ends. And the observation of this furnishes us with the same answer, to objections against the perfection of Christianity, as to objections of the like kind, against the constitution of nature. It shews the credibility, that the things objected against, how *foolish* [n] soever they appear to men, may be the very best means of accomplishing the very best ends. And their appearing *foolishness* is no presumption against this, in a scheme so greatly beyond our comprehension [o].

III. The credibility, that the Christian dispensation may have been, all along, carried on by general laws [p], no less than the course of nature, may require to be more distinctly made out. Consider then, upon what ground it is we say, that the whole common course of nature is carried on according to general fore-ordained laws. We know indeed several of the general laws of matter: and a great part of the natural behaviour of living agents is reducible to general laws. But we know in a manner nothing, by what laws, storms and tempests, earthquakes, famine, pestilence, become the instruments of destruction to mankind. And the laws, by which persons born into the world at such a time and place are of such capacities, geniuses, tempers; the laws, by which thoughts come into our mind, in a multitude of cases; and by which innumerable things happen, of the greatest influence upon the affairs and state of the world; these laws are so wholly unknown to

---

[m] P. 131, &c.   [n] 1 Cor. i.
[o] P. 135, &c.   [p] P. 137, 138.

us, that we call the events, which come to pass by them, accidental: though all reasonable men know certainly, that there cannot, in reality, be any such thing as chance; and conclude, that the things which have this appearance are the result of general laws, and may be reduced into them. It is then but an exceeding little way, and in but a very few respects, that we can trace up the natural course of things before us, to general laws. And it is only from analogy, that we conclude the whole of it to be capable of being reduced into them: only from our seeing, that part is so. It is from our finding, that the course of nature, in some respects and so far, goes on by general laws, that we conclude this of the rest. And if that be a just ground for such a conclusion, it is a just ground also, if not to conclude, yet to apprehend, to render it supposable and credible, which is sufficient for answering objections, that God's miraculous interpositions may have been, all along in like manner, by *general* laws of wisdom. Thus, that miraculous powers should be exerted, at such times, upon such occasions, in such degrees and manners, and with regard to such persons, rather than others; that the affairs of the world, being permitted to go on in their natural course so far, should, just at such a point, have a new direction given them by miraculous interpositions; that these interpositions should be exactly in such degrees and respects only; all this may have been by general laws. These laws are unknown indeed to us: but no more unknown, than the laws from whence it is, that some die as soon as they are born, and others live to extreme old age; that one man is so superior to another in understanding; with innumerable more things, which, as was before observed, we cannot reduce to any laws or rules at all, though it is taken for granted, they are as much reducible to general ones, as gravitation. Now, if the revealed dispensations of Providence, and miraculous interpositions, be by general laws, as well as God's ordinary government in the course of nature, made known by reason and experience; there is no more reason to expect, that every exigence, as it arises, should be provided for by these general laws or miraculous interpositions, than that every exigence in nature should, by the general laws of nature: yet there might be wise and good reasons, that miraculous interpositions should be by general laws; and that these laws should not be broken in upon, or deviated from, by other miracles.

Upon the whole then: the appearance of deficiencies and irregularities in nature is owing to its being a scheme but in part made known, and of such a certain particular kind in other respects. Now we see no more reason why the frame and course of nature should be such a scheme, than why Christianity should. And that the former is such a scheme, renders it credible, that the latter, upon supposition of its truth, may be so too. And as it is manifest, that Christianity is a scheme revealed but in part, and a scheme in which means are made use of to accomplish ends, like to that of nature: so the credibility, that it may have been all along carried on by general laws, no less than the course of nature, has been distinctly proved. And from all this it is beforehand credible that there might, I think probable that there would, be the like appearance of deficiencies and irregularities in Christianity, as in nature: i.e. that Christianity would be liable to the like objections, as the frame of nature. And these objections are answered by these observations concerning Christianity; as the like objections against the frame of nature are answered by the like observations concerning the frame of nature.

THE objections against Christianity, considered as a matter of fact [q], having, in general, been obviated in the preceding chapter; and the same, considered as made against the wisdom and goodness of it, having been obviated in this: the next thing, according to the method proposed, is to shew, that the principal objections, in particular, against Christianity, may be answered, by particular and full analogies in nature. And as one of them is made against the whole scheme of it together, as just now described, I choose to consider it here, rather than in a distinct chapter by itself. The thing objected against this scheme of the Gospel is, "that it seems to suppose God was reduced to the necessity of a long series of intricate means, in order to accomplish his ends, the recovery and salvation of the world: in like sort as men, for want of understanding or power, not being able to come at their ends directly, are forced to go roundabout ways, and make use of many perplexed contrivances to arrive at them." Now every thing which we see shews the folly of this, considered as an objection against the truth of Christianity. For, according to our manner of conception, God makes use of variety of means, what we often think tedious ones, in the natural course of providence, for the accomplishment of all his ends. Indeed it is certain there is somewhat in this matter quite beyond our comprehension: but the mystery

[q] P. 129. &c.

is as great in nature as in Christianity. We know what we ourselves aim at, as final ends: and what courses we take, merely as means conducing to those ends. But we are greatly ignorant how far things are considered by the Author of Nature, under the single notion of means and ends; so as that it may be said, this is merely an end, and that merely means, in his regard. And whether there be not some peculiar absurdity in our very manner of conception, concerning this matter, somewhat contradictory arising from our extremely imperfect views of things, it is impossible to say. However, thus much is manifest, that the whole natural world and government of it is a scheme or system; not a fixed, but a progressive one: a scheme, in which the operation of various means takes up a great length of time, before the ends they tend to can be attained. The change of seasons, the ripening of the fruits of the earth, the very history of a flower, is an instance of this: and so is human life. Thus vegetable bodies, and those of animals, though possibly formed at once, yet grow up by degrees to a mature state. And thus rational agents, who animate these latter bodies, are naturally directed to form each his own manners and character, by the gradual gaining of knowledge and experience, and by a long course of action. Our existence is not only successive, as it must be of necessity; but one state of our life and being is appointed by God, to be a preparation for another; and that, to be the means of attaining to another succeeding one: infancy to childhood; childhood to youth; youth to mature age. Men are impatient, and for precipitating things: but the Author of Nature appears deliberate throughout his operations; accomplishing his natural ends by slow successive steps. And there is a plan of things beforehand laid out, which, from the nature of it, requires various systems of means, as well as length of time, in order to the carrying on its several parts into execution. Thus, in the daily course of natural providence, God operates in the very same manner as in the dispensation of Christianity: making one thing subservient to another; this, to somewhat farther; and so on, through a progressive series of means, which extend, both backward and forward, beyond our utmost view. Of this manner of operation, every thing we see in the course of nature is as much an instance, as any part of the Christian dispensation.

CHAP. V.

Of the particular system of Christianity; the appointment of a Mediator, and the redemption of the world by him.

THERE is not, I think, any thing relating to Christianity, which has been more objected against, than the mediation of Christ, in some or other of its parts. Yet, upon thorough consideration, there seems nothing less justly liable to it. For,

I. The whole analogy of nature removes all imagined presumption against the general notion of *a Mediator between God and man*[a]. For we find all living creatures are brought into the world, and their life in infancy is preserved, by the instrumentality of others: and every satisfaction of it, some way or other, is bestowed by the like means. So that the visible government, which God exercises over the

[a] 1 Tim. ii. 5.

world, is by the instrumentality and mediation of others. And how far his invisible government be or be not so, it is impossible to determine at all by reason. And the supposition, that part of it is so, appears, to say the least, altogether as credible, as the contrary. There is then no sort of objection, from the light of nature, against the general notion of a mediator between God and man, considered as a doctrine of Christianity, or as an appointment in this dispensation: since we find by experience, that God does appoint mediators, to be the instruments of good and evil to us; the instruments of his justice and his mercy. And the objection here referred to is urged, not against mediation in that high, eminent, and peculiar sense, in which Christ is our mediator; but absolutely against the whole notion itself of a mediator at all.

II. As we must suppose, that the world is under the proper moral government of God, or in a state of religion, before we can enter into consideration of the revealed doctrine, concerning the redemption of it by Christ; so that supposition is here to be distinctly taken notice of. Now the Divine moral government which religion teaches us, implies, that the consequence of vice shall be misery, in some future state, by the righteous judgment of God. That such consequent punishment shall take effect by his appointment, is necessarily implied. But, as it is not in any sort to be supposed, that we are made acquainted with all the ends or reasons, for which it is fit future punishments should be inflicted, or why God has appointed such and such consequent misery should follow vice; and as we are altogether in the dark, how or in what manner it shall follow, by what immediate occasions, or by the instrumentality of what means; there is no absurdity in supposing it may follow in a way analogous to that, in which many miseries follow such and such courses of action at present; poverty, sickness, infamy, untimely death by diseases, death from the hands of civil justice. There is no absurdity in supposing future punishment may follow wickedness of course, as we speak, or in the way of natural consequence from God's original constitution of the world; from the nature he has given us, and from the condition in which he places us; or in a like manner, as a person rashly trifling upon a precipice, in the way of natural consequence, falls down; in the way of natural consequence, breaks his limbs, suppose; in the way of natural consequence of this, without help, perishes.

Some good men may perhaps be offended with hearing it spoken of as a supposable thing, that the future punishments of wickedness may be in the way of natural consequence: as if this were taking the execution of justice out of the hands of God, and giving it to nature. But they should remember, that when things come to pass according to the course of nature, this does not hinder them from being his doing, who is the God of nature: and that the Scripture ascribes those punishments to Divine justice, which are known to be natural; and which must be called so, when distinguished from such as are miraculous. But after all, this supposition, or rather this way of speaking, is here made use of only by way of illustration of the subject before us. For since it must be admitted, that the future punishment of wickedness is not a matter of arbitrary appointment, but of reason, equity, and justice; it comes, for ought I see, to the same thing, whether it is supposed to be inflicted in a way analogous to that, in which the temporal punishments of vice and folly are inflicted, or in any other way. And though there were a difference, it is allowable, in the present case, to make this supposition, plainly not an incredible one; that future punishment may follow wickedness in the way of natural consequence, or according to some general laws of government already established in the universe.

III. Upon this supposition, or even without it, we may observe somewhat, much to the present purpose, in the constitution of nature or appointments of Providence: the provision which is made, that all the bad natural consequences of men's actions should not always actually follow; or that such bad consequences, as, according to the settled course of things, would inevitably have followed if not prevented, should, in certain degrees, be prevented. We are apt presumptuously to imagine, that the world might have been so constituted, as that there would not have been any such thing as misery or evil. On the contrary we find the Author of Nature permits it: but then he has provided reliefs, and, in many cases, perfect remedies for it, after some pains and difficulties; reliefs and remedies even for that evil, which is the fruit of our own misconduct; and which, in the course of nature, would have continued, and ended in our destruction, but for such remedies. And this is an instance both of severity and indulgence, in the constitution of nature. Thus all the bad consequences, now mentioned, of a man's trifling upon a precipice, might be prevented. And though all were not, yet some of them might, by proper interposition, if not rejected: by another's coming to the rash man's relief, with his own laying hold on that relief, in such sort as the case required. Persons may do a great deal themselves towards preventing the bad consequences of their follies: and more may be done by themselves, together with the assistance of others their fellow-creatures; which assistance Nature requires and prompts us to. This is the general constitution of the world. Now suppose it had been so constituted, that after such actions were done, as were foreseen naturally to draw after them misery to the doer, it should have been no more in human power to have prevented that naturally consequent misery, in any instance, than it is, in all; no one can say, whether such a more severe constitution of things might not yet have been really good. But, that, on the contrary, provision is made by nature, that we may and do, to so great degree, prevent the bad natural effects of our follies; this may be called mercy or compassion in the original constitution of the world: compassion, as distinguished from goodness in general. And, the whole known constitution and course of things affording us instances of such compassion, it would be according to the analogy of nature, to hope, that, however ruinous the natural consequences of vice might be, from the general laws of God's government over the universe; yet provision might be made, possibly might have been originally made, for preventing those ruinous consequences from inevitably following: at least from following universally, and in all cases.

Many, I am sensible, will wonder at finding this made a question, or spoken of as in any degree doubtful. The generality of mankind are so far from having that awful sense of things, which the present state of vice and misery and darkness seems to make but reasonable, that they have scarce any apprehension or thought at all about this matter, any way: and some serious persons may have spoken unadvisedly concerning it. But let us observe, what we experience to be, and what, from the very constitution of nature, cannot but be, the consequences of irregular and disorderly behaviour; even of such rashness, wilfulness, neglects, as we scarce call vicious. Now it is natural to apprehend, that the bad consequences of irregularity will be greater, in proportion as the irregularity is so. And there is no comparison between these irregularities, and the greater instances of vice, or a dissolute profligate disregard to all religion; if there be any thing at all in religion. For consider what it is for creatures, moral agents, presumptuously to introduce that confusion and misery into the kingdom of God, which mankind have in fact introduced; to blaspheme the Sovereign Lord of all; to contemn his authority; to be injurious, to the degree they are, to their fellow-creatures, the creatures of God. Add that the effects of vice in the present world are often extreme misery, irretrievable ruin, and even death: and upon putting all this together, it will appear, that as no one can say, in what degree fatal the unprevented consequences of vice may be, according to the general rule of divine government; so it is by no means intuitively certain how far these consequences could possibly, in the nature of the thing, be prevented, consistently with the eternal rule of right, or with what is, in fact, the moral constitution of nature. However, there would be large ground to hope, that the universal government was not so severely strict, but that there was room for pardon, or for having those penal consequences prevented. Yet,

IV. There seems no probability, that any thing we could do would alone and of itself prevent them: prevent their following, or being inflicted. But one would think, at least, it were impossible that the contrary should be thought certain. For we are not acquainted with the whole of the case. We are not informed of all the reasons, which render it fit that future punishments should be inflicted: and therefore cannot know, whether any thing we could do would make such an alteration, as to render it fit that they should be remitted. We do not know what the whole natural or appointed consequences of vice are; nor in what way they would follow, if not prevented: and therefore can in no sort say, whether we could do any thing which would be sufficient to prevent them. Our ignorance being thus manifest, let us recollect the analogy of Nature or Providence. For, though this may be but a slight ground to raise a positive opinion upon, in this matter; yet it is sufficient to answer a mere arbitrary assertion, without any kind of evidence, urged by way of objection against a doctrine, the proof of which is not reason, but revelation. Consider then: people ruin their fortunes by extravagance; they bring diseases upon themselves by excess; they incur the penalties of civil laws; and surely civil government is natural; will sorrow for these follies past, and behaving well for the future, alone and of itself prevent the natural consequences of them? On the contrary, men's natural abilities of helping themselves are often impaired: or if not, yet they are forced to be beholden to the assistance of others, upon several accounts, and in different ways; assistance which they would have had no occasion for, had it not been for their misconduct; but which, in the disadvantageous condition they have reduced themselves to, is absolutely necessary to their recovery, and retrieving their affairs. Now since this is our case, considering ourselves merely as inhabitants of this world, and as having a temporal interest here, under the natural government of God, which however has a great deal moral in it; why is it not supposable that this may be our case also, in our more important capacity, as under his perfect moral government, and having a more general and future interest depending? If we have misbehaved in this higher capacity, and rendered ourselves obnoxious to the future punishment, which God has annexed to vice: it is plainly credible, that behaving well for the time to come may be—not useless, God forbid—but wholly insufficient, alone and of itself, to prevent that punishment; or to put us in the condition, which we should have been in, had we preserved our innocence.

And though we ought to reason with all reverence whenever we reason concerning the Divine conduct: yet it may be added, that it is clearly contrary to all our notions of government, as well as to what is, in fact, the general constitution of nature, to suppose, that doing well for the future should, in all cases, prevent all the judicial bad consequences of having done evil, or all the punishment annexed to disobedience. And we have manifestly nothing from whence to determine, in what degree, and in what cases, reformation would prevent this punishment, even supposing that it would in some. And though the efficacy of repentance itself alone, to prevent what mankind had rendered themselves obnoxious to, and recover what they had forfeited, is now insisted upon, in opposition to Christianity; yet, by the general prevalence of propitiatory sacrifices over the heathen world, this notion, of repentance alone being sufficient to expiate guilt, appears to be contrary to the general sense of mankind.

Upon the whole then; had the laws, the general laws of God's government been permitted to operate, without any interposition in our behalf, the future punishment, for aught we know to the contrary, or have any reason to think, must inevitably have followed, notwithstanding any thing we could have done to prevent it. Now,

V. In this darkness, or this light of nature, call it which you please, revelation comes in; confirms every doubting fear, which could enter into the heart of man, concerning the future unprevented consequence of wickedness; supposes the world to be in a state of ruin; (a supposition which seems the very ground of the Christian dispensation, and which, if not provable by reason, yet is in no wise contrary to it;) teaches us too, that the rules of Divine government are such, as not to admit of pardon immediately and directly upon repentance, or by the sole efficacy of it: but then teaches at the same time, what nature might justly have hoped, that the moral government of the universe was not so rigid, but that there was room for an interposition, to avert the fatal consequences of vice; which therefore, by this means, does admit of pardon. Revelation teaches us, that the unknown laws of God's more general government, no less than the particular laws by which we experience he governs us at present, are compassionate [b], as well as good in the more general notion of goodness: and that he hath mercifully provided, that there should be an interposition to prevent the destruction of human kind; whatever

[b] P. 208, &c.

that destruction unprevented would have been. *God so loved the world, that he gave his only begotten Son, that whosoever believeth,* not, to be sure, in a speculative, but in a practical sense, *that whosoever believeth in him, should not perish* [c]: gave his Son in the same way of goodness to the world, as he affords particular persons the friendly assistance of their fellow creatures; when, without it, their temporal ruin would be the certain consequence of their follies: in the same way of goodness, I say; though in a transcendent and infinitely higher degree. And the Son of God *loved us, and gave himself for us,* with a love, which he himself compares to that of human friendship: though, in this case, all comparisons must fall infinitely short of the thing intended to be illustrated by them. He interposed in such a manner as was necessary and effectual to prevent that execution of justice upon sinners, which God had appointed should otherwise have been executed upon them: or in such a manner, as to prevent that punishment from actually following, which, according to the general laws of Divine government, must have followed the sins of the world, had it not been for such interposition [d].

[c] John iii. 16.

[d] It cannot, I suppose, be imagined, even by the most cursory reader, that it is, in any sort, affirmed or implied in any thing said in this chapter, that none can have the benefit of the general redemption, but such as have the advantage of being made acquainted with it in the present life. But it may be needful to mention, that several questions, which have been brought into the subject before us, and determined, are not in the least entered into here: questions which have been, I fear, rashly determined, and perhaps with equal rashness contrary ways. For instance, whether God could have saved the world by other means than the death of Christ, consistently with the general laws of his government. And had not Christ come into the

If any thing here said should appear, upon first thought, inconsistent with Divine goodness; a second, I am persuaded, will entirely remove that appearance. For were we to suppose the constitution of things to be such, as that the whole creation must have perished, had it not been for somewhat, which God had appointed should be, in order to prevent that ruin: even this supposition would not be inconsistent, in any degree, with the most absolutely perfect goodness. But still it may be thought, that this whole manner of treating the subject before us supposes mankind to be naturally in a very strange state. And truly so it does. But it is not Christianity, which has put us into this state. Whoever will consider the manifold miseries, and the extreme wickedness of the world; that the best have great wrongnesses within themselves, which they complain of, and endeavour to amend; but that the generality grow more profligate and corrupt with age; that heathen moralists thought the present state to be a state of punishment: and, what might be added, that the earth our habitation has the appearances of being a ruin: whoever, I say, will consider all these, and some other obvious things, will think he has little reason to object against the Scripture account, that mankind is in a state of degradation; against this

world, what would have been the future condition of the better sort of men; those just persons over the face of the earth, for whom, Manasses in his prayer asserts, repentance was not appointed. The meaning of the first of these questions is greatly ambiguous: and neither of them can properly be answered, without going upon that infinitely absurd supposition, that we know the whole of the case. And perhaps the very inquiry, *What would have followed, if God had not done as he has*, may have in it some very great impropriety; and ought not to be carried on any further, than is necessary to help our partial and inadequate conceptions of things.

being the fact: how difficult soever he may think it to account for, or even to form a distinct conception of the occasions and circumstances of it. But that the crime of our first parents was the occasion of our being placed in a more disadvantageous condition, is a thing throughout and particularly analogous to what we see in the daily course of natural Providence; as the recovery of the world by the interposition of Christ has been shewn to be so in general.

VI. The particular manner in which Christ interposed in the redemption of the world, or his office as *Mediator*, in the largest sense, *between God and man*, is thus represented to us in the Scripture. *He is the light of the world* [c]; the revealer of the will of God in the most eminent sense. He is a propitiatory sacrifice [f]; *the Lamb of God* [g]*:* and, as he voluntarily offered himself up, he is styled our High Priest [h]. And, which seems of peculiar weight, he is described beforehand in the Old Testament, under the same characters of a priest, and an expiatory victim [i]. And whereas it is objected, that all this is merely by way of allusion to the sacrifices of the Mosaic Law, the Apostle on the contrary affirms, that the *Law was a shadow of good things to come, and not the very image of the things* [k]*:* and that *the priests that offer gifts according to the Law—serve unto the example and shadow of heavenly things, as*

---

[c] John i. and viii. 12.
[f] Rom. iii. 25. and v. 11; 1 Cor. v. 7; Eph. v. 2; 1 John ii. 2; Matth. xxvi. 28.
[g] John i. 29, 36, and throughout the Book of Revelation.
[h] Throughout the Epistle to the Hebrews.
[i] Isa. liii; Dan. ix. 24; Psalm cx. 4.
[k] Heb. x. 1.

Moses was admonished of God, when he was about to make the tabernacle. For see, saith he, that thou make all things according to the pattern shewed to thee in the mount[1]*:* i. e. the Levitical priesthood was a shadow of the priesthood of Christ; in like manner as the tabernacle made by Moses was according to that shewed him in the mount. The priesthood of Christ, and the tabernacle in the mount, were the originals: of the former of which the Levitical priesthood was a type; and of the latter the tabernacle made by Moses was a copy. The doctrine of this Epistle then plainly is, that the legal sacrifices were allusions to the great and final atonement to be made by the blood of Christ; and not that this was an allusion to those. Nor can any thing be more express or determinate than the following passage: *It is not possible that the blood of bulls and of goats should take away sin. Wherefore when he cometh into the world, he saith, Sacrifice and offering,* i. e. of bulls and of goats, *thou wouldest not, but a body hast thou prepared me—Lo, I come to do thy will, O God—By which will we are sanctified, through the offering of the body of Jesus Christ once for all*[m]. And to add one passage more of the like kind: *Christ was once offered to bear the sins of many; and unto them that look for him shall he appear the second time, without sin;* i. e. without bearing sin, as he did at his first coming, by being an offering for it; without having our *iniquities* again *laid upon him,* without being any more a sin-offering:—*unto them that look for him shall he appear the second time, without sin, unto salvation*[n]. Nor do the inspired writers at all confine themselves to this manner of speaking concerning the satisfac-

[l] Heb. viii. 4, 5.   [m] Heb. x. 4, 5, 7, 9, 10.   [n] Heb. ix. 28.

tion of Christ; but declare an efficacy in what he did and suffered for us, additional to and beyond mere instruction, example, and government, in great variety of expression : *That Jesus should die for that nation,* the Jews: *and not for that nation only, but that also,* plainly by the efficacy of his death, *he should gather together in one the children of God that were scattered abroad*[o]*:* that *he suffered for sins, the just for the unjust*[p]*:* that *he gave his life, himself, a ransom*[q]*:* that *we are bought, bought with a price*[r]*:* that *he redeemed us with his blood; redeemed us from the curse of the law, being made a curse for us*[s]*:* that he is our *advocate, intercessor,* and *propitiation*[t]*:* that *he was made perfect,* or consummate, *through sufferings: and being* thus *made perfect, he became the author of salvation*[u]*:* that *God was in Christ reconciling the world to himself; by the death of his Son, by the cross; not imputing their trespasses unto them*[w]*:* and lastly, that *through death he destroyed him that had the power of death*[x]. Christ then having thus *humbled himself, and become obedient to death, even the death of the cross; God also hath highly exalted him, and given him a name, which is above every name: hath given all things into his hands: hath committed all judgment unto him; that all men should honour the Son, even as they honour the Father*[y]. For, *worthy is the Lamb*

[o] John xi. 51, 52.   [p] 1 Pet. iii. 18.
[q] Matt. xx. 28; Mark x. 45; 1 Tim. ii. 6.
[r] 2 Pet. ii. 1; Rev. xiv. 4; 1 Cor. vi. 20.
[s] 1 Pet. i. 19; Rev. v. 9; Gal. iii. 13.
[t] Heb. vii. 25; 1 John ii. 1, 2.
[u] Heb. ii. 10. and v. 9.
[w] 2 Cor. v. 19; Rom. v. 10; Eph. ii. 16.
[x] Heb. ii. 14. See also a remarkable passage in the book of Job, xxxiii. 24.   [y] Phil. ii. 8, 9; John iii. 35, and v. 22, 23.

that was slain to receive power, and riches, and wisdom, and strength, and honour, and glory, and blessing. And every creature which is in heaven, and on the earth—heard I, saying, Blessing, and honour, and glory, and power, be unto him that sitteth upon the throne, and unto the Lamb for ever and ever[z].

These passages of Scripture seem to comprehend and express the chief parts of Christ's office, as Mediator between God and man, so far, I mean, as the nature of this his office is revealed; and it is usually treated of by divines under three heads:

First, He was, by way of eminence, the Prophet: *that Prophet that should come into the world*[a], to declare the Divine will. He published anew the law of nature, which men had corrupted; and the very knowledge of which, to some degree, was lost among them. He taught mankind, taught us authoritatively, to *live soberly, righteously, and godly in this present world*, in expectation of the future judgment of God. He confirmed the truth of this moral system of nature, and gave us additional evidence of it; the evidence of testimony[b]. He distinctly revealed the manner, in which God would be worshipped, the efficacy of repentance, and the rewards and punishments of a future life. Thus he was a prophet in a sense in which no other ever was. To which is to be added, that he set us a perfect *example, that we should follow his steps*.

Secondly, He has a *kingdom which is not of this world*. He founded a Church, to be to mankind a standing memorial of religion, and invitation to it; which he promised to be with always even to the end. He exercises an invisible government over it,

[z] Rev. v. 12, 13.   [a] John vi. 14.   [b] Page 154, &c.

himself, and by his Spirit: over that part of it, which is militant here on earth, a government of discipline, *for the perfecting of the saints, for the edifying his body: till we all come in the unity of the faith, and of the knowledge of the Son of God, unto a perfect man, unto the measure of the stature of the fulness of Christ*[c]. Of this Church, all persons scattered over the world, who live in obedence to his laws, are members. For these he is *gone to prepare a place,* and *will come again to receive them unto himself, that where he is, there they may be also; and reign with him for ever and ever*[d]: and likewise *to take vengeance on them that know not God, and obey not his Gospel*[e].

Against these parts of Christ's office I find no objections, but what are fully obviated in the beginning of this chapter.

Lastly, Christ offered himself a propitiatory sacrifice, and made atonement for the sins of the world; which is mentioned last, in regard to what is objected against it. Sacrifices of expiation were commanded the Jews, and obtained amongst most other nations, from tradition, whose original probably was revelation. And they were continually repeated, both occasionally, and at the returns of stated times: and made up great part of the external religion of mankind. *But now once in the end of the world Christ appeared to put away sin by the sacrifice of himself*[f]. And this sacrifice was, in the highest degree and with the most extensive influence, of that efficacy for obtaining pardon of sin, which the heathens may be supposed to have thought their sacrifices to have

[c] Eph. iv. 12, 13. [d] John xiv. 2, 3; Rev. iii. 21. and xi. 15.
[e] 2 Thess. i. 8. [f] Heb. ix. 26.

been, and which the Jewish sacrifices really were in some degree, and with regard to some persons.

How and in what particular way it had this efficacy, there are not wanting persons who have endeavoured to explain : but I do not find that the Scripture has explained it. We seem to be very much in the dark concerning the manner in which the ancients understood atonement to be made, i. e. pardon to be obtained by sacrifices. And if the Scripture has, as surely it has, left this matter of the satisfaction of Christ, mysterious, left somewhat in it unrevealed, all conjectures about it must be, if not evidently absurd, yet at least uncertain. Nor has any one reason to complain for want of farther information, unless he can shew his claim to it.

Some have endeavoured to explain the efficacy of what Christ has done and suffered for us, beyond what the Scripture has authorized : others, probably because they could not explain it, have been for taking it away, and confining his office as Redeemer of the world to his instruction, example, and government of the church. Whereas the doctrine of the Gospel appears to be, not only that he taught the efficacy of repentance, but rendered it of the efficacy which it is, by what he did and suffered for us: that he obtained for us the benefit of having our repentance accepted unto eternal life : not only that he revealed to sinners, that they were in a capacity of salvation, and how they might obtain it; but moreover that he put them into this capacity of salvation, by what he did and suffered for them; put us into a capacity of escaping future punishment, and obtaining future happiness. And it is our wisdom thankfully to accept the benefit, by performing the conditions, upon which it is offered, on our part, without disputing how it was procured on his. For,

VII. Since we neither know by what means punishment in a future state would have followed wickedness in this; nor in what manner it would have been inflicted, had it not been prevented; nor all the reasons why its infliction would have been needful; nor the particular nature of that state of happiness, which Christ is gone to prepare for his disciples: and since we are ignorant how far any thing which we could do, would, alone and of itself, have been effectual to prevent that punishment, to which we were obnoxious, and recover that happiness, which we had forfeited; it is most evident we are not judges, antecedently to revelation, whether a mediator was or was not necessary, to obtain those ends: to prevent That future punishment, and bring mankind to the final happiness of their nature. And for the very same reasons, upon supposition of the necessity of a mediator, we are no more judges, antecedently to revelation, of the whole nature of his office, or the several parts of which it consists; of what was fit and requisite to be assigned him, in order to accomplish the ends of Divine providence in the appointment. And from hence it follows, that to object against the expediency or usefulness of particular things, revealed to have been done or suffered by him, because we do not see how they were conducive to those ends, is highly absurd. Yet nothing is more common to be met with, than this absurdity. But if it be acknowledged beforehand, that we are not judges in the case, it is evident that no objection can, with any shadow of reason, be urged against any particular part of Christ's mediatorial office revealed in Scripture, till it can be shewn positively not to be requisite or conducive to the ends proposed to be accomplished; or that it is in itself unreasonable.

And there is one objection made against the satisfaction of Christ, which looks to be of this positive kind: that the doctrine of his being appointed to suffer for the sins of the world, represents God as being indifferent whether he punished the innocent or the guilty. Now from the foregoing observations we may see the extreme slightness of all such objections; and (though it is most certain all who make them do not see the consequence) that they conclude altogether as much against God's whole original constitution of nature, and the whole daily course of Divine providence in the government of the world, i. e. against the whole scheme of Theism and the whole notion of Religion, as against Christianity. For the world is a constitution or system, whose parts have a mutual reference to each other: and there is a scheme of things gradually carrying on, called the course of nature, to the carrying on of which God has appointed us, in various ways, to contribute. And when, in the daily course of natural providence, it is appointed that innocent people should suffer for the faults of the guilty, this is liable to the very same objection, as the instance we are now considering. The infinitely greater importance of that appointment of Christianity, which is objected against, does not hinder but it may be, as it plainly is, an appointment of the very same kind, with what the world affords us daily examples of. Nay, if there were any force at all in the objection, it would be stronger, in one respect, against natural providence, than against Christianity: because under the former we are in many cases commanded, and even necessitated whether we will or no, to suffer for the faults of others; whereas the sufferings of Christ were voluntary. The world's being under the righteous government of God does indeed imply, that finally and upon the whole every one shall receive according to his personal deserts: and the general doctrine of the whole Scripture is, that this shall be the completion of the Divine government. But during the progress, and, for ought we know, even in order to the completion of this moral scheme, vicarious punishments may be fit, and absolutely necessary. Men by their follies run themselves into extreme distress; into difficulties which would be absolutely fatal to them, were it not for the interposition and assistance of others. God commands by the law of nature, that we afford them this assistance, in many cases where we cannot do it without very great pains, and labour, and sufferings to ourselves. And we see in what variety of ways one person's sufferings contribute to the relief of another: and how, or by what particular means, this comes to pass, or follows, from the constitution and laws of nature, which come under our notice: and, being familiarized to it, men are not shocked with it. So that the reason of their insisting upon objections of the foregoing kind against the satisfaction of Christ is, either that they do not consider God's settled and uniform appointments as his appointments at all; or else they forget that vicarious punishment is a providential appointment of every day's experience: and then, from their being unacquainted with the more general laws of nature or Divine government over the world, and not seeing how the sufferings of Christ could contribute to the redemption of it, unless by arbitrary and tyrannical will; they conclude his sufferings could not contribute to it any other way. And yet, what has been often alleged in justification of this doctrine, even from the apparent natural tendency of this method of our redemption; its tendency to vindicate the authority of God's laws, and deter his creatures from sin; this has never yet been answered, and is, I think, plainly unanswerable: though I am far from thinking it an account of the whole of the case. But without taking this into consideration, it abundantly appears, from the observations above made, that this objection is, not an objection against Christianity, but against the whole general constitution of nature. And if it were to be considered as an objection against Christianity, or considering it as it is, an objection against the constitution of nature; it amounts to no more in conclusion than this, that a Divine appointment cannot be necessary or expedient, because the objector does not discern it to be so: though he must own that the nature of the case is such, as renders him incapable of judging, whether it be so or not; or of seeing it to be necessary, though it were so.

It is indeed a matter of great patience to reasonable men, to find people arguing in this manner: objecting against the credibility of such particular things revealed in Scripture, that they do not see the necessity or expediency of them. For though it is highly right, and the most pious exercise of our understanding, to inquire with due reverence into the ends and reasons of God's dispensations: yet when those reasons are concealed, to argue from our ignorance, that such dispensations cannot be from God, is infinitely absurd. The presumption of this kind of objections seems almost lost in the folly of them. And the folly of them is yet greater, when they are urged, as usually they are, against things in Christianity analogous or like to those natural dispensations of Providence, which are matter of experience. Let reason be kept to: and if any part of the Scripture account of the redemption of the world by Christ can be shewn to be really contrary to it, let the Scripture, in the name of God, be given up: but let not such poor creatures as we go on objecting against an infinite scheme, that we do not see the necessity or usefulness of all its parts, and call this reasoning; and, which still farther heightens the absurdity in the present case, parts which we are not actively concerned in. For it may be worth mentioning,

Lastly, That not only the reason of the thing, but the whole analogy of nature, should teach us, not to expect to have the like information concerning the Divine conduct, as concerning our own duty. God instructs us by experience, (for it is not reason, but experience which instructs us,) what good or bad consequences will follow from our acting in such and such manners: and by this he directs us, how we are to behave ourselves. But, though we are sufficiently instructed for the common purposes of life: yet it is but an almost infinitely small part of natural providence, which we are at all let into. The case is the same with regard to revelation. The doctrine of a mediator between God and man, against which it is objected, that the expediency of some things in it is not understood, relates only to what was done on God's part in the appointment, and on the mediator's in the execution of it. For what is required of us, in consequence of this gracious dispensation, is another subject, in which none can complain for want of information. The constitution of the world, and God's natural government over it, is all mystery, as much as the Christian dispensation. Yet under the first he has given men all things pertaining to life; and under the other, all things pertaining unto godliness. And it may be added, that there is nothing hard to be accounted for in any of the common precepts of Christianity: though if there were, surely, a Divine command is abundantly sufficient to lay us under the strongest obligations to obedience. But the fact is, that the reasons of all the Christian precepts are evident. Positive institutions are manifestly necessary to keep up and propagate religion amongst mankind. And our duty to Christ, the internal and external worship of him; this part of the religion of the Gospel manifestly arises out of what he has done and suffered, his authority and dominion, and the relation which he is revealed to stand in to us[g].

CHAP. VI.

Of the want of universality in revelation: and of the supposed deficiency in the proof of it.

It has been thought by some persons, that if the evidence of revelation appears doubtful, this itself turns into a positive argument against it: because it cannot be supposed, that, if it were true, it would be left to subsist upon doubtful evidence. And the objection against revelation from its not being universal is often insisted upon as of great weight.

[g] P. 161, &c.

Now the weakness of these opinions may be shewn, by observing the suppositions on which they are founded: which are really such as these; that it cannot be thought God would have bestowed any favour at all upon us, unless in the degree, which, we think, he might, and which, we imagine, would be most to our particular advantage; and also that it cannot be thought he would bestow a favour upon any, unless he bestowed the same upon all: suppositions, which we find contradicted, not by a few instances in God's natural government of the world, but by the general analogy of nature together.

Persons who speak of the evidence of religion as doubtful, and of this supposed doubtfulness as a positive argument against it, should be put upon considering, what that evidence indeed is, which they act upon with regard to their temporal interests. For, it is not only extremely difficult, but in many cases absolutely impossible, to balance pleasure and pain, satisfaction and uneasiness, so as to be able to say on which side the overplus is. There are the like difficulties and impossibilities in making the due allowances for a change of temper and taste, for satiety, disgusts, ill health: any of which render men incapable of enjoying, after they have obtained what they most eagerly desired. Numberless too are the accidents, besides that one of untimely death, which may even probably disappoint the best concerted schemes: and strong objections are often seen to lie against them, not to be removed or answered, but which seem overbalanced by reasons on the other side; so as that the certain difficulties and dangers of the pursuit are, by every one, thought justly disregarded, upon account of the appearing greater advantages in case of success, though there be but little probability of it. Lastly, every one observes our liableness, if we be not upon our guard, to be deceived by the falsehood of men, and the false appearances of things: and this danger must be greatly increased, if there be a strong bias within, suppose from indulged passion, to favour the deceit. Hence arises that great uncertainty and doubtfulness of proof, wherein our temporal interest really consists; what are the most probable means of attaining it; and whether those means will eventually be successful. And numberless instances there are, in the daily course of life, in which all men think it reasonable to engage in pursuits, though the probability is greatly against succeeding; and to make such provision for themselves, as it is supposable they may have occasion for, though the plain acknowledged probability is, that they never shall. Then those who think the objection against revelation, from its light not being universal, to be of weight, should observe, that the Author of Nature, in numberless instances, bestows That upon some, which he does not upon others, who seem equally to stand in need of it. Indeed he appears to bestow all his gifts with the most promiscuous variety among creatures of the same species: health and strength, capacities of prudence and of knowledge, means of improvement, riches, and all external advantages. And as there are not any two men found, of exactly like shape and features; so it is probable there are not any two, of an exactly like constitution, temper and situation, with regard to the goods and evils of life. Yet, notwithstanding these uncertainties and varieties, God does exercise a natural government over the world: and there is such a thing as a prudent and imprudent institution of life, with regard to our health and our affairs, under that his natural government.

As neither the Jewish nor Christian revelation have been universal; and as they have been afforded to a greater or less part of the world, at different times; so likewise, at different times, both revelations have had different degrees of evidence. The Jews who lived during the succession of prophets, that is, from Moses till after the Captivity, had higher evidence of the truth of religion, than those had, who lived in the interval between the last-mentioned period and the coming of Christ. And the first Christians had higher evidence of the miracles wrought in attestation of Christianity, than what we have now. They had also a strong presumptive proof of the truth of it, perhaps of much greater force, in way of argument, than many think, of which we have very little remaining; I mean the presumptive proof of its truth, from the influence which it had upon the lives of the generality of its professors. And we, or future ages, may possibly have a proof of it, which they could not have, from the conformity between the prophetic history, and the state of the world and of Christianity. And farther: if we were to suppose the evidence, which some have of religion, to amount to little more than seeing that it may be true; but that they remain in great doubts and uncertainties about both its evidence and its nature, and great perplexities concerning the rule of life: others to have a full conviction of the truth of religion, with a distinct knowledge of their duty; and others severally to have all the intermediate degrees of religious light and evidence, which lie between these two—if we put the case, that for the present, it was intended, revelation should be no more than a small light, in the midst of a world greatly overspread, notwithstanding it, with ignorance and darkness: that certain glimmerings of this light should extend, and be directed, to remote distances, in such a manner as that those who really partook of it should not discern from whence it originally came: that some in a nearer situation to it should have its light obscured, and, in different ways and degrees, intercepted: and that others should be placed within its clearer influence, and be much more enlivened, cheered, and directed by it; but yet that even to these it should be no more than *a light shining in a dark place:* all this would be perfectly uniform, and of a piece with the conduct of Providence, in the distribution of its other blessings. If the fact of the case really were, that some have received no light at all from the Scripture; as many ages and countries in the heathen world: that others, though they have, by means of it, had essential or natural religion enforced upon their consciences, yet have never had the genuine Scripture-revelation, with its real evidence, proposed to their consideration; and the ancient Persians and modern Mahometans may possibly be instances of people in a situation somewhat like to this: that others, though they have had the Scripture laid before them as of Divine revelation, yet have had it with the system and evidence of Christianity so interpolated, the system so corrupted, the evidence so blended with false miracles, as to leave the mind in the utmost doubtfulness and uncertainty about the whole; which may be the state of some thoughtful men, in most of those nations who call themselves Christian : and lastly, that others have had Christianity offered to them in its genuine simplicity, and with its proper evidence, as persons in countries and churches of civil and of Christian liberty; but however that even these persons are left in great ignorance in many respects, and have by no means light afforded them enough to satisfy their curiosity, but only to regulate their life, to teach them their duty, and encourage them in the careful discharge of it: I say, if we were to suppose this somewhat of a general true account of the degrees of moral and religious light and evidence, which were intended to be afforded mankind, and of what has actually been and is their situation, in their moral and religious capacity; there would be nothing in all this ignorance, doubtfulness and uncertainty, in all these varieties, and supposed disadvantages of some in comparison of others, respecting religion, but may be paralleled by manifest analogies in the natural dispensations of Providence at present, and considering ourselves merely in our temporal capacity.

Nor is there any thing shocking in all this, or which would seem to bear hard upon the moral administration in nature, if we would really keep in mind, that every one shall be dealt equitably with: instead of forgetting this, or explaining it away, after it is acknowledged in words. All shadow of injustice, and indeed all harsh appearances, in this various economy of Providence, would be lost; if we would keep in mind, that every merciful allowance shall be made, and no more be required of any one, than what might have been equitably expected of him, from the circumstances in which he was placed; and not what might have been expected, had he been placed in other circumstances : i. e. in Scripture language, that every man shall be *accepted according to what he had, not according to what he had not*[a]. This however doth not by any means imply, that all persons' condition here is equally advantageous with respect to futurity. And Providence's designing to place some in greater darkness with respect to religious knowledge, is no more a reason why they should not endeavour to get out of that darkness, and others to bring them out of it; than why ignorant and slow people in matters of other knowledge should not endeavour to learn, or should not be instructed.

It is not unreasonable to suppose, that the same wise and good principle, whatever it was, which disposed the Author of nature to make different kinds and orders of creatures, disposed him also to place creatures of like kinds in different situations: and that the same principle which disposed him to make creatures of different moral capacities, disposed him also to place creatures of like moral capacities in different religious situations; and even the same creatures, in different periods of their being. And the account or reason of this is also most probably the account why the constitution of things is such, as that creatures of moral natures or capacities, for a considerable part of that duration in which they are living agents, are not at all subjects of morality and religion; but grow up to be so, and grow up to be so more and more, gradually from childhood to mature age.

What, in particular, is the account or reason of these things we must be greatly in the dark, were it only that we know so very little even of our own

[a] 2 Cor. viii. 12.

case. Our present state may possibly be the consequence of somewhat past, which we are wholly ignorant of: as it has a reference to somewhat to come, of which we know scarce any more than is necessary for practice. A system or constitution, in its notion, implies variety; and so complicated an one as this world, very great variety. So that were revelation universal, yet, from men's different capacities of understanding, from the different lengths of their lives, their different educations and other external circumstances, and from their difference of temper and bodily constitution; their religious situations would be widely different, and the disadvantage of some in comparison of others, perhaps, altogether as much as at present. And the true account, whatever it be, why mankind, or such a part of mankind, are placed in this condition of ignorance, must be supposed also the true account of our farther ignorance, in not knowing the reasons why, or whence it is, that they are placed in this condition. But the following practical reflections may deserve the serious consideration of those persons, who think the circumstances of mankind or their own, in the forementioned respects, a ground of complaint.

First, The evidence of Religion not appearing obvious, may constitute one particular part of some men's trial in the religious sense: as it gives scope, for a virtuous exercise or vicious neglect of their understanding, in examining or not examining into that evidence. There seems no possible reason to be given, why we may not be in a state of moral —probation, with regard to the exercise of our understanding upon the subject of religion, as we are with regard to our behaviour in common affairs. The former is as much a thing within our power and choice as the latter. And I suppose it is to be laid down for certain, that the same character, the same inward principle, which, after a man is convinced of the truth of religion, renders him obedient to the precepts of it, would, were he not thus convinced, set him about an examination of it, upon its system and evidence being offered to his thoughts: and that in the latter state his examination would be with an impartiality, seriousness, and solicitude, proportionable to what his obedience is in the former. And as inattention, negligence, want of all serious concern, about a matter of such a nature and such importance, when offered to men's consideration, is, before a distinct conviction of its truth, as real immoral depravity and dissoluteness; as neglect of religious practice after such conviction: so active solicitude about it, and fair impartial consideration of its evidence before such conviction, is as really an exercise of a morally right temper; as is religious practice after. Thus, that religion is not intuitively true, but a matter of deduction and inference; that a conviction of its truth is not forced upon every one, but left to be, by some, collected with heedful attention to premises; this as much constitutes religious probation, as much affords sphere, scope, opportunity, for right and wrong behaviour, as any thing whatever does. And their manner of treating this subject, when laid before them, shews what is in their heart, and is an exertion of it.

Secondly, It appears to be a thing as evident, though it is not so much attended to, that if, upon consideration of religion, the evidence of it should seem to any persons doubtful, in the highest supposable degree; even this doubtful evidence will, however, put them into a *general state of probation* in the moral and religious sense. For, suppose a man to be really in doubt, whether such a person had not done him the greatest favour; or, whether his whole temporal interest did not depend upon that person: no one, who had any sense of gratitude and of prudence, could possibly consider himself in the same situation, with regard to such person, as if he had no such doubt. In truth, it is as just to say, that certainty and doubt are the same; as to say, the situations now mentioned would leave a man as entirely at liberty in point of gratitude or prudence, as he would be, were he certain he had received no favour from such person, or that he no way depended upon him. And thus, though the evidence of religion which is afforded to some men should be little more than that they are given to see the system of Christianity, or religion in general, to be supposable and credible; this ought in all reason to beget a serious practical apprehension, that it may be true. And even this will afford matter of exercise for religious suspense and deliberation, for moral resolution and self-government; because the apprehension that religion may be true does as really lay men under obligations, as a full conviction that it is true. It gives occasion and motives to consider farther the important subject; to preserve attentively upon their minds a general implicit sense that they may be under Divine moral government, an awful solicitude about religion, whether natural or revealed. Such apprehension ought to turn men's eyes to every degree of new light which may be had, from whatever side it comes; and induce them to refrain, in the mean time, from all immoralities, and live in the conscientious practice of every common virtue. Especially are they bound to keep at the greatest distance from all dissolute profaneness; for this the very nature of the case forbids; and to treat with highest reverence a matter, upon which their own whole interest and being, and the fate of nature, depends. This behaviour, and an active endeavour to maintain within themselves this temper, is the business, the duty, and the wisdom of those persons, who complain of the doubtfulness of religion: is what they are under the most proper obligations to. And such behaviour is an exertion of, and has a tendency to improve in them, that character, which the practice of all the several duties of religion, from a full conviction of its truth, is an exertion of, and has a tendency to improve in others: others, I say, to whom God has afforded such conviction. Nay, considering the infinite importance of religion, revealed as well as natural, I think it may be said in general that whoever will weigh the matter thoroughly may see, there is not near so much difference, as is commonly imagined, between what ought in reason to be the rule of life, to those persons who are fully convinced of its truth, and to those who have only a serious doubting apprehension, that it may be true. Their hopes and fears and obligations, will be in various degrees: but, as the subject-matter of their hopes and fears is the same; so the subject-matter of their obligations, what they are bound to do and to refrain from, is not so very unlike.

It is to be observed farther, that, from a character of understanding, or a situation of influence in the world, some persons have it in their power to do infinitely more harm or good, by setting an example of profaneness and avowed disregard to all religion, or, on the contrary, of a serious, though perhaps doubting, apprehension of its truth, and of a reverend regard to it under this doubtfulness; than they can do, by acting well or ill in all the common intercourses amongst mankind. And consequently they are most highly accountable for a behaviour, which, they may easily foresee, is of such importance, and in which there is most plainly a right and a wrong; even admitting the evidence of religion to be as doubtful as is pretended.

The ground of these observations, and that which renders them just and true, is, that doubting necessarily implies some degree of evidence for that, of which we doubt. For no person would be in doubt concerning the truth of a number of facts so and so circumstanced, which should accidentally come into his thoughts, and of which he had no evidence at all. And though in the case of an even chance, and where consequently we were in doubt, we should in common language say, that we had no evidence at all for either side; yet that situation of things, which renders it an even chance and no more, that such an event will happen, renders this case equivalent to all others, where there is such evidence on both sides of a question[b], as leaves the mind in doubt concerning the truth. Indeed in all these cases, there is no more evidence on one side than on the other; but there is (what is equivalent to) much more for either, than for the truth of a number of facts, which come into one's thoughts at random. And thus, in all these cases, doubt as much presupposes evidence, lower degrees of evidence, as belief presupposes higher, and certainty higher still. Any one, who will a little attend to the nature of evidence, will easily carry this observation on, and see, that between

[b] Introduction.

no evidence at all, and that degree of it which affords ground of doubt, there are as many intermediate degrees, as there are, between that degree which is the ground of doubt, and demonstration. And though we have not faculties to distinguish these degrees of evidence with any sort of exactness; yet, in proportion as they are discerned, they ought to influence our practice. For it is as real an imperfection in the moral character, not to be influenced in practice by a lower degree of evidence when discerned, as it is in the understanding, not to discern it. And as, in all subjects which men consider, they discern the lower as well as higher degrees of evidence, proportionably to their capacity of understanding; so, in practical subjects, they are influenced in practice, by the lower as well as higher degrees of it, proportionably to their fairness and honesty. And as, in proportion to defects in the understanding, men are unapt to see lower degrees of evidence, are in danger of overlooking evidence when it is not glaring, and are easily imposed upon in such cases; so, in proportion to the corruption of the heart, they seem capable of satisfying themselves with having no regard in practice to evidence acknowledged real, if it be not overbearing. From these things it must follow, that doubting concerning religion implies such a degree of evidence for it, as, joined with the consideration of its importance, unquestionably lays men under the obligations before mentioned, to have a dutiful regard to it in all their behaviour.

Thirdly, The difficulties in which the evidence of religion is involved, which some complain of, is no more a just ground of complaint, than the external circumstances of temptation, which others are placed in; or than difficulties in the practice of it, after a full conviction of its truth. Temptations render our state a more improving state of discipline [c], than it would be otherwise: as they give occasion for a more attentive exercise of the virtuous principle, which confirms and strengthens it more, than an easier or less attentive exercise of it could. Now speculative difficulties are, in this respect, of the very same nature with these external temptations. For the evidence of religion not appearing obvious, is to some persons a temptation to reject it, without any consideration at all; and therefore requires such an attentive exercise of the virtuous principle, seriously to consider that evidence, as there would be no occasion for, but for such temptation. And the supposed doubtfulness of its evidence, after it has been in some sort considered, affords opportunity to an unfair mind of explaining away, and deceitfully hiding from itself, that evidence which it might see; and also for men's encouraging themselves in vice, from hopes of impunity, though they do clearly see thus much at least, that these hopes are uncertain: in like manner as the common temptation to many instances of folly, which end in temporal infamy and ruin, is, the ground for hope of not being detected, and of escaping with impunity; i. e. the doubtfulness of the proof beforehand, that such foolish behaviour will thus end in infamy and ruin. On the contrary, supposed doubtfulness in the evidence of religion calls for a more careful and attentive exercise of the virtuous principle, in fairly yielding themselves up to the proper influence of any real evidence, though doubtful; and in practising conscientiously all virtue, though under some uncertainty, whether the government in the universe

[c] Part I. chap. v.

may not possibly be such, as that vice may escape with impunity. And in general, temptation, meaning by this word the lesser allurements to wrong and difficulties in the discharge of our duty, as well as the greater ones; temptation, I say, as such and of every kind and degree, as it calls forth some virtuous efforts, additional to what would otherwise have been wanting, cannot but be an additional discipline and improvement of virtue, as well as probation of it in the other senses of that word[d]. So that the very same account is to be given, why the evidence of religion should be left in such a manner, as to require, in some, an attentive, solicitous, perhaps painful exercise of their understanding about it; as why others should be placed in such circumstances, as that the practice of its common duties, after a full conviction of the truth of it, should require attention, solicitude, and pains: or, why appearing doubtfulness should be permitted to afford matter of temptation to some; as why external difficulties and allurements should be permitted to afford matter of temptation to others. The same account also is to be given, why some should be exercised with temptations of both these kinds; as why others should be exercised with the latter in such very high degrees, as some have been, particularly as the primitive Christians were.

Nor does there appear any absurdity in supposing, that the speculative difficulties, in which the evidence of religion is involved, may make even the principal part of some persons' trial. For as the chief temptations of the generality of the world are the ordinary motives to injustice or unrestrained pleasure; or to live in the neglect of religion from

[d] Part I. chap. iv. and p. 109, 110.

that frame of mind, which renders many persons almost without feeling as to any thing distant, or which is not the object of their senses: so there are other persons without this shallowness of temper, persons of a deeper sense as to what is invisible and future; who not only see, but have a general practical feeling, that what is to come will be present, and that things are not less real for their not being the objects of sense; and who, from their natural constitution of body and of temper, and from their external condition, may have small temptations to behave ill, small difficulty in behaving well, in the common course of life. Now when these latter persons have a distinct full conviction of the truth of religion, without any possible doubts or difficulties, the practice of it is to them unavoidable, unless they will do a constant violence to their own minds; and religion is scarce any more a discipline to them, than it is to creatures in a state of perfection. Yet these persons may possibly stand in need of moral discipline and exercise in a higher degree, than they would have by such an easy practice of religion. Or it may be requisite, for reasons unknown to us, that they should give some further manifestation [c] what is their moral character, to the creation of God, than such a practice of it would be. Thus in the great variety of religious situations in which men are placed, what constitutes, what chiefly and peculiarly constitutes, the probation, in all senses, of some persons, may be the difficulties in which the evidence of religion is involved: and their principal and distinguished trial may be, how they will behave under and with respect to these difficulties. Circumstances in men's situation, in their

[c] P. 109, 110.

temporal capacity, analogous in good measure to this respecting religion, are to be observed. We find some persons are placed in such a situation in the world, as that their chief difficulty with regard to conduct, is not the doing what is prudent when it is known; for this, in numberless cases, is as easy as the contrary: but to some the principal exercise is, recollection and being upon their guard against deceits, the deceits suppose of those about them; against false appearances of reason and prudence. To persons in some situations, the principal exercise with respect to conduct is, attention in order to inform themselves what is proper, what is really the reasonable and prudent part to act.

But as I have hitherto gone upon supposition, that men's dissatisfaction with the evidence of religion is not owing to their neglects or prejudices; it must be added, on the other hand, in all common reason, and as what the truth of the case plainly requires should be added, that such dissatisfaction possibly may be owing to those, possibly may be men's own fault. For,

If there are any persons, who never set themselves heartily and in earnest to be informed in religion; if there are any, who secretly wish it may not prove true; and are less attentive to evidence than to difficulties, and more to objections than to what is said in answer to them: these persons will scarce be thought in a likely way of seeing the evidence of religion, though it were most certainly true, and capable of being ever so fully proved. If any accustom themselves to consider this subject usually in the way of mirth and sport: if they attend to forms and representations, and inadequate manners of expression, instead of the real things intended by them : (for signs often can be no more than inadequately expressive of the things signified :) or if they substitute human errors in the room of Divine truth ; why may not all, or any of these things, hinder some men from seeing that evidence, which really is seen by others; as a like turn of mind, with respect to matters of common speculation and practice, does, we find by experience, hinder them from attaining that knowledge and right understanding, in matters of common speculation and practice, which more fair and attentive minds attain to? And the effect will be the same, whether their neglect of seriously considering the evidence of religion, and their indirect behaviour with regard to it, proceed from mere carelessness, or from the grosser vices; or whether it be owing to this, that forms and figurative manners of expression, as well as errors, administer occasions of ridicule, when the things intended, and the truth itself, would not. Men may indulge a ludicrous turn so far as to lose all sense of conduct and prudence in worldly affairs, and even, as it seems, to impair their faculty of reason. And in general, levity, carelessness, passion, and prejudice, *do* hinder us from being rightly informed, with respect to common things : and they *may*, in like manner, and perhaps in some farther providential manner, with respect to moral and religious subjects: may hinder evidence from being laid before us, and from being seen when it is. The Scripture [f] does declare, that

[f] Dan. xii. 10. See also Is. xxix. 13, 14; Matth. vi. 23. and xi. 25. and xiii. 11, 12 ; John iii. 19. and v. 44 ; 1 Cor. ii. 14. and 2 Cor. iv. 4 ; 2 Tim. iii. 13 ; and that affectionate as well as authoritative admonition, so very many times inculcated, *He that hath ears to hear, let him hear.* Grotius saw so strongly the thing intended in

every one *shall not understand.* And it makes no difference, by what providential conduct this comes to pass: whether the evidence of Christianity was, originally and with design, put and left so, as that those who are desirous of evading moral obligations should not see it; and that honest-minded persons should: or, whether it comes to pass by any other means.

Farther: The general proof of natural religion and of Christianity does, I think, lie level to common men; even those, the greatest part of whose time, from childhood to old age, is taken up with providing for themselves and their families the common conveniences, perhaps necessaries, of life: those, I mean, of this rank, who ever think at all of asking after proof, or attending to it. Common men, were they as much in earnest about religion, as about their temporal affairs, are capable of being convinced upon real evidence, that there is a God who governs the world: and they feel themselves to be of a moral nature, and accountable creatures. And as Christianity entirely falls in with this their natural sense of things, so they are capable, not only of being persuaded, but of being made to see, that there is evidence of miracles wrought in attestation of it, and many appearing completions of prophecy. But though this proof is real and conclusive, yet it is liable to objections and may be run up into difficulties; which, however, persons who are capable, not only of talking of, but of really seeing, are capable also of seeing through: i. e. not of clearing up

these and other passages of Scripture of the like sense, as to say, that the proof given us of Christianity was less than it might have been, for this very purpose: *Ut ita sermo Evangelii tanquam lapis esset Lydius ad quem ingenia sanabilia explorarentur.* De Ver. R. C. lib. ii. towards the end.

and answering them, so as to satisfy their curiosity, for of such knowledge we are not capable with respect to any one thing in nature; but capable of seeing that the proof is not lost in these difficulties, or destroyed by these objections. But then a thorough examination into religion, with regard to these objections, which cannot be the business of every man, is a matter of pretty large compass, and, from the nature of it, requires some knowledge, as well as time and attention; to see, how the evidence comes out, upon balancing one thing with another, and what, upon the whole, is the amount of it. Now if persons who have picked up these objections from others, and take for granted they are of weight, upon the word of those from whom they received them, or, by often retailing of them, come to see, or fancy they see them to be of weight; will not prepare themselves for such an examination, with a competent degree of knowledge; or will not give that time and attention to the subject, which, from the nature of it, is necessary for attaining such information: in this case, they must remain in doubtfulness, ignorance, or error; in the same way as they must, with regard to common sciences, and matters of common life, if they neglect the necessary means of being informed in them.

But still perhaps it will be objected, that if a prince or common master were to send directions to a servant, he would take care, that they should always bears the certain mark, who they came from, and that their sense should be always plain: so as that there should be no possible doubt, if he could help it, concerning the authority or meaning of them. Now the proper answer to all this kind of objections is, that, wherever the fallacy lies, it is even certain we cannot argue thus with respect to Him, who is the governor of the world: and particularly that he does not afford us such information, with respect to our temporal affairs and interests, as experience abundantly shews. However, there is a full answer to this objection, from the very nature of religion. For, the reason why a prince would give his directions in this plain manner is, that he absolutely desires such an external action should be done, without concerning himself with the motive or principle upon which it is done: i. e. he regards only the external event, or the thing's being done; and not at all, properly speaking, the doing of it, or the action. Whereas the whole of morality and religion consisting merely in action itself, there is no sort of parallel between the cases. But if the prince be supposed to regard only the action: i. e. only to desire to exercise, or in any sense prove, the understanding or loyalty of a servant; he would not always give his orders in such a plain manner. It may be proper to add, that the will of God, respecting morality and religion, may be considered either as absolute, or as only conditional. If it be absolute, it can only be thus, that we should act virtuously in such given circumstances; not that we should be brought to act so, by his changing of our circumstances. And if God's will be thus absolute, then it is in our power, in the highest and strictest sense, to do or to contradict his will; which is a most weighty consideration. Or his will may be considered only as conditional, that if we act so and so, we shall be rewarded; if otherwise, punished: of which conditional will of the Author of Nature, the whole constitution of it affords most certain instances.

Upon the whole: that we are in a state of religion necessarily implies, that we are in a state of probation: and the credibility of our being at all in such a state being admitted, there seems no peculiar difficulty in supposing our probation to be, just as it is, in those respects which are above objected against. There seems no pretence, from *the reason of the thing*, to say, that the trial cannot equitably be any thing, but whether persons will act suitably to certain information, or such as admits no room for doubt; so as that there can be no danger of miscarriage, but either from their not attending to what they certainly know, or from overbearing passion hurrying them on to act contrary to it. For, since ignorance and doubt afford scope for probation in all senses, as really as intuitive conviction or certainty: and since the two former are to be put to the same account as difficulties in practice; men's moral probation may also be, whether they will take due care to inform themselves by impartial consideration and, afterwards whether they will act as the case requires, upon the evidence which they have, however doubtful. And this, we find by *experience*, is frequently our probation g, in our temporal capacity. For, the information which we want with regard to our worldly interests is by no means always given us of course, without any care of our own. And we are greatly liable to self-deceit from inward secret prejudices, and also to the deceits of others. So that to be able to judge what is the prudent part, often requires much and difficult consideration. Then after we have judged the very best we can, the evidence upon which we must act, if we will live and act at all, is perpetually doubtful to a very high

g P. 41, 239, 242, 243.

degree. And the constitution and course of the world in fact is such, as that want of impartial consideration what we have to do, and venturing upon extravagant courses because it is doubtful what will be the consequence, are often naturally, i. e. providentially, altogether as fatal, as misconduct occasioned by heedless inattention to what we certainly know, or disregarding it from overbearing passion.

Several of the observations here made may well seem strange, perhaps unintelligible, to many good men. But if the persons for whose sake they are made think so; persons who object as above, and throw off all regard to religion under pretence of want of evidence; I desire them to consider again, whether their thinking so be owing to any thing unintelligible in these observations, or to their own not having such a sense of religion and serious solicitude about it, as even their state of scepticism does in all reason require? It ought to be forced upon the reflection of these persons, that our nature and condition necessarily require us, in the daily course of life, to act upon evidence much lower than what is commonly called probable; to guard, not only against what we fully believe will, but also against what we think it supposable may, happen; and to engage in pursuits when the probability is greatly against success, if it be credible, that possibly we may succeed in them.

CHAP. VII.

Of the particular evidence for Christianity.

THE presumptions against revelation, and objections against the general scheme of Christianity, and particular things relating to it, being removed; there remains to be considered, what positive evidence we have for the truth of it: chiefly in order to see, what the analogy of nature suggests with regard to that evidence, and the objections against it: or to see what is, and is allowed to be, the plain natural rule of judgment and of action, in our temporal concerns, in cases where we have the same kind of evidence, and the same kind of objections against it, that we have in the case before us.

Now in the evidence of Christianity there seem to be several things of great weight, not reducible to the head, either of miracles, or the completion of prophecy, in the common acceptation of the words. But these two are its direct and fundamental proofs: and those other things, however considerable they are, yet ought never to be urged apart from its direct proofs, but always to be joined with them. Thus the evidence of Christianity will be a long series of things, reaching, as it seems, from the beginning of the world to the present time, of great variety and compass, taking in both the direct, and also the collateral, proofs; and making up, all of them together, one argument: the conviction arising from which kind of proof may be compared to what they call *the effect* in architecture or other works of art; a result from a great number of things so and so disposed, and taken into one view. I shall therefore, first, make some observations relating to miracles, and the appearing completions of prophecy; and consider what analogy suggests, in answer to the objections brought against this evidence. And, secondly, I shall endeavour to give some account of the general argument now mentioned, consisting both of the direct and collateral evidence, considered as making up one argument: this being the kind of proof, upon which we determine most questions of difficulty, concerning common facts, alleged to have happened, or seeming likely to happen; especially questions relating to conduct.

First, I shall make some observations upon the direct proof of Christianity from miracles and prophecy, and upon the objections alleged against it.

I. Now the following observations relating to the historical evidence of miracles wrought in attestation of Christianity, appear to be of great weight.

1. The Old Testament affords us the same historical evidence of the miracles of Moses and of the prophets, as of the common civil history of Moses and the kings of Israel; or, as of the affairs of the Jewish nation. And the *Gospels* and the *Acts* afford us the same historical evidence of the miracles of Christ and the Apostles, as of the common matters related in them. This indeed could not have been affirmed by any reasonable man, if the authors of these books, like many other historians, had appeared to make an entertaining manner of writing their aim; though they had interspersed miracles in their works, at proper distances and upon proper occasions. These might have animated a dull relation, amused the reader, and engaged his attention. And the same account would naturally have been given of them, as of the speeches and descriptions of such authors: the same account, in a manner, as is to be

given, why the poets make use of wonders and prodigies. But the facts, both miraculous and natural, in Scripture, are related in plain unadorned narratives: and both of them appear, in all respects, to stand upon the same foot of historical evidence. Farther: some parts of Scripture, containing an account of miracles fully sufficient to prove the truth of Christianity, are quoted as genuine, from the age in which they are said to be written, down to the present: and no other parts of them, material in the present question, are omitted to be quoted in such manner, as to afford any sort of proof of their not being genuine. And, as common history, when called in question in any instance, may often be greatly confirmed by cotemporary or subsequent events more known and acknowledged; and as the common Scripture-history, like many others, is thus confirmed; so likewise is the miraculous history of it, not only in particular instances, but in general. For, the establishment of the Jewish and Christian religions, which were events cotemporary with the miracles related to be wrought in attestation of both, or subsequent to them, these events are just what we should have expected, upon supposition such miracles were really wrought to attest the truth of those religions. These miracles are a satisfactory account of those events: of which no other satisfactory account can be given; nor any account at all, but what is imaginary merely, and invented. It is to be added, that the most obvious, the most easy and direct account of this history, how it came to be written and to be received in the world, as a true history, is, that it really is so: nor can any other account of it be easy and direct. Now, though an account, not at all obvious, but very far-fetched and indirect, may indeed be, and often is, the true account of a matter; yet it cannot be admitted on the authority of its being asserted. Mere guess, supposition, and possibility, when opposed to historical evidence, prove nothing, but that historical evidence is not demonstrative.

Now the just consequence from all this, I think, is, that the Scripture-history in general is to be admitted as an authentic genuine history, till somewhat positive be alleged sufficient to invalidate it. But no man will deny the consequence to be, that it cannot be rejected, or thrown by as of no authority, till it can be proved to be of none: even though the evidence now mentioned for its authority were doubtful. This evidence may be confronted by historical evidence on the other side, if there be any: or general incredibility in the things related, or inconsistence in the general turn of the history, would prove it to be of no authority. But since, upon the face of the matter, upon a first and general view, the appearance is, that it is an authentic history; it cannot be determined to be fictitious without some proof that it is so. And the following observations in support of these, and coincident with them, will greatly confirm the historical evidence for the truth of Christianity.

2. The Epistles of St. Paul, from the nature of epistolary writing, and moreover from several of them being written, not to particular persons, but to churches, carry in them evidences of their being genuine, beyond what can be in a mere historical narrative, left to the world at large. This evidence, joined with that which they have in common with the rest of the New Testament, seems not to leave so much as any particular pretence for denying

their genuineness, considered as an ordinary matter of fact, or of criticism : I say *particular* pretence, for *denying* it ; because any single fact, of such a kind and such antiquity, may have *general doubts* raised concerning it, from the very nature of human affairs and human testimony. There is also to be mentioned a distinct and particular evidence of the genuineness of the Epistle chiefly referred to here, the first to the Corinthians; from the manner in which it is quoted by Clemens Romanus, in an epistle of his own to that church [a]. Now these epistles afford a proof of Christianity, detached from all others, which is, I think, a thing of weight; and also a proof of a nature and kind peculiar to itself. For,

In them the author declares, that he received the Gospel in general, and the institution of the Communion in particular, not from the rest of the Apostles, or jointly together with them, but alone, from Christ himself; whom he declares likewise, conformably to the history in the Acts, that he saw after his ascension [b]. So that the testimony of St. Paul is to be considered, as detached from that of the rest of the Apostles.

And he declares farther, that he was endued with a power of working miracles, as what was publicly known to those very people, speaks of frequent and great variety of miraculous gifts as then subsisting in those very churches, to which he was writing; which he was reproving for several irregularities; and where he had personal opposers : he mentions these gifts incidentally, in the most easy manner, and without effort; by way of reproof to those who

[a] Clem. Rom. Ep. i. c. 47.
[b] Gal. i; 1 Cor. xi. 23, &c.; 1 Cor. xv. 8.

had them, for their indecent use of them; and by way of depreciating them, in comparison of moral virtues: in short he speaks to these churches, of these miraculous powers, in the manner, any one would speak to another of a thing, which was as familiar and as much known in common to them both, as any thing in the world [c]. And this, as hath been observed by several persons, is surely a very considerable thing.

3. It is an acknowledged historical fact, that Christianity offered itself to the world, and demanded to be received, upon the allegation, i.e. as unbelievers would speak, upon the pretence, of miracles, publicly wrought to attest the truth of it, in such an age; and that it was actually received by great numbers in that very age, and upon the professed belief of the reality of these miracles. And Christianity, including the dispensation of the Old Testament, seems distinguished by this from all other religions. I mean, that this does not appear to be the case with regard to any other: for surely it will not be supposed to lie upon any person, to prove by positive historical evidence, that it was not. It does in no sort appear that Mahometanism was first received in the world upon the foot of supposed miracles [d], i.e. public ones: for, as revelation is itself miraculous, all pretence to it must necessarily imply some pretence of miracles. And it is a known fact, that it was immediately, at the first, propagated by other means. And as particular institutions, whether in Paganism or Popery, said to be confirmed by miracles after those insti-

[c] Rom. xv. 19; 1 Cor. xii. 8, 9, 10—28, &c. and xiii. 1, 2, 8, and the whole xivth chapter; 2 Cor. xii. 12, 13; Gal. iii. 2, 5.

[d] See the Koran, c. xiii. and c. xvii.

tutions had obtained, are not to the purpose: so, were there what might be called historical proof, that any of them were introduced by a supposed divine command, believed to be attested by miracles; these would not be in any wise parallel. For single things of this sort are easy to be accounted for, after parties are formed, and have power in their hands; and the leaders of them are in veneration with the multitude; and political interests are blended with religious claims and religious distinctions. But before any thing of this kind, for a few persons, and those of the lowest rank, all at once, to bring over such great numbers to a new religion, and get it to be received upon the particular evidence of miracles; this is quite another thing. And I think it will be allowed by any fair adversary that the fact now mentioned, taking in all the circumstances of it, is peculiar to the Christian religion. However, the fact itself is allowed, that Christianity obtained, i. e. was professed to be received in the world, upon the belief of miracles, immediately in the age in which it is said those miracles were wrought: or that this is what its first converts would have alleged, as the reason for their embracing it. Now certainly it is not to be supposed, that such numbers of men, in the most distant parts of the world, should forsake the religion of their country, in which they had been educated; separate themselves from their friends, particularly in their festival shows and solemnities, to which the common people are so greatly addicted, and which were of a nature to engage them much more, than any thing of that sort amongst us; and embrace a religion, which could not but expose them to many inconveniences, and indeed must have been a giving up the world in a great degree, even from the very first, and before the empire engaged in form against them: it cannot be supposed, that such numbers should make so great, and, to say the least, so inconvenient a change in their whole institution of life, unless they were really convinced of the truth of those miracles, upon the knowledge or belief of which they professed to make it. And it will, I suppose, readily be acknowledged, that the generality of the first converts to Christianity must have believed them: that as by becoming Christians they declared to the world, they were satisfied of the truth of those miracles; so this declaration was to be credited. And this their testimony is the same kind of evidence for those miracles, as if they had put it in writing, and these writings had come down to us. And it is real evidence, because it is of facts, which they had capacity and full opportunity to inform themselves of. It is also distinct from the direct or express historical evidence, though it is of the same kind; and it would be allowed to be distinct in all cases. For were a fact expressly related by one or more ancient historians, and disputed in after-ages; that this fact is acknowledged to have been believed by great numbers of the age in which the historian says it was done, would be allowed an additional proof of such fact, quite distinct from the express testimony of the historian. The credulity of mankind is acknowledged: and the suspicions of mankind ought to be acknowledged too; and their backwardness even to believe, and greater still to practise, what makes against their interest. And it must particularly be remembered, that education and prejudice and authority, were against Christianity, in the age I am speaking of. So that the immediate conversion of such numbers is a real presumption of somewhat more than human in this matter: I say presumption, for it is not alleged as a proof alone and by itself. Nor need any one of the things mentioned in this chapter be considered as a proof by itself: and yet all of them together may be one of the strongest [c].

Upon the whole: as there is large historical evidence, both direct and circumstantial, of miracles wrought in attestation of Christianity, collected by those who have writ upon the subject; it lies upon unbelievers to shew, why this evidence is not to be credited. This way of speaking is, I think, just; and what persons who write in defence of religion naturally fall into. Yet, in a matter of such unspeakable importance, the proper question is, not whom it lies upon, according to the rules of argument, to maintain or confute objections: but whether there really are any, against this evidence, sufficient, in reason, to destroy the credit of it. However, unbelievers seem to take upon them the part of shewing that there are.

They allege, that numberless enthusiastic people, in different ages and countries, expose themselves to the same difficulties which the primitive Christians did; and are ready to give up their lives for the most idle follies imaginable. But it is not very clear, to what purpose this objection is brought. For every one, surely, in every case, must distinguish between opinions and facts. And though testimony is no proof of enthusiastic opinions, or of any opinions at all; yet it is allowed, in all other cases, to be a proof of facts. And a person's laying down

[c] Page 290, &c.

his life in attestation of facts or of opinions, is the strongest proof of his believing them. And if the Apostles and their cotemporaries did believe the facts, in attestation of which they exposed themselves to sufferings and death; this their belief, or rather knowledge, must be a proof of those facts: for they were such as came under the observation of their senses. And though it is not of equal weight, yet it is of weight, that the martyrs of the next age, notwithstanding they were not eyewitnesses of those facts, as were the Apostles and their cotemporaries, had, however, full opportunity to inform themselves, whether they were true or not, and gave equal proof of their believing them to be true.

But enthusiasm, it is said, greatly weakens the evidence of testimony even for facts, in matters relating to religion: some seem to think it totally and absolutely destroys the evidence of testimony upon this subject. And indeed the powers of enthusiasm, and of diseases too, which operate in a like manner, are very wonderful, in particular instances. But if great numbers of men, not appearing in any peculiar degree weak, nor under any peculiar suspicion of negligence, affirm that they saw and heard such things plainly with their eyes and their ears, and are admitted to be in earnest; such testimony is evidence of the strongest kind we can have, for any matter of fact. Yet possibly it may be overcome, strong as it is, by incredibility in the things thus attested, or by contrary testimony. And in an instance where one thought it was so overcome, it might be just to consider, how far such evidence could be accounted for, by enthusiasm; for it seems as if no other imaginable account were to be given of it. But till such incredibility be shewn, or contrary testimony produced, it cannot surely be expected, that so far-fetched, so indirect and wonderful an account of such testimony, as that of enthusiasm must be; an account so strange, that the generality of mankind can scarce be made to understand what is meant by it: it cannot, I say, be expected, that such account will be admitted of such evidence; when there is this direct, easy, and obvious account of it, that people really saw and heard a thing not incredible, which they affirm sincerely and with full assurance, they did see and hear. Granting then that enthusiasm is not (strictly speaking) an absurd, but a possible account of such testimony; it is manifest, that the very mention of it goes upon the previous supposition that the things so attested are incredible: and therefore need not be considered, till they are shewn to be so. Much less need it be considered, after the contrary has been proved. And I think it has been proved, to full satisfaction, that there is no incredibility in a revelation, in general; or in such an one as the Christian, in particular. However; as religion is supposed peculiarly liable to enthusiasm, it may just be observed, that prejudices almost without number, and without name, romance, affectation, humour, a desire to engage attention, or to surprise, the party-spirit, custom, little competitions, unaccountable likings and dislikings; these influence men strongly in common matters. And as these prejudices are often scarce known or reflected upon by the persons themselves who are influenced by them, they are to be considered as influences of a like kind to enthusiasm. Yet human testimony in common matters is naturally and justly believed notwithstanding.

It is intimated farther, in a more refined way of

observation, that though it should be proved, that the Apostles and first Christians could not, in some respects, be deceived themselves, and, in other respects, cannot be thought to have intended to impose upon the world; yet it will not follow, that their general testimony is to be believed, though truly handed down to us: because they might still in part, i. e. in other respects, be deceived themselves, and in part also designedly impose upon others; which, it is added, is a thing very credible, from that mixture of real enthusiasm, and real knavery, to be met with in the same characters. And, I must confess, I think the matter of fact contained in this observation upon mankind is not to be denied; and that somewhat very much akin to it is often supposed in Scripture as a very common case, and most severely reproved. But it were to have been expected, that persons capable of applying this observation as applied in the objection, might also frequently have met with the like mixed character, in instances where religion was quite out of the case. The thing plainly is, that mankind are naturally endued with reason, or a capacity of distinguishing between truth and falsehood; and as naturally they are endued with veracity, or a regard to truth in what they say: but from many occasions they are liable to be prejudiced and biassed and deceived themselves, and capable of intending to deceive others, in every different degree: insomuch that, as we are all liable to be deceived by prejudice, so likewise it seems to be not an uncommon thing, for persons, who, from their regard to truth, would not invent a lie entirely without any foundation at all, to propagate it with heightening circumstances, after it is once invented and set.agoing. And others, though they would not *propagate* a lie, yet, which is a lower degree of falsehood, will let it pass without contradiction. But, notwithstanding all this, human testimony remains still a natural ground of assent; and this assent a natural principle of action.

It is objected farther, that however it has happened, the *fact* is, that mankind have, in different ages, been strangely deluded with pretences to miracles and wonders. But it is by no means to be admitted, that they have been oftener, or are at all more liable to be deceived by these pretences, than by others.

It is added, that there is a very considerable degree of historical evidence for miracles, which are, on all hands, acknowledged to be fabulous. But suppose there were even *the like* historical evidence for these, to what there is for those alleged in proof of Christianity, which yet is in no wise allowed, but suppose this; the consequence would not be, that the evidence of the latter is not to be admitted. Nor is there a man in the world, who, in common cases, would conclude thus. For what would such a conclusion really amount to but this, that evidence, confuted by contrary evidence, or any way overbalanced, destroys the credibility of other evidence, neither confuted nor overbalanced? To argue, that because there is, if there were, like evidence from testimony, for miracles acknowledged false, as for those in attestation of Christianity, therefore the evidence in the latter case is not to be credited; this is the same as to argue, that if two men of equally good reputation had given evidence in different cases no way connected, and one of them had been convicted of perjury, this confuted the testimony of the other.

Upon the whole then, the general observation, that human creatures are so liable to be deceived, from enthusiasm in religion, and principles equivalent to enthusiasm in common matters, and in both from negligence; and that they are so capable of dishonestly endeavouring to deceive others; this does indeed weaken the evidence of testimony in all cases, but does not destroy it in any. And these things will appear, to different men, to weaken the evidence of testimony in different degrees: in degrees proportionable to the observations they have made, or the notions they have any way taken up, concerning the weakness and negligence and dishonesty of mankind; or concerning the powers of enthusiasm, and prejudices equivalent to it. But it seems to me, that people do not know what they say, who affirm these things to destroy the evidence from testimony, which we have of the truth of Christianity. Nothing can destroy the evidence of testimony in any case, but a proof or probability, that persons are not competent judges of the facts to which they give testimony; or that they are actually under some indirect influence in giving it, in such particular case. Till this be made out, the *natural* laws of human actions require, that testimony be admitted. It can never be sufficient to overthrow direct historical evidence, indolently to say, that there are so many principles, from whence men are liable to be deceived themselves, and disposed to deceive others, especially in matters of religion, that one knows not what to believe. And it is surprising persons can help reflecting, that this very manner of speaking supposes they are not satisfied that there is nothing in the evidence, of which they speak thus; or that they can avoid observing, if they do make this reflection, that it is, on such a subject, a very material one [f].

And over against all these objections is to be set the importance of Christianity, as what must have engaged the attention of its first converts, so as to have rendered them less liable to be deceived from carelessness, than they would in common matters; and likewise the strong obligations to veracity, which their religion laid them under: so that the first and most obvious presumption is, that they could not be deceived themselves, nor would deceive others. And this presumption, in this degree, is peculiar to the testimony we have been considering.

In argument, assertions are nothing in themselves, and have an air of positiveness, which sometimes is not very easy: yet they are necessary, and necessary to be repeated; in order to connect a discourse, and distinctly to lay before the view of the reader, what is proposed to be proved, and what is left as proved. Now the conclusion from the foregoing observations is, I think, beyond all doubt, this: that unbelievers must be forced to admit the external evidence for Christianity, i.e. the proof of miracles wrought to attest it, to be of real weight and very considerable; though they cannot allow it to be sufficient, to convince them of the reality of those miracles. And as they must, in all reason, admit this; so it seems to me, that upon consideration they would, in fact, admit it; those of them, I mean, who know any thing at all of the matter: in like manner as persons, in many cases, own they see strong evidence from testimony, for the truth of things, which yet they cannot be convinced are true: cases, suppose, where there is contrary testi-

[f] See the foregoing chapter.

mony; or things which they think, whether with or without reason, to be incredible. But there is no testimony contrary to that which we have been considering: and it has been fully proved, that there is no incredibility in Christianity in general, or in any part of it.

II. As to the evidence for Christianity from prophecy, I shall only make some few general observations, which are suggested by the Analogy of Nature; i. e. by the acknowledged natural rules of judging in common matters, concerning evidence of a like kind to this from prophecy.

1. The obscurity or unintelligibleness of one part of a prophecy does not, in any degree, invalidate the proof of foresight, arising from the appearing completion of those other parts which are understood. For the case is evidently the same, as if those parts, which are not understood, were lost, or not written at all, or written in an unknown tongue. Whether this observation be commonly attended to or not, it is so evident, that one can scarce bring oneself to set down an instance in common matters to exemplify it. However, suppose a writing, partly in cypher, and partly in plain words at length; and that in the part one understood, there appeared mention of several known facts; it would never come into any man's thoughts to imagine, that if he understood the whole, perhaps he might find, that those facts were not in reality known by the writer. Indeed, both in this example, and the thing intended to be exemplified by it, our not understanding the whole (the whole, suppose, of a sentence or a paragraph) might sometimes occasion a doubt, whether one understood the literal meaning of such a part: but this comes under another consideration.

For the same reason, though a man should be incapable, for want of learning, or opportunities of inquiry, or from not having turned his studies this way, even so much as to judge, whether particular prophecies have been throughout completely fulfilled; yet he may see, in general, that they have been fulfilled to such a degree, as, upon very good ground, to be convinced of foresight more than human in such prophecies, and of such events being intended by them. For the same reason also, though, by means of the deficiencies in civil history, and the different accounts of historians, the most learned should not be able to make out to satisfaction, that such parts of the prophetic history have been minutely and throughout fulfilled; yet a very strong proof of foresight may arise, from that general completion of them, which is made out: as much proof of foresight, perhaps, as the giver of prophecy intended should ever be afforded by such parts of prophecy.

2. A long series of prophecy being applicable to such and such events, is itself a proof that it was intended of them: as the rules, by which we naturally judge and determine, in common cases parallel to this, will shew. This observation I make in answer to the common objection against the application of the prophecies, that, considering each of them distinctly by itself, it does not at all appear, that they were intended of those particular events, to which they are applied by Christians; and therefore it is to be supposed, that, if they meant any thing, they were intended of other events unknown to us, and not of these at all.

Now there are two kinds of writing, which bear a great resemblance to prophecy, with respect to the matter before us: the mythological, and the satirical, where the satire is, to a certain degree, concealed. And a man might be assured, that he understood what an author intended by a fable or parable, related without any application or moral, merely from seeing it to be easily capable of such application, and that such a moral might naturally be deduced from it. And he might be fully assured, that such persons and events were intended in a satirical writing, merely from its being applicable to them. And, agreeably to the last observation, he might be in a good measure satisfied of it, though he were not enough informed in affairs, or in the story of such persons, to understand half the satire. For, his satisfaction, that he understood the meaning, the intended meaning, of these writings, would be greater or less in proportion as he saw the general turn of them to be capable of such application; and in proportion to the number of particular things capable of it. And thus, if a long series of prophecy is applicable to the present state of the church, and to the political situations of the kingdoms of the world, some thousand years after these prophecies were delivered, and a long series of prophecy delivered before the coming of Christ is applicable to him; these things are in themselves a proof, that the prophetic history was intended of him, and of those events: in proportion as the general turn of it is capable of such application, and to the number and variety of particular prophecies capable of it. And though, in all just way of consideration, the appearing completion of prophecies is to be allowed to be thus explanatory of, and to determine, their meaning; yet it is to be remembered farther, that the ancient Jews applied the prophecies to a Messiah before his coming, in much the same manner as

Christians do now: and that the primitive Christians interpreted the prophecies respecting the state of the church and of the world in the last ages, in the sense which the event seems to confirm and verify. And from these things it may be made appear:

3. That the shewing even to a high probability, if that could be, that the prophets thought of some other events, in such and such predictions, and not those at all which Christians allege to be completions of those predictions; or that such and such prophecies are capable of being applied to other events than those, to which Christians apply them—that this would not confute or destroy the force of the argument from prophecy, even with regard to those very instances. For, observe how this matter really is. If one knew such a person to be the sole author of such a book, and was certainly assured, or satisfied to any degree, that one knew the whole of what he intended in it; one should be assured or satisfied to such degree, that one knew the whole meaning of that book: for the meaning of a book is nothing but the meaning of the author. But if one knew a person to have compiled a book out of memoirs, which he received from another, of vastly superior knowledge in the subject of it, especially if it were a book full of great intricacies and difficulties; it would in no wise follow, that one knew the whole meaning of the book, from knowing the whole meaning of the compiler: for the original memoirs, i. e. the author of them, might have, and there would be no degree of presumption, in many cases, against supposing him to have, some farther meaning than the compiler saw. To say then, that the Scriptures, and the things contained in them, can have no other or farther meaning than those persons thought

or had, who first recited or wrote them ; is evidently saying, that those persons were the original, proper, and sole authors of those books, i. e. that they are not inspired: which is absurd, whilst the authority of these books is under examination ; i. e. till you have determined they are of no divine authority at all. Till this be determined, it must in all reason be supposed, not indeed that they have, for this is taking for granted that they are inspired; but that they may have, some farther meaning than what the compiler saw or understood. And, upon this supposition, it is supposable also, that this farther meaning may be fulfilled. Now events corresponding to prophecies, interpreted in a different meaning from that, in which the prophets are supposed to have understood them; this affords, in a manner, the same proof, that this different sense was originally intended, as it would have afforded, if the prophets had not understood their predictions in the sense it is supposed they did: because there is no presumption of their sense of them being the whole sense of them. And it has been already shewn, that the apparent completions of prophecy must be allowed to be explanatory of its meaning. So that the question is, whether a series of prophecy has been fulfilled, in a natural or proper, i. e. in any real, sense of the words of it. For such completion is equally a proof of foresight more than human, whether the prophets are, or are not, supposed to have understood it in a different sense. I say, supposed: for, though I think it clear, that the prophets did not understand the full meaning of their predictions; it is another question, how far they thought they did, and in what sense they understood them.

Hence may be seen, to how little purpose those

persons busy themselves, who endeavour to prove, that the prophetic history is applicable to events of the age in which it was written, or of ages before it. Indeed to have proved this, before there was any appearance of a farther completion of it, might have answered some purpose; for it might have prevented the expectation of any such farther completion. Thus could Porphyry have shewn, that some principal parts of the book of Daniel, for instance, the seventh verse of the seventh chapter, which the Christians interpreted of the latter ages, was applicable to events, which happened before or about the age of Antiochus Epiphanes; this might have prevented them from expecting any farther completion of it. And, unless there was then, as I think there must have been, external evidence concerning that book, more than is come down to us; such a discovery might have been a stumblingblock in the way of Christianity itself: considering the authority which our Saviour has given to the book of Daniel, and how much the general scheme of Christianity presupposes the truth of it. But even this discovery, had there been any such[g], would be of very little weight with reasonable men now; if this passage, thus applicable to events before the age of Porphyry, appears to be applicable also to events which succeeded the dissolution of the Roman empire. I mention this, not at all as intending to

---

[g] It appears that Porphyry did nothing worth mentioning in this way. For Jerom on the place says, *Duas posteriores bestias—in uno Macedonum regno ponit.* And as to the ten Kings; *Decem reges enumerat, qui fuerunt sævissimi: ipsosque reges non unius ponit regni, verbi gratia, Macedoniæ, Syriæ, Asiæ, et Ægypti; sed de diversis regnis unum efficit regum ordinem.* And in this way of interpretation anything may be made of any thing.

insinuate, that the division of this empire into ten parts, for it plainly was divided into about that number, were, alone and by itself, of any moment in verifying the prophetic history: but only as an example of the thing I am speaking of. And thus upon the whole, the matter of inquiry evidently must be, as above put, Whether the prophecies are applicable to Christ, and to the present state of the world, and of the church; applicable in such a degree, as to imply foresight: not whether they are capable of any other application; though I know no pretence for saying the general turn of them is capable of any other.

These observations are, I think, just; and the evidence referred to in them real: though there may be people who will not accept of such imperfect information from Scripture. Some too have not integrity and regard enough to truth, to attend to evidence, which keeps the mind in doubt, perhaps perplexity, and which is much of a different sort from what they expected. And it plainly requires a degree of modesty and fairness, beyond what every one has, for a man to say, not to the world, but to himself, that there is a real appearance of somewhat of great weight in this matter, though he is not able thoroughly to satisfy himself about it; but it shall have its influence upon him, in proportion to its appearing reality and weight. It is much more easy, and more falls in with the negligence, presumption, and wilfulness of the generality, to determine at once, with a decisive air, There is nothing in it. The prejudices arising from that absolute contempt and scorn, with which this evidence is treated in the world, I do not mention. For what indeed can be said to persons, who are weak enough in their understandings to think this any presumption against it; or, if they do not, are yet weak enough in their temper to be influenced by such prejudices, upon such a subject?

I shall now, secondly, endeavour to give some account of the general argument for the truth of Christianity, consisting both of the direct and circumstantial evidence, considered as making up one argument. Indeed to state and examine this argument fully, would be a work much beyond the compass of this whole treatise; nor is so much as a proper abridgement of it to be expected here. Yet the present subject requires to have some brief account of it given. For it is the kind of evidence, upon which most questions of difficulty, in common practice, are determined: evidence arising from various coincidences, which support and confirm each other, and in this manner prove, with more or less certainty, the point under consideration. And I choose to do it also: first, because it seems to be of the greatest importance, and not duly attended to by every one, that the proof of revelation is, not some direct and express things only, but a great variety of circumstantial things also; and that though each of these direct and circumstantial things is indeed to be considered separately, yet they are afterwards to be joined together; for that the proper force of the evidence consists in the result of those several things, considered in their respects to each other, and united into one view: and in the next place, because it seems to me, that the matters of fact here set down, which are acknowledged by unbelievers, must be acknowledged by them also to contain together a degree of evidence of great weight, if they could be brought to lay these several things before themselves distinctly, and then with attention consider them together; instead of that cursory thought of them, to which we are familiarized. For being familiarized to the cursory thought of things as really hinders the weight of them from being seen, as from having its due influence upon practice.

The thing asserted, and the truth of which is to be inquired into, is this: That over and above our reason and affections, which God has given us for the information of our judgment and the conduct of our lives, he has also, by external revelation, given us an account of himself and his moral government over the world, implying a future state of rewards and punishments; i.e. hath revealed the system of natural religion: for natural religion may be externally [h] revealed by God, as the ignorant may be taught it by mankind their fellow-creatures —that God, I say, has given us the evidence of revelation, as well as the evidence of reason, to ascertain this moral system; together with an account of a particular dispensation of Providence, which reason could no way have discovered, and a particular institution of religion founded on it, for the recovery of mankind out of their present wretched condition, and raising them to the perfection and final happiness of their nature.

This revelation, whether real or supposed, may be considered as wholly historical. For prophecy is nothing but the history of events before they come to pass; doctrines also are matters of fact; and precepts come under the same notion. And the general design of Scripture, which contains in it this revelation, thus considered as historical, may be said to be, to give us an account of the world, in this

[h] P. 153. &c.

one single view, as God's world: by which it appears essentially distinguished from all other books, so far as I have found, except such as are copied from it. It begins with an account of God's creation of the world, in order to ascertain, and distinguish from all others, who is the object of our worship, by what he has done: in order to ascertain, who he is, concerning whose providence, commands, promises, and threatenings, this sacred book, all along, treats; the Maker and Proprietor of the world, he whose creatures we are, the God of nature: in order likewise to distinguish him from the idols of the nations, which are either imaginary beings, i.e. no beings at all; or else part of that creation, the historical relation of which is here given. And St. John, not improbably, with an eye to this Mosaic account of the creation, begins his Gospel with an account of our Saviour's pre-existence, and that *all things were made by him; and without him was not any thing made that was made*[i]: agreeably to the doctrine of St. Paul, that *God created all things by Jesus Christ*[k]. This being premised, the Scripture, taken together, seems to profess to contain a kind of an abridgment of the history of the world, in the view just now mentioned: that is, a general account of the condition of religion and its professors, during the continuance of that apostasy from God, and state of wickedness, which it every where supposes the world to lie in. And this account of the state of religion carries with it some brief account of the political state of things, as religion is affected by it. Revelation indeed considers the common affairs of this world, and what is going on in it, as a mere scene of distraction; and cannot be supposed to

[i] John i. 3. [k] Eph. iii. 9.

concern itself with foretelling at what time Rome, or Babylon, or Greece, or any particular place, should be the most conspicuous seat of that tyranny and dissoluteness, which all places equally aspire to be; cannot, I say, be supposed to give any account of this wild scene for its own sake. But it seems to contain some very general account of the chief governments of the world, as the general state of religion has been, is, or shall be, affected by them, from the first transgression, and during the whole interval of the world's continuing in its present state, to a certain future period, spoken of both in the Old and New Testament, very distinctly, and in great variety of expression: *The times of the restitution of all things*[1]: when *the mystery of God shall be finished, as he hath declared to his servants the prophets*[m]: when *the God of heaven shall set up a kingdom, which shall never be destroyed: and the kingdom shall not be left to other people*[n], as it is represented to be during this apostasy, but *judgment shall be given to the saints*[o], *and they shall reign*[p]: *and the kingdom and dominion, and the greatness of the kingdom under the whole heaven, shall be given to the people of the saints of the Most High*[q].

Upon this general view of the Scripture, I would remark, how great a length of time the whole relation takes up, near six thousand years of which are past; and how great a variety of things it treats of; the natural and moral system or history of the world, including the time when it was formed, all contained in the very first book, and evidently written in a rude and unlearned age; and in subsequent books, the various common and prophetic history,

[1] Acts iii. 21.   [m] Rev. x. 7.   [n] Dan. ii. 44.   [o] Dan. vii. 22.
[p] Rev. xxii. 5.   [q] Dan. vii. 27.

and the particular dispensation of Christianity. Now all this together gives the largest scope for criticism; and for confutation of what is capable of being confuted, either from reason, or from common history, or from any inconsistence in its several parts: And it is a thing which deserves, I think, to be mentioned, that whereas some imagine the supposed doubtfulness of the evidence for revelation implies a positive argument that it is not true; it appears, on the contrary, to imply a positive argument that it is true. For, could any common relation, of such antiquity, extent, and variety, (for in these things the stress of what I am now observing lies,) be proposed to the examination of the world: that it could not, in an age of knowledge and liberty, be confuted, or shewn to have nothing in it, to the satisfaction of reasonable men; this would be thought a strong presumptive proof of its truth. And indeed it must be a proof of it, just in proportion to the probability, that if it were false, it might be shewn to be so: and this, I think, is scarce pretended to be shewn, but upon principles and in ways of arguing, which have been clearly obviated [r]. Nor does it at all appear, that any set of men, who believe natural religion, are of the opinion, that Christianity has been thus confuted. But to proceed:

Together with the moral system of the world, the Old Testament contains a chronological account of the beginning of it, and from thence, an unbroken genealogy of mankind for many ages before common history begins; and carried on as much farther as to make up a continued thread of history of the length of between three and four thousand years. It contains an account of God's making a covenant with

[r] Chap. ii, iii, &c.

a particular nation, that they should be his people, and he would be their God, in a peculiar sense; of his often interposing miraculously in their affairs; giving them the promise, and, long after, the possession, of a particular country; assuring them of the greatest national prosperity in it, if they would worship him, in opposition to the idols which the rest of the world worshipped, and obey his commands; and threatening them with unexampled punishments, if they disobeyed him, and fell into the general idolatry: insomuch that this one nation should continue to be the observation and the wonder of all the world. It declares particularly, that *God would scatter them among all people, from one end of the earth unto the other:* but that *when they should return unto the Lord their God, he would have compassion upon them, and gather them from all the nations, whither he had scattered them:* that *Israel should be saved in the Lord, with an everlasting salvation; and not be ashamed or confounded world without end.* And as some of these promises are conditional, others are as absolute, as any thing can be expressed: that the time should come, when *the people should be all righteous, and inherit the land for ever:* that *though God would make a full end of all nations whither he had scattered them, yet would he not make a full end of them:* that *he would bring again the captivity of his people Israel, and plant them upon their land, and they should be no more pulled up out of their land: that the seed of Israel should not cease from being a nation for ever*[*]. It foretells, that God would raise them up a particular Person, in whom all his promises should finally be fulfilled; the Messiah,

---

[*] Deut. xxviii. 64. xxx. 2, 3; Isa. xlv. 17. lx. 21; Jer. xxx. 11. xlvi. 28; Amos ix. 14. 15; Jer. xxxi. 36.

who should be, in an high and eminent sense, their anointed Prince and Saviour. This was foretold in such a manner, as raised a general expectation of such a person in the nation, as appears from the New Testament, and is an acknowledged fact; an expectation of his coming at such a particular time before any one appeared claiming to be that person, and when there was no ground for such an expectation, but from the prophecies: which expectation, therefore, must in all reason be presumed to be explanatory of those prophecies, if there were any doubt about their meaning. It seems moreover to foretell, that this person should be rejected by that nation, to whom he had been so long promised, and though he was so much desired by them[t]. And it expressly foretells, that he should be the Saviour of the Gentiles; and even that the completion of the scheme, contained in this book, and then begun, and in its progress, should be somewhat so great, that, in comparison with it, the restoration of the Jews alone would be but of small account[u]. *It is a light thing that thou shouldest be my servant to raise up the tribes of Jacob, and to restore the preserved of Israel: I will also give thee for a light to the Gentiles, that thou mayest be my salvation unto the end of the earth.* And, *In the last days, the mountain of the Lord's house shall be established in the top of the mountains, and shall be exalted above the hills; and all nations shall flow into it—for out of Zion shall go forth the law, and the word of the Lord*

---

[t] Is. viii. 14, 15. xlix. 5. ch. liii; Mal. i. 10, 11. and ch. iii.

[u] Is. xlix. 6. ch. ii. ch. xi. ch. lvi. 7; Mal. i. 11. To which must be added, the other prophecies of the like kind, several in the New Testament, and very many in the Old; which describe what shall be the completion of the revealed plan of Providence.

from Jerusalem. And he shall judge among the nations—and the Lord alone shall be exalted in that day, and the idols he shall utterly abolish. The Scripture farther contains an account, that at the time the Messiah was expected, a person rose up, in this nation, claiming to be that Messiah, to be the Person whom all the prophecies referred to, and in whom they should centre: that he spent some years in a continued course of miraculous works; and endued his immediate disciples and followers with a power of doing the same, as a proof of the truth of that religion which he commissioned them to publish: that, invested with this authority and power, they made numerous converts in the remotest countries, and settled and established his religion in the world; to the end of which the Scripture professes to give a prophetic account of the state of this religion amongst mankind.

Let us now suppose a person utterly ignorant of history, to have all this related to him out of the Scripture. Or suppose such an one, having the Scripture put into his hands, to remark these things in it, not knowing but that the whole, even its civil history, as well as the other parts of it, might be, from beginning to end, an entire invention; and to ask, What truth was in it, and whether the revelation here related was real, or a fiction? And, instead of a direct answer, suppose him, all at once, to be told the following confessed facts; and then to unite them into one view.

Let him first be told, in how great a degree the profession and establishment of natural religion, the belief that there is one God to be worshipped, that virtue is his law, and that mankind shall be rewarded and punished hereafter, as they obey and disobey it here; in how very great a degree, I say, the profession and establishment of this moral system in the world is owing to the revelation, whether real or supposed, contained in this book: the establishment of this moral system, even in those countries which do not acknowledge the proper authority of the Scripture[x]. Let him be told also, what number of nations do acknowledge its proper authority. Let him then take in the consideration, of what importance religion is to mankind. And upon these things he might, I think, truly observe, that this supposed revelation's obtaining and being received in the world, with all the circumstances and effects of it, considered together as one event, is the most conspicuous and important event in the history of mankind: that a book of this nature, and thus promulged and recommended to our consideration, demands, as if by a voice from heaven, to have its claims most seriously examined into: and that, before such examination, to treat it with any kind of scoffing and ridicule, is an offence against natural piety. But it is to be remembered, that how much soever the establishment of natural religion in the world is owing to the Scripture-revelation, this does not destroy the proof of religion from reason, any more than the proof of Euclid's Elements is destroyed, by a man's knowing or thinking, that he should never have seen the truth of the several propositions contained in it, nor had those propositions come into his thoughts, but for that mathematician.

Let such a person as we are speaking of be, in the next place, informed of the acknowledged antiquity of the first parts of this book; and that its

[x] Page 231.

chronology, its account of the time when the earth, and the several parts of it, were first peopled with human creatures, is no way contradicted, but is really confirmed, by the natural and civil history of the world, collected from common historians, from the state of the earth, and from the late invention of arts and sciences. And as the Scripture contains an unbroken thread of common and civil history, from the creation to the captivity, for between three and four thousand years; let the person we are speaking of be told, in the next place, that this general history, as it is not contradicted, but is confirmed by profane history as much as there would be reason to expect, upon supposition of its truth; so there is nothing in the whole history *itself*, to give any reasonable ground of suspicion of its not being, in the general, a faithful and literally true genealogy of men, and series of things. I speak here only of the common Scripture-history, or of the course of ordinary events related in it, as distinguished from miracles, and from the prophetic history. In all the Scripture-narrations of this kind, following events arise out of foregoing ones, as in all other histories. There appears nothing related as done in any age, not conformable to the manners of that age: nothing in the account of a succeeding age, which, one would say, could not be true, or was improbable, from the account of things in the preceding one. There is nothing in the characters, which would raise a thought of their being feigned; but all the internal marks imaginable of their being real. It is to be added also, that mere genealogies, bare narratives of the number of years, which persons called by such and such names lived, do not carry the face of fiction; perhaps do carry some presumption of veracity: and all unadorned narratives, which have nothing to surprise, may be thought to carry somewhat of the like presumption too. And the domestic and the political history is plainly credible. There may be incidents in Scripture, which, taken alone in the naked way they are told, may appear strange; especially to persons of other manners, temper, education: but there are also incidents of undoubted truth, in many or most persons' lives, which, in the same circumstances, would appear to the full as strange. There may be mistakes of transcribers, there may be other real or seeming mistakes, not easy to be particularly accounted for: but there are certainly no more things of this kind in the Scripture, than what were to have been expected in books of such antiquity; and nothing, in any wise, sufficient to discredit the general narrative. Now, that a history, claiming to commence from the creation, and extending in one continued series, through so great a length of time, and variety of events, should have such appearances of reality and truth in its whole contexture, is surely a very remarkable circumstance in its favour. And as all this is applicable to the common history of the New Testament, so there is a farther credibility, and a very high one, given to it by profane authors: many of these writing of the same time, and confirming the truth of customs and events, which are incidentally as well as more purposely mentioned in it. And this credibility of the common Scripture-history gives some credibility to its miraculous history: especially as this is interwoven with the common, so as that they imply each other, and both together make up one relation.

Let it then be more particularly observed to this

person, that it is an acknowledged matter of fact, which is indeed implied in the foregoing observation, that there was such a nation as the Jews, of the greatest antiquity, whose government and general polity was founded on the law, here related to be given them by Moses as from heaven : that natural religion, though with rites additional yet no way contrary to it, was their established religion, which cannot be said of the Gentile world : and that their very being as a nation, depended upon their acknowledgment of one God, the God of the universe. For, suppose in their captivity, in Babylon, they had gone over to the religion of their conquerors, there would have remained no bond of union, to keep them a distinct people. And whilst they were under their own kings, in their own country, a total apostasy from God would have been the dissolution of their whole government. They in such a sense nationally acknowledged and worshipped the Maker of heaven and earth, when the rest of the world were sunk in idolatry, as rendered them, in fact, the peculiar people of God. And this so remarkable an establishment and preservation of natural religion amongst them, seems to add some peculiar credibility to the historical evidence for the miracles of Moses and the Prophets : because these miracles are a full satisfactory account of this event, which plainly wants to be accounted for, and cannot otherwise.

Let this person, supposed wholly ignorant of history, be acquainted farther, that one claiming to be the Messiah, of Jewish extraction, rose up at the time when this nation, from the prophecies above mentioned, expected the Messiah : that he was rejected, as it seemed to have been foretold he should, by the body of the people, under the direction of their rulers: that in the course of a very few years, he was believed on and acknowledged as the promised Messiah, by great numbers among the Gentiles, agreeably to the prophecies of Scripture, yet not upon the evidence of prophecy, but of miracles [y], of which miracles we also have strong historical evidence, (by which I mean here no more than must be acknowledged by unbelievers; for let pious frauds and follies be admitted to weaken, it is absurd to say they destroy, our evidence of miracles wrought in proof of Christianity [z]:) that this religion approving itself to the reason of mankind, and carrying its own evidence with it, so far as reason is a judge of its system, and being no way contrary to reason in those parts of it which require to be believed upon the mere authority of its Author; that this religion, I say, gradually spread and supported itself for some hundred years, not only without any assistance from temporal power, but under constant discouragements, and often the bitterest persecutions from it; and then became the religion of the world: that in the mean time, the Jewish nation and government were destroyed in a very remarkable manner, and the people carried away captive and dispersed through the most distant countries; in which state of dispersion they have remained fifteen hundred years: and that they remain a numerous people, united amongst themselves, and distinguished from the rest of the world, as they were in the days of Moses, by the profession of his law; and every where looked upon in a manner, which one scarce knows how distinctly to express, but in the words of the prophetic account of it, given so many ages before it came to pass; *Thou shalt become an astonishment, a proverb,*

[y] P. 255, &c.   [z] P. 262, &c.

and a byword, among all nations whither the Lord shall lead thee[a].

The appearance of a standing miracle, in the Jews remaining a distinct people in their dispersion, and the confirmation which this event appears to give to the truth of revelation, may be thought to be answered, by their religion's forbidding them intermarriages with those of any other, and prescribing them a great many peculiarities in their food, by which they are debarred from the means of incorporating with the people in whose countries they live. This is not, I think, a satisfactory account of that which it pretends to account for. But what does it pretend to account for? The correspondence between this event and the prophecies; or the coincidence of both, with a long dispensation of Providence of a peculiar nature, towards that people formerly? No. It is only the event itself, which is offered to be thus accounted for; which single event, taken alone, abstracted from all such correspondence and coincidence, perhaps would not have appeared miraculous: but that correspondence and coincidence may be so, though the event itself be supposed not. Thus the concurrence of our Saviour's being born at Bethlehem, with a long foregoing series of prophecy and other coincidences, is doubtless miraculous; the series of prophecy, and other coincidences, and the event, being admitted: though the event itself, his birth at that place, appears to have been brought about in a natural way; of which, however, no one can be certain.

And as several of these events seem, in some degree expressly, to have verified the prophetic history already; so likewise they may be considered

[a] Deut. xxviii. 37.

farther, as having a peculiar aspect towards the full completion of it; as affording some presumption that the whole of it shall, one time or other, be fulfilled. Thus, that the Jews have been so wonderfully preserved in their long and wide dispersion; which is indeed the direct fulfilling of some prophecies, but is now mentioned only as looking forward to somewhat yet to come : that natural religion came forth from Judea, and spread, in the degree it has done over the world, before lost in idolatry; which, together with some other things, have distinguished that very place, in like manner as the people of it are distinguished: that this great change of religion over the earth was brought about under the profession and acknowledgment, that Jesus was the promised Messiah : things of this kind naturally turn the thoughts of serious men towards the full completion of the prophetic history, concerning the final restoration of that people ; concerning the establishment of the everlasting kingdom among them, the kingdom of the Messiah ; and the future state of the world, under this sacred government. Such circumstances and events, compared with these prophecies, though no completions of them, yet would not, I think, be spoken of as nothing in the argument, by a person upon his first being informed of them. They fall in with the prophetic history of things still future, give it some additional credibility, have the appearance of being somewhat in order to the full completion of it.

Indeed it requires a good degree of knowledge, and great calmness and consideration, to be able to judge thoroughly of the evidence for the truth of Christianity, from that part of the prophetic history which relates to the situation of the kingdoms of the world, and to the state of the Church, from the establishment of Christianity to the present time. But it appears, from a general view of it, to be very material. And those persons who have thoroughly examined it, and some of them were men of the coolest tempers, greatest capacities, and least liable to imputations of prejudice, insist upon it as determinately conclusive.

Suppose now a person quite ignorant of history, first to recollect the passages above mentioned out of Scripture, without knowing but that the whole was a late fiction, then to be informed of the correspondent facts now mentioned, and to unite them all into one view: that the profession and establishment of natural religion in the world, is greatly owing, in different ways, to this book, and the supposed revelation which it contains; that it is acknowledged to be of the earliest antiquity; that its chronology and common history are entirely credible; that this ancient nation, the Jews, of whom it chiefly treats, appear to have been, in fact, the people of God, in a distinguished sense; that, as there was a national expectation amongst them, raised from the prophecies, of a Messiah to appear at such a time, so one at this time appeared claiming to be that Messiah; that he was rejected by this nation, but received by the Gentiles, not upon the evidence of prophecy, but of miracles; that the religion he taught supported itself under the greatest difficulties, gained ground, and at length became the religion of the world; that in the mean time the Jewish polity was utterly destroyed, and the nation dispersed over the face of the earth; that notwithstanding this, they have remained a distinct numerous people for so many centuries, even to this day; which not only appears to be the express completion of several prophecies concerning them, but also renders it, as one may speak, a visible and easy possibility that the promises made to them as a nation may yet be fulfilled. And to these acknowledged truths, let the person we have been supposing add, as I think he ought, whether every one will allow it or no, the obvious appearances which there are, of the state of the world, in other respects besides what relates to the Jews, and of the Christian Church, having so long answered, and still answering to the prophetic history. Suppose, I say, these facts set over against the things before mentioned out of the Scripture, and seriously compared with them; the joint view of both together must, I think, appear of very great weight to a considerate reasonable person: of much greater indeed, upon having them first laid before him, than is easy for us, who are so familiarized to them, to conceive, without some particular attention for that purpose.

All these things, and the several particulars contained under them, require to be distinctly and most thoroughly examined into; that the weight of each may be judged of, upon such examination, and such conclusion drawn as results from their united force. But this has not been attempted here. I have gone no farther than to shew, that the general imperfect view of them now given, the confessed historical evidence for miracles, and the many obvious appearing completions of prophecy, together with the collateral things[b] here mentioned, and there are several others of the like sort; that all this together,

---

[b] All the particular things mentioned in this chapter, not reducible to the head of certain miracles, or determinate completions of prophecy. See pp. 250, 251.

which, being fact, must be acknowledged by unbelievers, amounts to real evidence of somewhat more than human in this matter: evidence much more important, than careless men, who have been accustomed only to transient and partial views of it, can imagine; and indeed abundantly sufficient to act upon. And these things, I apprehend, must be acknowledged by unbelievers. For though they may say, that the historical evidence of miracles wrought in attestation of Christianity, is not sufficient to convince them that such miracles were really wrought; they cannot deny, that there is such historical evidence, it being a known matter of fact that there is. They may say, the conformity between the prophecies and events is by accident: but there are many instances in which such conformity itself cannot be denied. They may say, with regard to such kind of collateral things as those above mentioned, that any odd accidental events, without meaning, will have a meaning found in them by a fanciful people: and that such as are fanciful in any one certain way, will make out a thousand coincidences which seem to favour their peculiar follies. Men, I say, may talk thus: but no one who is serious, can possibly think these things to be nothing, if he considers the importance of collateral things, and even of lesser circumstances, in the evidence of probability, as distinguished, in nature, from the evidence of demonstration. In many cases indeed it seems to require the truest judgment, to determine with exactness the weight of circumstantial evidence: but it is very often altogether as convincing, as that which is the most express and direct.

This general view of the evidence for Christianity,

considered as making one argument, may also serve to recommend to serious persons, to set down every thing which they think may be of any real weight at all in proof of it, and particularly the many seeming completions of prophecy: and they will find, that, judging by the natural rules, by which we judge of probable evidence in common matters, they amount to a much higher degree of proof, upon such a joint review, than could be supposed upon considering them separately, at different times; how strong soever the proof might before appear to them, upon such separate views of it. For probable proofs, by being added, not only increase the evidence, but multiply it. Nor should I dissuade any one from setting down, what he thought made for the contrary side. But then it is to be remembered, not in order to influence his judgment, but his practice, that a mistake on one side may be, in its consequences, much more dangerous, than a mistake on the other. And what course is most safe, and what most dangerous, is a consideration thought very material, when we deliberate, not concerning events, but concerning conduct in our temporal affairs. To be influenced by this consideration in our judgment, to believe or disbelieve upon it, is indeed as much prejudice, as any thing whatever. And, like other prejudices, it operates contrary ways, in different men; for some are inclined to believe what they hope, and others what they fear. And it is manifest unreasonableness to apply to men's passions in order to gain their assent. But in deliberations concerning conduct, there is nothing which reason more requires to be taken into the account, than the importance of it. For, suppose it doubtful, what would be the consequence of acting in this, or in a contrary manner: still, that taking one side could be attended with little or no bad consequence, and taking the other might be attended with the greatest, must appear, to unprejudiced reason, of the highest moment towards determining how we are to act. But the truth of our religion, like the truth of common matters, is to be judged of by all the evidence taken together. And unless the whole series of things which may be alleged in this argument, and every particular thing in it, can reasonably be supposed to have been by accident; (for here the stress of the argument for Christianity lies;) then is the truth of it proved: in like manner, as if in any common case, numerous events acknowledged, were to be alleged in proof of any other event disputed; the truth of the disputed event would be proved, not only if any one of the acknowledged ones did of itself clearly imply it, but, though no one of them singly did so, if the whole of the acknowledged events taken together could not in reason be supposed to have happened, unless the disputed one were true.

It is obvious, how much advantage the nature of this evidence gives to those persons who attack Christianity, especially in conversation. For it is easy to shew, in a short and lively manner, that such and such things are liable to objection, that this and another thing is of little weight in itself; but impossible to shew, in like manner, the united force of the whole argument in one view.

However, lastly, as it has been made appear, that there is no presumption against a revelation as miraculous; that the general scheme of Christianity, and the principal parts of it, are conformabl to the experienced constitution of things, and the whole perfectly credible: so the account now given of the positive evidence for it, shews, that this evidence is such, as, from the nature of it, cannot be destroyed, though it should be lessened.

CHAP. VIII.

Of the objections which may be made against arguing from the analogy of nature, to religion.

IF every one would consider, with such attention as they are bound, even in point of morality, to consider, what they judge and give characters of; the occasion of this chapter would be, in some good measure at least, superseded. But since this is not to be expected; for some we find do not concern themselves to understand even what they write against: since this treatise, in common with most others, lies open to objections, which may appear very material to thoughtful men at first sight; and, besides that, seems peculiarly liable to the objections of such as can judge without thinking, and of such as can censure without judging; it may not be amiss to set down the chief of these objections which occur to me, and consider them to their hands. And they are such as these:

"That it is a poor thing to solve difficulties in revelation, by saying, that there are the same in natural religion; when what is wanting is to clear both of them of these their common, as well as other their respective, difficulties: but that it is a strange way indeed of convincing men of the obligations of religion, to shew them, that they have as little reason for their worldly pursuits: and a strange way of vindicating the justice and goodness of the Author of nature, and of removing the objections against both, to which the system of religion lies open, to shew, that the like objections lie against natural providence; a way of answering objections against religion, without so much as pretending to make out, that the system of it, or the particular things in it objected against, are reasonable— especially, perhaps some may be inattentive enough to add, must this be thought strange, when it is confessed that analogy is no answer to such objections: that when this sort of reasoning is carried to the utmost length it can be imagined capable of, it will yet leave the mind in a very unsatisfied state: and that it must be unaccountable ignorance of mankind, to imagine they will be prevailed with to forego their present interests and pleasures, from regard to religion, upon doubtful evidence."

Now, as plausible as this way of talking may appear, that appearance will be found in a great measure owing to half-views, which shew but part of an object, yet shew that indistinctly, and to undeterminate language. By these means weak men are often deceived by others, and ludicrous men, by themselves. And even those, who are serious and considerate, cannot always readily disentangle, and at once clearly see through the perplexities, in which subjects themselves are involved; and which are heightened by the deficiencies and the abuse of words. To this latter sort of persons, the following reply to each part of this objection severally, may be of some assistance; as it may also tend a little to stop and silence others.

First, The thing wanted, i.e. what men require, is to have all difficulties cleared. And this is, or, at least for any thing we know to the contrary, it may be, the same, as requiring to comprehend the Divine nature, and the whole plan of Providence from everlasting to everlasting. But it hath always been allowed to argue, from what is acknowledged, to what is disputed. And it is in no other sense a poor thing, to argue from natural religion to revealed, in the manner found fault with, than it is to argue in numberless other ways of probable deduction and inference, in matters of conduct, which we are continually reduced to the necessity of doing. Indeed the epithet *poor* may be applied, I fear, as properly to great part or the whole of human life, as it is to the things mentioned in the objection. Is it not a poor thing, for a physician to have so little knowledge in the cure of diseases, as even the most eminent have? to act upon conjecture and guess, where the life of man is concerned? Undoubtedly it is: but not in comparison of having no skill at all in that useful art, and being obliged to act wholly in the dark.

Further: since it is as unreasonable, as it is common, to urge objections against revelation, which are of equal weight against natural religion; and those who do this, if they are not confused themselves, deal unfairly with others, in making it seem, that they are arguing only against revelation, or particular doctrines of it, when in reality they are arguing against moral providence; it is a thing of consequence to shew, that such objections are as much levelled against natural religion as against revealed. And objections, which are equally applicable to both, are properly speaking answered, by its being shewn that they are so, provided the former be admitted to be true. And, without taking in the consideration how distinctly this is admitted, it is plainly very material to observe, that as the things objected against in natural religion are of the same kind with what is certain matter of experience in the course of providence, and in the information which God affords us concerning our temporal interest under his government; so the objections against the system of Christianity, and the evidence of it, are of the very same kind with those which are made against the system and evidence of natural religion. However, the reader upon review may see, that most of the analogies insisted upon, even in the latter part of this treatise, do not necessarily require to have more taken for granted than is in the former; that there is an Author of nature, or natural Governor of the world: and Christianity is vindicated, not from its analogy to natural religion, but chiefly from its analogy to the experienced constitution of nature.

Secondly, Religion is a practical thing, and consists in such a determinate course of life, as being what, there is reason to think, is commanded by the Author of nature, and will, upon the whole, be our happiness under his government. Now if men can be convinced, that they have the like reason to believe this, as to believe, that taking care of their temporal affairs will be to their advantage; such conviction cannot but be an argument to them for the practice of religion. And if there be really any reason for believing one of these, and endeavouring to preserve life, and secure ourselves the necessaries and conveniences of it; then there is reason also for believing the other, and endeavouring to secure the interest it proposes to us. And if the interest, which religion proposes to us, be infinitely greater than our whole temporal interest; then there must be proportionably greater reason for endeavouring to secure one, than the other; since, by the supposition, the probability of our securing one is equal to the probability of our securing the other. This seems plainly unanswerable; and has a tendency to influence fair minds, who consider what our condition really is, or upon what evidence we are naturally appointed to act; and who are disposed to acquiesce in the terms upon which we live, and attend to and follow that practical instruction, whatever it be, which is afforded us.

But the chief and proper force of the argument referred to in the objection, lies in another place. For, it is said that the proof of religion is involved in such inextricable difficulties, as to render it doubtful; and that it cannot be supposed, that, if it were true, it would be left upon doubtful evidence. Here then, over and above the force of each particular difficulty or objection, these difficulties and objections taken together are turned into a positive argument against the truth of religion; which argument would stand thus: If religion were true, it would not be left doubtful, and open to objections to the degree in which it is: therefore that it is thus left, not only renders the evidence of it weak, and lessens its force, in proportion to the weight of such objections; but also shews it to be false, or is a general presumption of its being so. Now the observation, that, from the natural constitution and course of things, we must in our temporal concerns, almost continually, and in matters of great consequence, act upon evidence of a like kind and degree to the evidence of religion, is an answer to this argument; because it shews, that it is according to the conduct and character of the Author of nature to appoint we should act upon evidence like to that, which this argument presumes he cannot be supposed to appoint we should act upon : it is an instance, a general one made up of numerous particular ones, of somewhat in his dealing with us, similar to what is said to be incredible. And as the force of this answer lies merely in the parallel, which there is between the evidence for religion and for our temporal conduct; the answer is equally just and conclusive, whether the parallel be made out, by shewing the evidence of the former to be higher, or the evidence of the latter to be lower.

Thirdly, The design of this treatise is not to vindicate the character of God, but to shew the obligations of men : it is not to justify his providence, but to shew what belongs to us to do. These are two subjects, and ought not to be confounded. And though they may at length run up into each other, yet observations may immediately tend to make out the latter, which do not appear, by any immediate connection, to the purpose of the former; which is less our concern, than many seem to think. For, first, it is not necessary we should justify the dispensations of Providence against objections, any farther than to shew, that the things objected against may, for ought we know, be consistent with justice and goodness. Suppose then, that there are things in the system of this world, and plan of Providence relating to it, which taken alone would be unjust : yet it has been shewn unanswerably, that if we could take in the reference, which these things may have to other things present, past, and to come : to the whole scheme, which the things objected against are parts of; these very things might, for ought we know, be found to be, not only consistent with justice, but instances of it. Indeed it has been shewn, by the analogy of what we see, not only possible that this may be the case, but credible that it is. And thus objections, drawn from such things, are answered, and Providence is vindicated, as far as religion makes its vindication necessary. Hence it appears, secondly, that objections against the Divine justice and goodness are not endeavoured to be removed, by shewing that the like objections, allowed to be really conclusive, lie against natural providence: but those objections being supposed and shewn not to be conclusive, the things objected against, considered as matters of fact, are farther shewn to be credible, from their conformity to the constitution of nature; for instance, that God will reward and punish men for their actions hereafter, from the observation, that he does reward and punish them for their actions here. And this, I apprehend, is of weight. And I add, thirdly, it would be of weight, even though those objections were not answered. For, there being the proof of religion above set down; and religion implying several facts; for instance again, the fact last mentioned, that God will reward and punish men for their actions hereafter; the observation, that his present method of government is by rewards and punishments, shews that future fact not to be incredible: whatever objections men may think they have against it, as unjust or unmerciful, according to their notions of justice and mercy; or as improbable from their belief of necessity. I say, *as improbable:* for it is evident no objection against it, *as unjust,* can be urged from necessity; since this notion as much destroys injustice, as it does justice. Then, fourthly, Though objections against the reasonableness of the system of religion cannot indeed be answered without entering into consideration of its reasonableness; yet objections against the credibility or truth of it may. Because the system of it is reducible into what is properly matter of fact: and the truth, the probable truth, of facts may be shewn without consideration of their reasonableness. Nor is it necessary, though, in some cases and respects, it is highly useful and proper, yet it is not necessary, to give a proof of the reasonableness of every precept enjoined us, and of every particular dispensation of Providence, which comes into the system of religion. Indeed the more thoroughly a person of a right disposition is convinced of the perfection of the Divine nature and conduct, the farther he will advance towards that perfection of religion, which St. John speaks of [a]. But the general obligations of religion are fully made out, by proving the reasonableness of the practice of it. And that the practice of religion *is* reasonable, may be shewn, though no more could be proved, than that the system of it *may be* so, for ought we know to the contrary: and even without entering into the distinct consideration of this. And from hence, fifthly, it is easy to see, that though the analogy of nature is not an immediate answer to objections, against the wisdom, the justice, or goodness, of any doctrine or precept of religion: yet it may be, as it is, an immediate and direct answer to what is really intended by such objections; which is, to shew that the things objected against are incredible.

Fourthly, It is most readily acknowledged, that the foregoing treatise is by no means satisfactory; very far indeed from it: but so would any natural

[a] 1 John iv. 18.

institution of life appear, if reduced into a system, together with its evidence. Leaving religion out of the case, men are divided in their opinions, whether our pleasures overbalance our pains: and whether it be, or be not, eligible to live in this world. And were all such controversies settled, which perhaps, in speculation, would be found involved in great difficulties; and were it determined upon the evidence of reason, as nature has determined it to our hands, that life is to be preserved: yet still, the rules which God has been pleased to afford us, for escaping the miseries of it, and obtaining its satisfactions, the rules, for instance, of preserving health, and recovering it when lost, are not only fallible and precarious, but very far from being exact. Nor are we informed by nature, in future contingencies and accidents, so as to render it at all certain, what is the best method of managing our affairs. What will be the success of our temporal pursuits, in the common sense of the word Success, is highly doubtful. And what will be the success of them in the proper sense of the word; i. e. what happiness or enjoyment we shall obtain by them, is doubtful in a much higher degree. Indeed the unsatisfactory nature of the evidence, with which we are obliged to take up, in the daily course of life, is scarce to be expressed. Yet men do not throw away life, or disregard the interests of it, upon account of this doubtfulness. The evidence of religion then being admitted real, those who object against it, as not satisfactory, i. e. as not being what they wish it, plainly forget the very condition of our being: for satisfaction, in this sense, does not belong to such a creature as man. And, which is more material, they forget also the very nature of religion. For, religion presupposes, in all those who will embrace it, a certain degree of integrity and honesty; which it was intended to try whether men have or not, and to exercise in such as have it, in order to its improvement. Religion presupposes this as much, and in the same sense, as speaking to a man presupposes he understands the language in which you speak; or as warning a man of any danger presupposes that he hath such a regard to himself, as that he will endeavour to avoid it. And therefore the question is not at all, Whether the evidence of religion be satisfactory; but Whether it be, in reason, sufficient to prove and discipline that virtue, which it presupposes. Now the evidence of it is fully sufficient for all those purposes of probation; how far soever it is from being satisfactory, as to the purposes of curiosity, or any other: and indeed it answers the purposes of the former in several respects, which it would not do, if it were as overbearing as is required. One might add farther; that whether the motives or the evidence for any course of action be satisfactory, meaning here, by that word what satisfies a man, that such a course of action will in event be for his good; this need never be, and I think, strictly speaking, never is, the practical question in common matters. But the practical question in all cases is, Whether the evidence for a course of action be such, as, taking in all circumstances, makes the faculty within us, which is the guide and judge of conduct[b], determine that course of action to be prudent. Indeed, satisfaction that it will be for our interest or happiness, abundantly determines an action to be prudent: but evidence almost infinitely lower than this, determines actions to be so too; even in the conduct of every day.

[b] See Dissert. II.

Fifthly, As to the objection concerning the influence which this argument, or any part of it, may, or may not, be expected to have upon men; I observe, as above, that religion being intended for a trial and exercise of the morality of every person's character, who is a subject of it; and there being, as I have shewn, such evidence for it, as is sufficient, in reason, to influence men to embrace it: to object, that it is not to be imagined mankind will be influenced by such evidence, is nothing to the purpose of the foregoing treatise. For the purpose of it is not to inquire, what sort of creatures mankind are; but what the light and knowledge, which is afforded them, requires they should be: to shew how, in reason, they ought to behave; not how, in fact, they will behave. This depends upon themselves, and is their own concern; the personal concern of each man in particular. And how little regard the generality have to it, experience indeed does too fully shew. But religion, considered as a probation, has had its end upon all persons, to whom it has been proposed with evidence sufficient in reason to influence their practice: for by this means they have been put into a state of probation; let them behave as they will in it. And thus, not only revelation, but reason also, teaches us, that by the evidence of religion being laid before men, the designs of Providence are carrying on, not only with regard to those who will, but likewise with regard to those who will not, be influenced by it. However, lastly, the objection here referred to, allows the things insisted upon in this treatise to be of some weight: and if so, it may be hoped it will have some influence. And if there be a probability that it will have any at all, there is the same reason in kind, though not in degree, to lay it before men, as there would be, if it were likely to have a greater influence.

And farther, I desire it may be considered, with respect to the whole of the foregoing objections, that in this treatise I have argued upon the principles of others[c], not my own: and have omitted what I think true, and of the utmost importance, because by others thought unintelligible, or not true. Thus I have argued upon the principles of the Fatalists, which I do not believe: and have omitted a thing of the utmost importance which I do believe, the moral fitness and unfitness of actions, prior to all will whatever; which I apprehend as certainly to determine the Divine conduct, as speculative truth and falsehood necessarily determine the Divine judgment. Indeed the principle of liberty, and that of moral fitness, so force themselves upon the mind, that moralists, the ancients as well as moderns, have formed their language upon it. And probably it may appear in mine: though I have endeavoured to avoid it; and, in order to avoid it, have sometimes been obliged to express myself in a manner, which will appear strange to such as do not observe the reason for it: but the general argument here pursued does not at all suppose or proceed upon these principles. Now, these two abstract principles of liberty and moral fitness being omitted, religion can be considered in no other view, than merely as a question of fact: and in this view it is here considered. It is obvious, that Christianity, and the proof of it,

---

[c] By *arguing upon the principles of others*, the reader will observe is meant; not proving any thing *from* those principles, but *notwithstanding* them. Thus religion is proved, not *from* the opinion of necessity; which is absurd: but, *notwithstanding* or *even though* that opinion were admitted to be true.

are both historical. And even natural religion is, properly, a matter of fact. For, that there is a righteous Governor of the world, is so: and this proposition contains the general system of natural religion. But then, several abstract truths, and in particular those two principles, are usually taken into consideration in the proof of it: whereas it is here treated of only as a matter of fact. To explain this: that the three angles of a triangle are equal to two right ones, is an abstract truth: but that they appear so to our mind, is only a matter of fact. And this last must have been admitted, if any thing was, by those ancient sceptics, who would not have admitted the former: but pretended to doubt, Whether there were any such thing as truth, or Whether we could certainly depend upon our faculties of understanding for the knowledge of it in any case. So likewise, that there is, in the nature of things, an original standard of right and wrong in actions, independent upon all will, but which unalterably determines the will of God, to exercise that moral government over the world, which religion teaches, i. e. finally and upon the whole to reward and punish men respectively as they act right or wrong; this assertion contains an abstract truth, as well as matter of fact. But suppose, in the present state, every man, without exception, was rewarded and punished, in exact proportion as he followed or transgressed that sense of right and wrong, which God has implanted in the nature of every man: this would not be at all an abstract truth, but only a matter of fact. And though this fact were acknowledged by every one; yet the very same difficulties might be raised as are now, concerning the abstract questions of liberty and moral fitness: and we should have a proof, even the certain one of experience, that the government of the world was perfectly moral, without taking in the consideration of those questions: and this proof would remain, in what way soever they were determined. And thus, God having given mankind a moral faculty, the object of which is actions, and which naturally approves some actions as right, and of good desert, and condemns others as wrong, and of ill desert; that he will, finally and upon the whole, reward the former and punish the latter, is not an assertion of an abstract truth, but of what is as mere a fact, as his doing so at present would be. This future fact I have not indeed proved with the force with which it might be proved, from the principles of liberty and moral fitness; but without them have given a really conclusive practical proof of it, which is greatly strengthened by the general analogy of nature: a proof easily cavilled at, easily shewn not to be demonstrative, for it is not offered as such; but impossible, I think, to be evaded, or answered. And thus the obligations of religion are made out, exclusively of the questions concerning liberty and moral fitness; which have been perplexed with difficulties and abstruse reasonings, as every thing may.

Hence therefore may be observed distinctly, what is the force of this treatise. It will be, to such as are convinced of religion upon the proof arising out of the two last-mentioned principles, an additional proof and a confirmation of it: to such as do not admit those principles, an original proof of it[d], and a confirmation of that proof. Those who believe will here find the scheme of Christianity cleared of objections, and the evidence of it in a peculiar manner strengthened: those who do not believe will at least

[d] P. 120, &c.

be shewn the absurdity of all attempts to prove Christianity false, the plain undoubted credibility of it; and, I hope, a good deal more.

And thus, though some perhaps may seriously think, that analogy, as here urged, has too great stress laid upon it; and ridicule, unanswerable ridicule, may be applied, to show the argument from it in a disadvantageous light: yet there can be no question, but that it is a real one. For religion, both natural and revealed, imply in it numerous facts; analogy, being a confirmation of all facts to which it can be applied, as it is the only proof of most, cannot but be admitted by every one to be a material thing, and truly of weight on the side of religion, both natural and revealed: and it ought to be particularly regarded by such as profess to follow nature, and to be less satisfied with abstract reasonings.

CONCLUSION.

WHATEVER account may be given of the strange inattention and disregard, in some ages and countries, to a matter of such importance as Religion; it would, before experience, be incredible, that there should be the like disregard in those, who have had the moral system of the world laid before them, as it is by Christianity, and often inculcated upon them: because this moral system carries in it a good degree of evidence for its truth, upon its being barely proposed to our thoughts. There is no need of abstruse reasonings and distinctions, to convince an unprejudiced understanding, that there is a God who made and governs the world, and will judge it in righteousness; though they may be necessary to answer abstruse difficulties, when once such are raised: when the very meaning of those words, which express most intelligibly the general doctrine of religion, is pretended to be uncertain; and the clear truth of the thing itself is obscured by the intricacies of speculation. But to an unprejudiced mind ten thousand thousand instances of design cannot but prove a designer. And it is intuitively manifest, that creatures ought to live under a dutiful sense of their Maker; and that justice and charity must be his laws, to creatures whom he has made social, and placed in society. Indeed the truth of revealed religion, peculiarly so called, is not self-evident, but requires external proof, in order to its being received. Yet inattention, among us, to revealed religion, will be found to imply the same dissolute immoral temper of mind, as inattention to natural religion: because, when both are laid before us, in the manner they are in Christian countries of liberty, our obligations to inquire into both, and to embrace both upon supposition of their truth, are obligations of the same nature. For, revelation claims to be the voice of God: and our obligation to attend to his voice is surely moral in all cases. And as it is insisted, that its evidence is conclusive, upon thorough consideration of it; so it offers itself to us with manifest obvious appearances of having something more than human in it, and therefore in all reason requires to have its claims most seriously examined into. It is to be added, that though light and knowledge, in what manner soever afforded us, is equally from God; yet a miraculous revelation has a peculiar tendency, from the first principles of our nature, to awaken mankind, and inspire them with reverence and awe: and this is a peculiar obligation, to attend to what claims to be so with such appearances of truth. It is therefore most certain, that our obligations to inquire seriously into the evidence of Christianity, and, upon supposition of its truth, to embrace it, are of the utmost importance, and moral in the highest and most proper sense. Let us then suppose, that the evidence of religion in general, and of Christianity, has been seriously inquired into, by all reasonable men among us. Yet we find many professedly to reject both, upon speculative principles of infidelity. And all of them do not content themselves with a bare neglect of religion, and enjoying their imaginary freedom from its restraints. Some go much beyond this. They deride God's moral government over the world. They renounce his protection, and defy his justice. They ridicule and vilify Christianity, and blaspheme the Author of it; and take all occasions to manifest a scorn and contempt of revelation. This amounts to an active setting themselves against religion; to what may be considered as a positive principle of irreligion; which they cultivate within themselves, and, whether they intend this effect or not, render habitual, as a good man does the contrary principle. And others, who are not chargeable with all this profligateness, yet are in avowed opposition to religion, as if discovered to be groundless. Now admitting, which is the supposition we go upon, that these persons act upon what they think principles of reason, and otherwise they are not to be argued with; it is really inconceivable, that they should imagine they clearly see the whole evidence of it, considered in itself, to be nothing at all: nor do they pretend this. They are far indeed from having a just notion of its evidence: but they would not say its evidence was nothing, if they thought the system of it, with all its circumstances, were credible, like other matters of science or history. So that their manner of treating it must proceed, either from such kind of objections against all religion, as have been answered or obviated in the former part of this treatise; or else from objections, and difficulties, supposed more peculiar to Christianity. Thus, they entertain prejudices against the whole notion of a revelation, and miraculous interpositions. They find things in Scripture, whether in incidental passages, or in the general scheme of it, which appear to them unreasonable. They take for granted, that if Christianity were true, the light of it must have been more general, and the evidence of it more satisfactory, or rather overbearing: that it must and would have been, in some way, otherwise put and left, than it is. Now this is not imagining they see the evidence itself to be nothing, or inconsiderable; but quite another thing. It is being fortified against the evidence, in some degree acknowledged, by thinking they see the system of Christianity, or somewhat which appears to them necessarily connected with it, to be incredible or false; fortified against that evidence, which might, otherwise, make great impression upon them. Or, lastly, if any of these persons are, upon the whole, in doubt concerning the truth of Christianity; their behaviour seems owing to their taking for granted, through strange inattention, that such doubting is, in a manner, the same thing, as being certain against it.

To these persons, and to this state of opinion concerning religion, the foregoing treatise is adapted.

For, all the general objections against the moral system of nature having been obviated, it is shewn, that there is not any peculiar presumption at all against Christianity, either considered as not discoverable by reason, or as unlike to what is so discovered; nor any worth mentioning against it as miraculous, if any at all; none, certainly, which can render it in the least incredible. It is shewn, that, upon supposition of a divine revelation, the analogy of nature renders it beforehand highly credible, I think probable, that many things in it, must appear liable to great objections; and that we must be incompetent judges of it, to a great degree. This observation is, I think, unquestionably true, and of the very utmost importance: but it is urged, as I hope it will be understood, with great caution of not vilifying the faculty of reason, which is *the candle of the Lord within us* [a]; though it can afford no light, where it does not shine; nor judge, where it has no principles to judge upon. The objections here spoken of, being first answered in the view of objections against Christianity as a matter of fact, are in the next place considered as urged more immediately against the wisdom, justice, and goodness of the Christian dispensation. And it is fully made out, that they admit of exactly the like answer, in every respect, to what the like objections against the constitution of nature admit of: that, as partial views give the appearance of wrong to things, which, upon farther consideration and knowledge of their relations to other things, are found just and good; so it is perfectly credible, that the things objected against the wisdom and goodness of the Christian dispensation, may be rendered instances of wisdom and good-

[a] Prov. xx. 27.

ness, by their reference to other things beyond our view: because Christianity is a scheme as much above our comprehension, as that of nature; and like that, a scheme in which means are made use of to accomplish ends, and which, as is most credible, may be carried on by general laws. And it ought to be attended to, that this is not an answer taken merely or chiefly from our ignorance; but from somewhat positive, which our observation shews us. For, to like objections, the like answer is experienced to be just, in numberless parallel cases. The objections against the Christian dispensation, and the method by which it is carried on, having been thus obviated, in general and together; the chief of them are considered distinctly, and the particular things objected to are shewn credible, by their perfect analogy, each apart, to the constitution of nature. Thus, if man be fallen from his primitive state, and to be restored, and infinite wisdom and power engages in accomplishing our recovery: it were to have been expected, it is said, that this should have been effected at once; and not by such a long series of means, and such a various economy of persons and things; one dispensation preparatory to another, this to a farther one, and so on through an indefinite number of ages, before the end of the scheme proposed can be completely accomplished; a scheme conducted by infinite wisdom, and executed by almighty power. But now, on the contrary, our finding that every thing in the constitution and course of nature is thus carried on, shews such expectations concerning revelation to be highly unreasonable; and is a satisfactory answer to them, when urged as objections against the credibility, that the great scheme of Providence in the redemption of the world may be of this kind, and to be accomplished in this manner. As to the particular method of our redemption, the appointment of a Mediator between God and man: this has been shewn to be most obviously analogous to the general conduct of nature, i. e. the God of nature, in appointing others to be the instruments of his mercy, as we experience in the daily course of providence. The condition of this world, which the doctrine of our redemption by Christ presupposes, so much falls in with natural appearances, that heathen moralists inferred it from those appearances: inferred, that human nature was fallen from its original rectitude, and, in consequence of this, degraded from its primitive happiness. Or, however this opinion came into the world, these appearances must have kept up the tradition, and confirmed the belief of it. And as it was the general opinion under the light of nature, that repentance and reformation, alone and by itself, was not sufficient to do away sin, and procure a full remission of the penalties annexed to it; and as the reason of the thing does not at all lead to any such conclusion; so every day's experience shews us, that reformation is not, in any sort, sufficient to prevent the present disadvantages and miseries, which, in the natural course of things, God has annexed to folly and extravagance. Yet there may be ground to think, that the punishments, which, by the general laws of Divine government, are annexed to vice, may be prevented: that provision may have been, even originally, made, that they should be prevented by some means or other, though they could not by reformation alone. For we have daily instances of *such mercy*, in the general conduct of nature: compassion provided for misery[b], medicines for

[b] Serm. at the Rolls, p. 106.

diseases, friends against enemies. There is provision made, in the original constitution of the world, that much of the natural bad consequences of our follies, which persons themselves alone cannot prevent, may be prevented by the assistance of others; assistance, which nature enables, and disposes, and appoints them to afford. By a method of goodness analogous to this, when the world lay in wickedness, and consequently in ruin, *God so loved the world, that he gave his only-begotten Son to save it:* and *he being made perfect by suffering, became the author of eternal salvation to all them that obey him*[c]. Indeed neither reason nor analogy would lead us to think, in particular, that the interposition of Christ, in the manner in which he did interpose, would be of that efficacy for recovery of the world, which the Scripture teaches us it was: but neither would reason nor analogy lead us to think, that other particular means would be of the efficacy, which experience shews they are, in numberless instances. And therefore, as the case before us does not admit of experience; so, that neither reason nor analogy can shew how, or in what particular way, the interposition of Christ, as revealed in Scripture, is of that efficacy, which it is there represented to be; this is no kind nor degree of presumption against its being really of that efficacy. Farther: the objections against Christianity, from the light of it not being universal, nor its evidence so strong as might possibly be given us, have been answered by the general analogy of nature. That God has made such variety of creatures, is indeed an answer to the former: but that he dispenses his gifts in such variety, both of degrees and kinds, amongst creatures of the same species, and even

[c] John iii. 16: Heb. v. 9.

to the same individuals at different times; is a more obvious and full answer to it. And it is so far from being the method of Providence in other cases, to afford us such overbearing evidence, as some require in proof of Christianity; that, on the contrary, the evidence upon which we are naturally appointed to act in common matters, throughout a very great part of life, is doubtful in a high degree. And admitting the fact, that God has afforded to some no more than doubtful evidence of religion; the same account may be given of it, as of difficulties and temptations with regard to practice. But as it is not impossible[d], surely, that this alleged doubtfulness may be men's own fault; it deserves their most serious consideration, whether it be not so. However, it is certain, that doubting implies a degree of evidence for that of which we doubt: and that this degree of evidence as really lays us under obligations, as demonstrative evidence.

The whole then of religion is throughout credible: nor is there, I think, any thing relating to the revealed dispensation of things, more different from the experienced constitution and course of nature, than some parts of the constitution of nature are from other parts of it. And if so, the only question which remains is, what positive evidence can be alleged for the truth of Christianity. This too in general has been considered, and the objections against it estimated. Deduct, therefore, what is to be deducted from that evidence, upon account of any weight which may be thought to remain in these objections, after what the analogy of nature has suggested in answer to them: and then consider, what are the practical consequences from all this, upon the

[d] Page 243, &c.

most sceptical principles one can argue upon: (for I am writing to persons who entertain these principles:) and upon such consideration it will be obvious, that immorality, as little excuse as it admits of in itself, is greatly aggravated, in persons who have been made acquainted with Christianity, whether they believe it or not: because the moral system of nature, or natural religion, which Christianity lays before us, approves itself, almost intuitively, to a reasonable mind, upon seeing it proposed. In the next place, with regard to Christianity, it will be observed; that there is a middle between a full satisfaction of the truth of it, and a satisfaction of the contrary. The middle state of mind between these two consists in a serious apprehension, that it may be true, joined with doubt whether it be so. And this, upon the best judgment I am able to make, is as far towards speculative infidelity, as any sceptic can at all be supposed to go, who has had true Christianity, with the proper evidence of it, laid before him, and has in any tolerable measure considered them. For I would not be mistaken to comprehend all who have ever heard of it: because it seems evident, that in many countries called Christian, neither Christianity, nor its evidence, are fairly laid before men. And in places where both are, there appear to be some, who have very little attended to either, and who reject Christianity with a scorn proportionate to their inattention; and yet are by no means without understanding in other matters. Now it has been shewn, that a serious apprehension that Christianity may be true, lays persons under the strictest obligations of a serious regard to it, throughout the whole of their life: a regard not the same exactly, but in many respects nearly the same, with what a full conviction of its truth would lay them under. Lastly, it will appear, that blasphemy and profaneness, I mean with regard to Christianity, are absolutely without excuse. For there is no temptation to it, but from the wantonness of vanity or mirth: and these, considering the infinite importance of the subject, are no such temptations as to afford any excuse for it. If this be a just account of things, and yet men can go on to vilify or disregard Christianity, which is to talk and act as if they had a demonstration of its falsehood; there is no reason to think they would alter their behaviour to any purpose, though there were a demonstration of its truth.

THE END OF THE SECOND PART.

TWO BRIEF DISSERTATIONS.

I. OF PERSONAL IDENTITY.
II. OF THE NATURE OF VIRTUE.

ADVERTISEMENT.

In the first copy of these Papers, I had inserted the two following Dissertations into the chapters, *Of a future life*, and, *Of the moral government of God;* with which they are closely connected. But as they do not directly fall under the *title* of the foregoing Treatise, and would have kept the subject of it too long out of sight; it seemed more proper to place them by themselves.

DISSERTATION I.

OF PERSONAL IDENTITY.

WHETHER we are to live in a future state, as it is the most important question which can possibly be asked, so it is the most intelligible one which can be expressed in language. Yet strange perplexities have been raised about the meaning of that identity, or sameness of person, which is implied in the notion of our living now and hereafter, or in any two successive moments. And the solution of these difficulties hath been stranger than the difficulties themselves. For personal identity has been explained so by some, as to render the inquiry concerning a future life of no consequence at all to us the persons who are making it. And though few men can be misled by such subtleties; yet it may be proper a little to consider them.

Now when it is asked, wherein personal identity consists, the answer should be the same, as if it were asked, wherein consists similitude, or equality; that all attempts to define would but perplex it. Yet there is no difficulty at all in ascertaining the idea. For as, upon two triangles being compared or viewed together, there arises to the mind the idea of similitude; or upon twice two and four, the idea of equality: so likewise, upon comparing the consciousnesses of one's self, or one's own existence, in any two moments, there as immediately arises to the mind the idea of personal identity. And as the two former comparisons not only give us the ideas of similitude and equality; but also shew us, that two triangles are alike, and twice two and four are equal: so the latter comparison not only gives us the idea of personal identity, but also shews us the identity of ourselves in those two moments; the present, suppose, and that immediately past; or the present, and that a month, a year, or twenty years past. Or in other words, by reflecting upon that, which is myself now, and that, which was myself twenty years ago, I discern they are not two, but one and the same self.

But though consciousness of what is past does thus ascertain our personal identity to ourselves, yet to say, that it makes personal identity, or is necessary to our being the same persons, is to say, that a person has not existed a single moment, nor done one action, but what he can remember; indeed none but what he reflects upon. And one should really think it self-evident, that consciousness of personal identity presupposes, and therefore cannot constitute, personal identity; any more than knowledge, in any other case, can constitute truth, which it presupposes.

This wonderful mistake may possibly have arisen from hence; that to be endued with consciousness is inseparable from the idea of a person, or intelligent being. For, this might be expressed inaccurately thus, that consciousness makes personality: and from hence it might be concluded to make personal identity. But though present consciousness of what we at present do and feel is necessary to our being the persons we now are; yet present consciousness of past actions or feelings is not necessary to our being the same persons who performed those actions, or had those feelings.

The inquiry, what makes vegetables the same in the common acceptation of the word, does not appear to have any relation to this of personal identity: because the word *same*, when applied to them and to person, is not only applied to different subjects, but it is also used in different senses. For when a man swears to the same tree, as having stood fifty years in the same place, he means only the same as to all the purposes of property and uses of common life, and not that the tree has been all that time the same in the strict philosophical sense of the word. For he does not know, whether any one particle of the present tree be the same with any one particle of the tree which stood in the same place fifty years ago. And if they have not one common particle of matter, they cannot be the same tree in the proper philosophic sense of the word *same:* it being evidently a contradiction in terms, to say they are, when no part of their substance, and no one of their properties is the same: no part of their substance, by the supposition; no one of their properties, because it is allowed, that the same property cannot be transferred from one substance to another. And therefore, when we say the identity or sameness of a plant consists in a continuation of the same life, communicated under the same organization, to a number of particles of matter, whether the same or not; the word *same*, when applied to life and to organization, cannot possibly be understood to signify, what it signifies in this very sentence, when applied to matter. In a loose and popular sense then, the life and the organization and the plant are justly said to be the same, notwithstanding the perpetual change of the parts. But in a strict and philosophical manner of speech, no man, no being, no mode of being, no anything, can be the same with that, with which it hath indeed nothing the same. Now sameness is used in this latter sense, when applied to persons. The identity of these, therefore, cannot subsist with diversity of substance.

The thing here considered, and demonstratively, as I think, determined, is proposed by Mr. Locke in these words, *Whether it*, i. e. the same self or person, *be the same identical substance?* And he has suggested what is a much better answer to the question, than that which he gives it in form. For he defines Person, *a thinking intelligent being*, &c., and personal identity, *the sameness of a rational being*[a]. The question then is, whether the same rational being is the same substance: which needs no answer, because Being and Substance, in this place, stand for the same idea. The ground of the doubt, whether the same person be the same substance, is said to be this; that the consciousness of our own existence, in youth and in old age, or in any two joint successive moments, is not the *same individual action*[b], i. e. not the same consciousness, but different successive consciousnesses. Now it is strange that this should have occasioned such perplexities. For it is surely conceivable, that a person may have a capacity of knowing some object or other to be the same now, which it was when he contemplated it formerly: yet in this case, where, by the supposition, the object is perceived to be the same, the perception of it in any two moments cannot be one and the same perception. And thus though the successive consciousnesses, which we have of our own existence, are not the same, yet are they consciousnesses of one and the same thing or object; of the same person, self,

[a] Locke's Works, vol. i. p. 146. [b] Locke, pp. 146, 147.

or living agent. The person, of whose existence the consciousness is felt now, and was felt an hour or a year ago, is discerned to be, not two persons, but one and the same person; and therefore is one and the same.

Mr. Locke's observations upon this subject appear hasty: and he seems to profess himself dissatisfied with suppositions, which he has made relating to it[c]. But some of those hasty observations have been carried to a strange length by others; whose notion, when traced and examined to the bottom, amounts, I think, to this[d]: "That Personality is not a permanent, but a transient thing: that it lives and dies, begins and ends continually: that no one can any more remain one and the same person two moments together, than two successive moments can be one and the same moment: that our substance is indeed continually changing; but whether this be so or not, is, it seems, nothing to the purpose; since it is not substance, but consciousness alone, which constitutes personality: which consciousness, being successive, cannot be the same in any two moments, nor consequently the personality constituted by it." And from hence it must follow, that it is a fallacy upon ourselves, to charge our present selves with any thing we did, or to imagine our present selves interested in any thing which befell us yesterday; or that our present self will be interested in what will befall us to-morrow: since our present self is not, in reality, the same with the self of yesterday, but another like self or person coming in its room, and mistaken for it; to which another self will succeed

[c] Locke, p. 152.
[d] See an Answer to Dr. Clarke's Third Defence of his Letter to Mr. Dodwell, 2nd edit. pp. 44, 56, &c.

to-morrow. This, I say, must follow: for if the self or person of to-day, and that of to-morrow, are not the same, but only like persons; the person of to-day is really no more interested in what will befall the person of to-morrow, than in what will befall any other person. It may be thought, perhaps, that this is not a just representation of the opinion we are speaking of: because those who maintain it allow, that a person is the same as far back as his remembrance reaches. And indeed they do use the words, *identity* and *same* person. Nor will language permit these words to be laid aside; since if they were, there must be I know not what ridiculous periphrasis substituted in the room of them. But they cannot, consistently with themselves, mean, that the person is really the same. For it is self-evident, that the personality cannot be really the same, if, as they expressly assert, that in which it consists is not the same. And as, consistently with themselves, they cannot, so, I think it appears, they do not, mean, that the person is *really* the same, but only that he is so in a fictitious sense: in such a sense only as they assert, for this they do assert, that any number of persons whatever may be the same person. The bare unfolding this notion, and laying it thus naked and open, seems the best confutation of it. However, since great stress is said to be put upon it, I add the following things.

First, This notion is absolutely contradictory to that certain conviction, which necessarily and every moment rises within us, when we turn our thoughts upon ourselves, when we reflect upon what is past, and look forward upon what is to come. All imagination of a daily change of that living agent which each man calls himself, for another, or of any such change throughout our whole present life, is entirely borne down by our natural sense of things. Nor is it possible for a person in his wits to alter his conduct, with regard to his health or affairs, from a suspicion, that, though he should live to-morrow, he should not, however, be the same person he is to-day. And yet, if it be reasonable to act, with respect to a future life, upon this notion, that personality is transient; it is reasonable to act upon it, with respect to the present. Here then is a notion equally applicable to religion and to our temporal concerns; and every one sees and feels the inexpressible absurdity of it in the latter case; if, therefore, any can take up with it in the former, this cannot proceed from the reason of the thing, but must be owing to an inward unfairness, and secret corruption of heart.

Secondly, It is not an idea, or abstract notion, or quality, but a being only, which is capable of life and action, of happiness and misery. Now all beings confessedly continue the same, during the whole time of their existence. Consider then a living being now existing, and which has existed for any time alive: this living being must have done and suffered and enjoyed, what it has done and suffered and enjoyed formerly, (this living being, I say, and not another,) as really as it does and suffers and enjoys, what it does and suffers and enjoys this instant. All these successive actions, enjoyments, and sufferings, are actions, enjoyments, and sufferings, of the same living being. And they are so, prior to all consideration of its remembering or forgetting: since remembering or forgetting can make no alteration in the truth of past matter of fact. And suppose this being endued with limited powers of knowledge and memory, there is no more difficulty in conceiving it to have a power of knowing itself to be the same living being which it was some time ago, of remembering some of its actions, sufferings, and enjoyments, and forgetting others, than in conceiving it to know or remember or forget anything else.

Thirdly, Every person is conscious, that he is now the same person or self he was as far back as his remembrance reaches: since when any one reflects upon a past action of his own, he is just as certain of the person who did that action, namely, himself, the person who now reflects upon it, as he is certain that the action was at all done. Nay, very often a person's assurance of an action having been done, of which he is absolutely assured, arises wholly from the consciousness that he himself did it. And this he, person, or self, must either be a substance, or the property of some substance. If he, if person, be a substance; then consciousness that he is the same person is consciousness that he is the same substance. If the person, or he, be the property of a substance, still consciousness that he is the same property is as certain a proof that his substance remains the same, as consciousness that he remains the same substance would be: since the same property cannot be transferred from one substance to another.

But though we are thus certain that we are the same agents, living beings, or substances, now which we were as far back as our remembrance reaches; yet it is asked, whether we may not possibly be deceived in it? And this question may be asked at the end of any demonstration whatever: because it is a question concerning the truth of perception by memory. And he who can doubt, whether perception by memory can in this case be depended upon, may doubt also, whether perception by deduction and reasoning, which also include memory, or indeed whether intuitive perception can. Here then we can go no farther. For it is ridiculous to attempt to prove the truth of those perceptions, whose truth we can no otherwise prove, than by other perceptions of exactly the same kind with them, and which there is just the same ground to suspect; or to attempt to prove the truth of our faculties, which can no otherwise be proved, than by the use or means of those very suspected faculties themselves.

DISSERTATION II.

OF THE NATURE OF VIRTUE.

THAT which renders beings capable of moral government, is their having a moral nature, and moral faculties of perception and of action. Brute creatures are impressed and actuated by various instincts and propensions: so also are we. But additional to this, we have a capacity of reflecting upon actions and characters, and making them an object to our thought: and on doing this, we naturally and unavoidably approve some actions, under the peculiar view of their being virtuous and of good desert; and disapprove others, as vicious and of ill-desert. That we have this moral approving and disapproving[a] faculty, is certain from our experiencing it in ourselves, and recognising it in

---

[a] This way of speaking is taken from Epictetus*, and is made use of as seeming the most full, and least liable to cavil. And the moral faculty may be understood to have these two epithets, δοκιμαστικὴ and ἀποδοκιμαστικὴ, upon a double account; because, upon a survey of actions, whether before or after they are done, it determines them to be good or evil; and also because it determines itself to be the guide of action and of life, in contradistinction from all other faculties, or natural principles of action: in the very same manner as speculative reason *directly* and naturally judges of speculative truth and falsehood; and at the same time is attended with a consciousness upon *reflection*, that the natural right to judge of them belongs to it.

* Arr. Epict. lib. i. cap. I.

each other. It appears from our exercising it unavoidably, in the approbation and disapprobation even of feigned characters: from the words *right* and *wrong*, *odious* and *amiable*, *base* and *worthy*, with many others of like signification in all languages, applied to actions and characters: from the many written systems of morals which suppose it; since it cannot be imagined, that all these authors, throughout all these treatises, had absolutely no meaning at all to their words, or a meaning merely chimerical: from our natural sense of gratitude, which implies a distinction between merely being the instrument of good, and intending it: from the like distinction, every one makes, between injury and mere harm, which, Hobbes says, is peculiar to mankind; and between injury and just punishment, a distinction plainly natural, prior to the consideration of human laws. It is manifest great part of common language, and of common behaviour over the world, is formed upon supposition of such a moral faculty; whether called conscience, moral reason, moral sense, or Divine reason; whether considered as a sentiment of the understanding, or as a preception of the heart; or, which seems the truth, as including both. Nor is it at all doubtful in the general, what course of action this faculty, or practical discerning power within us, approves, and what it disapproves. For, as much as it has been disputed wherein virtue consists, or whatever ground for doubt there may be about particulars; yet, in general, there is in reality an universally acknowledged standard of it. It is that, which all ages and all countries have made profession of in public: it is that, which every man you meet puts on the show of: it is that, which the primary and fundamental laws of all civil constitutions over the face of the earth make it their business and endeavour to enforce the practice of upon mankind: namely, justice, veracity, and regard to common good. It being manifest then, in general, that we have such a faculty or discernment as this, it may be of use to remark some things more distinctly concerning it.

First, It ought to be observed, that the object of this faculty is actions[b], comprehending under that name active or practical principles: those principles from which men would act, if occasions and circumstances gave them power; and which, when fixed and habitual in any person, we call his character. It does not appear, that brutes have the least reflex sense of actions, as distinguished from events: or that will and design, which constitute the very nature of actions as such, are at all an object to their perception. But to ours they are: and they are the object, and the only one, of the approving and disapproving faculty. Acting, conduct, behaviour, abstracted from all regard to what is, in fact and event, the consequence of it, is itself the natural object of the moral discernment; as speculative truth and falsehood is of speculative reason. Intention of such and such consequences, indeed, is always included; for it is part of the action itself: but though the intended good or bad consequences do not follow, we have exactly the same sense of the action as if they did. In like manner we think well or ill of characters, abstracted from all consideration of the good or the evil, which persons of such characters have it actually in their power to do. We never, in the moral way, applaud or blame either ourselves or others,

---

[b] Οὐδὲ ἡ ἀρετὴ καὶ κακία—ἐν πείσει, ἀλλὰ ἐνεργείᾳ, M. Anton. lib. ix. 16. Virtutis laus omnis in actione consistit. Cic. Off. lib. i. cap. 6.

for what we enjoy or what we suffer, or for having impressions made upon us which we consider as altogether out of our power: but only for what we do, or would have done, had it been in our power; or for what we leave undone, which we might have done, or would have left undone, though we could have done it.

Secondly, Our sense or discernment of actions as morally good or evil, implies in it a sense or discernment of them as of good or ill desert. It may be difficult to explain this perception, so as to answer all the questions which may be asked concerning it: but every one speaks of such and such actions as deserving punishment; and it is not, I suppose, pretended, that they have absolutely no meaning at all to the expression. Now the meaning plainly is not, that we conceive it for the good of society, that the doer of such actions should be made to suffer. For if unhappily it were resolved, that a man, who, by some innocent action, was infected with the plague, should be left to perish, lest, by other people's coming near him, the infection should spread; no one would say he deserved this treatment. Innocence and ill-desert are inconsistent ideas. Ill-desert always supposes guilt: and if one be not part of the other, yet they are evidently and naturally connected in our mind. The sight of a man in misery raises our compassion towards him; and, if this misery be inflicted on him by another, our indignation against the author of it. But when we are informed, that the sufferer is a villain, and is punished only for his treachery or cruelty; our compassion exceedingly lessens, and in many instances our indignation wholly subsides. Now what produces this effect is the conception of that in the sufferer, which we call ill-desert. Upon considering then, or viewing together, our notion of vice and that of misery, there results a third, that of ill-desert. And thus there is in human creatures an association of the two ideas, natural and moral evil, wickedness and punishment. If this association were merely artificial or accidental, it were nothing: but being most unquestionably natural, it greatly concerns us to attend to it, instead of endeavouring to explain it away.

It may be observed farther, concerning our perception of good and of ill-desert, that the former is very weak with respect to common instances of virtue. One reason of which may be, that it does not appear to a spectator, how far such instances of virtue proceed from a virtuous principle, or in what degree this principle is prevalent: since a very weak regard to virtue may be sufficient to make men act well in many common instances. And on the other hand, our perception of ill-desert in vicious actions lessens, in proportion to the temptations men are thought to have had to such vices. For, vice in human creatures consisting chiefly in the absence or want of the virtuous principle; though a man be overcome, suppose, by tortures, it does not from thence appear to what degree the virtuous principle was wanting. All that appears is, that he had it not in such a degree, as to prevail over the temptation: but possibly he had it in a degree, which would have rendered him proof against common temptations.

Thirdly, Our perception of vice and ill-desert arises from, and is the result of, a comparison of actions with the nature and capacities of the agent. For the mere neglect of doing what we ought to do would, in many cases, be determined by all men to be in the highest degree vicious. And this determination must arise from such comparison, and be the result of it; because such neglect would not be vicious in creatures of other natures and capacities, as brutes. And it is the same also with respect to positive vices, or such as consist in doing what we ought not. For, every one has a different sense of harm done by an idiot, madman, or child, and by one of mature and common understanding; though the action of both, including the intention, which is part of the action, be the same: as it may be, since idiots and madmen, as well as children, are capable not only of doing mischief, but also of intending it. Now this difference must arise from somewhat discerned in the nature of capacities or one, which renders the action vicious; and the want of which, in the other, renders the same action innocent or less vicious: and this plainly supposes a comparison, whether reflected upon or not, between the action and capacities of the agent, previous to our determining an action to be vicious. And hence arises a proper application of the epithets, *incongruous, unsuitable, disproportionate, unfit*, to actions which our moral faculty determines to be vicious.

Fourthly, It deserves to be considered, whether men are more at liberty, in point of morals, to make themselves miserable without reason, than to make other people so: or dissolutely to neglect their own greater good, for the sake of a present lesser gratification, than they are to neglect the good of others, whom nature has committed to their care. It should seem, that a due concern about our own interest or happiness, and a reasonable endeavour to secure and promote it, which is, I think, very much the meaning of the word *prudence* in our language;

it should seem, that this is virtue, and the contrary behaviour faulty and blamable; since, in the calmest way of reflection, we approve of the first, and condemn the other conduct, both in ourselves and others. This approbation and disapprobation are altogether different from mere desire of our own, or of their happiness, and from sorrow upon missing it. For the object or occasion of this last kind of perception is satisfaction or uneasiness: whereas the object of the first is active behaviour. In one case, what our thoughts fix upon is our condition: in the other, our conduct. It is true indeed, that nature has not given us so sensible a disapprobation of imprudence and folly, either in *ourselves* or *others*, as of falsehood, injustice, and cruelty: I suppose, because that constant habitual sense of private interest and good, which we always carry about with us, renders such sensible disapprobation less necessary, less wanting, to keep us from imprudently neglecting our own happiness, and foolishly injuring ourselves, than it is necessary and wanting to keep us from injuring others, to whose good we cannot have so strong and constant a regard: and also because imprudence and folly, appearing to bring its own punishment more immediately and constantly than injurious behaviour, it less needs the additional punishment, which would be inflicted upon it by others, had they the same sensible indignation against it, as against injustice and fraud and cruelty. Besides, unhappiness being in itself the natural object of compassion; the unhappiness which people bring upon themselves, though it be wilfully, excites in us some pity for them: and this of course lessens our displeasure against them. But still it is matter of experience, that we are formed so as to reflect very severely upon the greater instances of imprudent neglects and foolish rashness, both in ourselves and others. In instances of this kind, men often say of themselves with remorse, and of others with some indignation, that they deserved to suffer such calamities, because they brought them upon themselves, and would not take warning. Particularly when persons come to poverty and distress by a long course of extravagance, and after frequent admonitions, though without falsehood or injustice; we plainly do not regard such people as alike objects of compassion with those, who are brought into the same condition by unavoidable accidents. From these things it appears, that prudence is a species of virtue, and folly of vice: meaning by *folly*, somewhat quite different from mere incapacity; a thoughtless want of that regard and attention to our own happiness, which we had capacity for. And this the word properly includes; and, as it seems, in its usual acceptation: for we scarce apply it to brute creatures.

However, if any person be disposed to dispute the matter, I shall very willingly give him up the words Virtue and Vice, as not applicable to prudence and folly: but must beg leave to insist, that the faculty within us, which is the judge of actions, approves of prudent actions, and disapproves imprudent ones; I say prudent and imprudent *actions* as such, and considered distinctly from the happiness or misery which they occasion. And, by the way, this observation may help to determine what justness there is in that objection against religion, that it teaches us to be interested and selfish.

Fifthly, Without inquiring how far, and in what sense, virtue is resolvable into benevolence, and vice into the want of it; it may be proper to observe, that benevolence, and the want of it, singly considered, are in no sort the whole of virtue and vice. For if this were the case, in the review of one's own character, or that of others, our moral understanding and moral sense would be indifferent to every thing but the degrees in which benevolence prevailed, and the degrees in which it was wanting. That is, we should neither approve of benevolence to some persons rather than to others, nor disapprove injustice and falsehood upon any other account, than merely as an overbalance of happiness was foreseen likely to be produced by the first, and of misery by the second. But now, on the contrary, suppose two men competitors for any thing whatever, which would be of equal advantage to each of them; though nothing indeed would be more impertinent, than for a stranger to busy himself to get one of them preferred to the other; yet such endeavour would be virtue, in behalf of a friend or benefactor, abstracted from all consideration of distant consequences: as that examples of gratitude, and the cultivation of friendship, would be of general good to the world. Again, suppose one man should, by fraud or violence, take from another the fruit of his labour, with intent to give it to a third, who, he thought, would have as much pleasure from it as would balance the pleasure which the first possessor would have had in the enjoyment, and his vexation in the loss of it; suppose also that no bad consequences would follow: yet such an action would surely be vicious. Nay farther, were treachery, violence and injustice, no otherwise vicious, than as foreseen likely to produce an overbalance of misery to society; then, if in any case a man could procure to himself as great advantage by an act of injustice, as the whole foreseen inconvenience, likely to be brought upon others by it, would amount to; such a piece of injustice would not be faulty or vicious at all: because it would be no more than, in any other case, for a man to prefer his own satisfaction to another's in equal degrees. The fact then appears to be, that we are constituted so as to condemn falsehood, unprovoked violence, injustice, and to approve of benevolence to some preferably to others, abstracted from all consideration, which conduct is likeliest to produce an overbalance of happiness or misery. And therefore, were the Author of nature to propose nothing to himself as an end but the production of happiness, were his moral character merely that of benevolence; yet ours is not so. Upon that supposition indeed, the only reason of his giving us the above-mentioned approbation of benevolence to some persons rather than others, and disapprobation of falsehood, unprovoked violence, and injustice, must be, that he foresaw this constitution of our nature would produce more happiness, than forming us with a temper of mere general benevolence. But still, since this is our constitution; falsehood, violence, injustice, must be vice in us, and benevolence to some, preferably to others, virtue; abstracted from all consideration of the overbalance of evil or good, which they may appear likely to produce.

Now if human creatures are endued with such a moral nature as we have been explaining, or with a moral faculty, the natural object of which is actions: moral government must consist in rendering them happy and unhappy, in rewarding and punishing them, as they follow, neglect, or depart from, the moral rule of action interwoven in their nature, or suggested and enforced by this moral faculty[c]; in

[c] Page 126.

rewarding and punishing them upon account of their so doing.

I am not sensible that I have, in this fifth observation, contradicted what any author designed to assert. But some of great and distinguished merit have, I think, expressed themselves in a manner, which may occasion some danger, to careless readers, of imagining the whole of virtue to consist in singly aiming, according to the best of their judgment, at promoting the happiness of mankind in the present state; and the whole of vice, in doing what they foresee, or might foresee, is likely to produce an overbalance of unhappiness in it: than which mistakes, none can be conceived more terrible. For it is certain, that some of the most shocking instances of injustice, adultery, murder, perjury, and even of persecution, may, in many supposable cases, not have the appearance of being likely to produce an overbalance of misery in the present state; perhaps sometimes may have the contrary appearance. For this reflection might easily be carried on, but I forbear—— The happiness of the world is the concern of him, who is the Lord and the Proprietor of it: nor do we know what we are about, when we endeavour to promote the good of mankind in any ways, but those which he has directed; that is indeed in all ways not contrary to veracity and justice. I speak thus upon supposition of persons really endeavouring, in some sort, to do good without regard to these. But the truth seems to be, that such supposed endeavours proceed, almost always, from ambition, the spirit of party, or some indirect principle, concealed perhaps in great measure from persons themselves. And though it is our business and our duty to endeavour, within the bounds of veracity and justice, to contribute to the ease, convenience, and even cheerfulness and diversion of our fellow-creatures; yet, from our short views, it is greatly uncertain, whether this endeavour will, in particular instances, produce an overbalance of happiness upon the whole; since so many and distant things must come into the account. And that which makes it our duty is, that there is some appearance that it will, and no positive appearance sufficient to balance this, on the contrary side; and also, that such benevolent endeavour is a cultivation of that most excellent of all virtuous principles, the active principle of benevolence.

However, though veracity, as well as justice, is to be our rule of life; it must be added, otherwise a snare will be laid in the way of some plain men, that the use of common forms of speech, generally understood, cannot be falsehood; and, in general, that there can be no designed falsehood without designing to deceive. It must likewise be observed, that in numberless cases, a man may be under the strictest obligations to what he foresees will deceive, without his intending it. For it is impossible not to foresee, that the words and actions of men, in different ranks and employments, and of different educations, will perpetually be mistaken by each other: and it cannot but be so, whilst they will judge with the utmost carelessness, as they daily do, of what they are not, perhaps, enough informed to be competent judges of, even though they considered it with great attention.

INDEX

TO BISHOP BUTLER'S ANALOGY,

Drawn up by Dr. Bentham, and revised and corrected by the Bishop himself. Printed from the original MS. now in the Bodleian Library.

Abstract notions, not to be applied to practical subjects without great cautiousness, 115, 120.
Accidental, in what respects events are so termed, 201.
Actions, to be distinguished from the moral quality ascribed to them, 54, 55.
Afflictions, how they produce the habit of pious resignation, 109.
Analogical reasoning, what, 2, 4, 5.
—— how to be conducted, 5, 6.
—— *Origen's* hint concerning it, 5.
—— how far intended to be here applied to religion, 6.
Analogy, how it becomes the ground of probability in different degrees, 2.
—— arguments drawn from it imply something similar and parallel in the cases, 31, 32, 176.
—— may reasonably be admitted to determine our judgments, 3.
—— afford sufficient proof to influence our practice, 10.
—— what it shows us concerning our ignorance, 141.
—— its use with regard to objections against natural and revealed religion, both as to their systems and evidence, 10.
—— how it assists us in judging of revelation, 183.

Analogy, how it may be applied to invalidate objections brought against the wisdom and goodness of the Divine government, 129, 130.
—— how it obviates objections against the credibility of future punishments, 40.
—— between our state of trial, in our temporal and religious capacity, 75, 76.
—— between the misconduct of mankind as to present and future interests, 79, 80.
—— the miserable consequences of men's neglecting moral improvement illustrated from it, 105, 106.
—— how it invalidates the plea which is urged in favour of vice, from passion, 147, 148.
—— what argument it suggests that the principles of Fatalism, if admitted to be true, do not destroy the proof of God's moral attributes, 118, 119.
—— suggests arguments sufficient to confute the Fatalist's plea for irreligion, 117, 118.
—— between the moral system of things as manifested by natural reason and by revelation, 9, 10.
—— between the light of nature and revelation, 190.

Analogy, how it obviates objections drawn from our ignorance of the manner or measure in which knowledge supernatural is communicated to mankind, 187.
—— as to the fitness of means to their respective ends, 200.
—— affords no argument against the general scheme of Christianity, 172.
—— affords no peculiar presumption against the reality of miracles, 174.
—— between the mysteriousness of the scheme of Christianity, and of God's natural government, 196, 197.
—— between the difficulty there is in accounting for some parts of God's ordinary Providence, and some particulars of Christianity, 181, 182.
—— the usefulness of arguing from the analogy of nature to religion, 266, 295.
—— what is taken for granted in this argument, 6.
—— between what *we see* contained in the natural government of God, and what *may be* contained in his moral, 135.
—— between what we at present experience concerning happiness, and what religion teaches us to expect, 34, 35.
—— affords no argument against the certainty of a future life, 16, 17.
—— how it confirms our apprehensions of future rewards and punishments, 123, 124.
—— between our state of probation, as to temporal and future welfare, 78, 84, 85, 94, 109, 110.
—— how it illustrates the Scriptural doctrine of the fall, 202, 214.
—— the Christian doctrine of a Mediator and Redeemer, 205, 213, &c.
—— how it obviates those objections against Christianity which are drawn from its supposed want of universality, 191, &c.
—— from its supposed want of wisdom and justice, 196, 197.
—— how it obviates the objection against the miraculousness of spiritual gifts in the first Christians, drawn from their disorderly use of them, 189.
Analogy, objections against the argument from analogy, drawn from the supposed small degree of influence which it is likely to have upon mankind, 302.
Attention, necessary when we consider Christianity, 273.

Benevolence, divine, towards us, how limited, 48.
Body, our existence may be considered without it, 19.
Brachmans: see *Death*.
Brutes, whether capable of immortality, and what kind, 25.

Chance, what is meant by it, 200.
Changes which things may undergo without destruction, 13.
Characters, what it is that renders some the object of approbation, others of dislike, 330.
Christ, his prophetical office, 219.
—— regal and priestly, 219, 220.
—— the apparent tendency of his sufferings justifies that method of our redemption, 224, 225.
—— his satisfaction, see *Mediator, Redemption, Sacrifices*.
—— a summary of the Bible history, as respecting the Messiah, 276, &c.
—— upon what evidence his Divine mission was acknowledged by the Gentiles, 284.
Christianity: see *Revelation, Objections*.
Christians, primitive, what argument their conversion and zeal afford of the reality of Christ's miracles, 258, 259.
Church, visible, the necessity of one to promote religion and virtue, 156, &c.
Conscience, what proof it affords of God's moral government, 49.
—— the dictates of it are to be considered as the laws of God, 122.
—— makes us proper subjects of moral government, 328.
—— regards chiefly, but not solely, the intention of the agent, 332.
Consciousness does not *make* personal identity, but ascertains it to ourselves, 320.
Contemplation, of itself, insufficient

to produce the habit of virtue, 88.
Conversation: see *Objections.*
Conviction [see *Evidence*], how it may arise from *analogy*, 2.
Creature, upright, and finitely perfect; the notion of such an one, 99.

Dangers of our miscarrying as to our religious interests, whence they chiefly arise, 79.
—— no impeachment [a] of God's goodness, 81, 82.
Daniel: the book of *D.* had probably greater external evidence of its authority formerly than what is come down to us, 270.
Death, the opinion of the *Brachmans* concerning it, 30.
—— the proper notion of it, 14, &c.
—— our imaginations apt to mislead us in considering it, 18.
—— not likely to destroy or suspend our powers of perception, 27, &c.
—— our state after *d.* not discoverable by reason, 31.
—— may be supposed to open our way into a better state, 30, &c.
Definitions sometimes serve only to perplex, 319.
Degradation: see *Fall.*
Difference of men's situations in religious matters [b], how to be accounted for, 232, 233.
—— whether a supposed universality of revelation would prevent it, 233.
Different degrees of evidence in religious matters, consistent with the justice of God's moral government, 232.
Difficulties in religion; unreasonable to expect to have them all cleared, 293, 294.
—— as to the *evidence* of religion, are analogous to those attending the practice of it, 239, 240.
Discipline, necessary [c] to our improvement in virtue, 96, 97.

Discipline, necessary [d] to our security against sin, 98.
—— the expediency of it to *creatures,* whether supposed upright or depraved, 101.
—— how this world is peculiarly fitted to be a state of discipline, 102.
Diseases of the *body* and *mind;* the analogy observable between the *remedies* which natural providence has furnished us with for the *former,* and those of revelation for the *latter,* 192, 193.
Doubting [see *Evidence*]; some *evidence* is implied wherever we *doubt,* 238, 276.
Duties to other beings arise from the relations in which they stand to us, 162, 163.
—— Christian *d.,* the reasons of them evident, 227.

Education: see *Youth.*
End: see *Means.*
Enthusiasm; the conversion and zeal of the first Christians not to be accounted for by *e.,* 259.
—— in what cases the pretence of enthusiasm may be urged in opposition to direct testimony, 259, 260.
—— religion not peculiarly liable to *e.,* 260.
—— sometimes mixed with knavery, 261.
—— how injudiciously *e.* is sometimes urged to discredit [e] the evidence of testimony in proof of Christianity, 262.
Evidence; the different sorts of *e.,* 1, &c.
—— probable *e.,* how distinguished from *demonstrative,* 1, 3.
—— probable *e.,* relative to beings of limited capacity, 3.
—— probable *e.,* even in a low degree, is a reasonable ground of action, 3.
—— what great force probable *e.* may receive from uniting several

---

[a] Credible from analogy that we are surrounded with these dangers, notwithstanding any objections which may be alleged against it from the goodness of God.—*Butler.*

[b] Probably to be accounted for in the same manner as their different situations in other respects.—*Butler.*

[c] Of great efficacy.—*Butler.* [d] Of great efficacy.—*Butler.*

[e] Destroy or overthrow.—*Butler.*

collateral things and circumstances into one view, 288, &c.

Evidence; the nature of that which directs us with regard to our temporal interests, 228.

Evidence, though not sufficient to exclude all doubt, affords rational ground to influence our conduct, 3, 272, 273, 295.

Evidence of testimony; upon what subjects it may be admitted as proof, 259.

—— the circumstances which strengthen this kind of *e.*, 260.

—— whether it may be invalidated, and how, 259, 260, 262, 263.

—— of *t.* of the first converts to Christianity has several presumptions in favour of it, 264.

—— of religion lies level to the apprehensions of all men,—why not attended to, 245, 246.

—— is the same kind as that which guides us in temporal matters, 297–301.

—— whether *Natural Religion* has any external *e.*, and what, 123, 124.

—— for Christianity represented, p. ii. c. vii. partly *direct* or fundamental, 250, 272.

—— partly collateral, 286, 287.

—— not to be truly judged of without careful consideration, 288.

—— the supposed doubtfulness of the *e.* of revelation is no argument against revelation, 227, 228.

—— of religion, though doubtful, *enforces* the obligation to behave religiously, 235–237.

—— why *e.* of religion has been left doubtful, 240, 241.

—— about the authority and meaning of divine commands, why it may in some cases have been designedly left doubtful, 246, 247, &c.

Evil, though the permission of it may be beneficial, yet it might have been better for the world if this or that particular evil had not been done, 136, 137, &c.

—— natural *e.*, the remedies which God has appointed for it, 208.

Existence, necessary, in what sense attributed to God, 118.

Faculties, the human, why not given us at our birth in their full maturity, 91.

Fall of man, whether nature suggests any appearances of it, 81.

—— does not afford just matter of complaint, 81, 82.

—— how conceivable, 97, 99.

—— not to be accounted for solely from the nature of liberty, 99.

—— how accounted for by particular affections, 99, 100.

—— the Scriptural account of it analogous[f] to what we see and experience, 215.

—— our not being able to account for it would not affect the certainty of the Christian dispensation, 215.

Falsehood, the several kinds of it, 261.

Fatalist, what is meant thereby, 112.

—— his argument against future rewards and punishments retorted, 127.

Fate, in what view considered in this treatise, 111.

—— if reconcilable with the present constitution of things, is so with religion, 112.

—— see *Necessity.*

Fear and Hope, proper motives to religious obedience, 106.

Final Cause, the notion thereof does not always imply that the end designed is answered, 105, 106.

Fitness, whether, and in what sense, it determines the will of God, 122, 123, 303, 304.

—— why the proof of religion from moral fitness is here omitted, 303.

Folly of mankind as to present and future interests, compared, 79, 80.

Future Life, the questions concerning it here considered, 29 *n.* 43 *n.*

—— implied in the notion of religion, 33.

—— belief of it disposes the mind to attend to the evidence of religion, 33.

—— the importance of it to us, and of our considering it, 34, 142, 143.

—— demonstrative proof of it not necessary to answer the purposes of religion, and to awaken our serious consideration, 33, 34.

[f] And conformable.—*Butler.*

Future Life is represented both by Reason and Scripture as a social state, 95.
—— not to be conceived without *particular* affections, 98.
—— this life a state of discipline for it, 147.
—— the security of our virtue in it may possibly be the effect of impressions acquired in this life, 103.
—— the certainty of it deducible from the imperfection of God's moral government in the present state of things, 49, 50.
—— the argument of it as drawn from analogy, 13, &c. 144, &c.
—— the absurdity of arguing against it upon principles of Atheism, 33.
Future Judgment, the supposal of one implies temptations, 76.
Future Punishments, the consideration of them, whether it belongs to Natural Religion, 43 *n*.
—— the certainty of them implied in our natural sense of actions as *ill-deserving*, 121.
—— may be presumed from God's rewarding or punishing us for our behaviour at present, 127.
—— the doctrine of religion concerning them is rendered credible by what we experience concerning the present distribution of happiness and misery, 34, &c. 40, 44.
—— the end for which and the manner in which they shall be inflicted, not fully discovered, 206, 211.
—— objections against the credibility of them obviated, 40, 41, 44.
Future Rewards, the certainty of them is implied in our natural sense of actions as *well-deserving*, 121.

General Laws; on what grounds we say that the course of nature is carried on by them, 200.
—— whether it be supposable that the Christian dispensation is so likewise, 200.
—— the use and application of this supposition, 201, 202.

General Laws, the manifest wisdom of carrying on the natural government of the world by them, 137, 138.
God; the being of G. why taken for granted in this treatise, 6.
—— is necessarily existent, 113.
—— his will may be considered as absolute or conditional, 247.
—— his will, how determined, 122 *n*.
—— his government, how exercised over us at present, 39.
—— his *natural government* over mankind, what, and how proved, 47, 75, 76.
—— carried on by general laws, 137, 138.
—— whether natural pleasure and pain may be considered as rewards and punishments from him, 38, 49, 128.
—— his *moral government*, what, and how proved, 47, 48, 53, 95, 143, 206.
——veracity and justice are the natural rule of God's government, 120.
—— the analogy between his natural and moral government, 130, 212.
—— his moral government not *perfectly* executed in this present state, 49.
—— the equitableness of it not yet fully discernible by us, 72.
—— whether the present course of nature, and the natural tendencies of virtue and vice, afford any probability that it will be perfectly equitable hereafter, 71, 72.
—— his *visible* government over the world is exercised by the *mediation* of others, 205, &c.
—— not incredible that his invisible may be so likewise, 206.
—— we may be certain that his government is *moral*, and yet be ignorant *how* it is carried on, 135.
—— his goodness; whether or how far the notion of it implies a disposition to confer happiness, 36.
—— his goodness with regard to the natural evils of life, 208.
—— it is no objection to God's goodness that he did not make us perfect creatures all at once g, 109, 110.

g The expectation that his goodness would have induced him to make us perfect creatures all at once, contradicted by the analogy of what we experience. —*Butler.*

God; the series of God's providential dispensations is *progressive,* 203.
—— his particular purposes not knowable to us antecedently to experience, 183, 184.
—— how God's moral government accounts for our being placed in a state of probation, 94.
—— upon what suppositions the objections against God's providence are usually founded, 133.
—— the dispensations of providence, how to be judged of, 159.
—— how far we are concerned to answer objections against God's providence, 294, 297, 298.
—— objections against the Divine government, how obviated by analogy, 129, 130, &c.
—— resignation to God's will is an essential part of virtue, 107.
—— what temper of mind in us corresponds to G.'s sovereignty, 109.
—— the heinousness[h] of disobeying G.'s commands, 153, 210.
—— whether disobedience[i] in any case admits of an excuse, and when, 143.
—— the duties to God *the Father,* whence their obligation arises, 161, &c.
—— those to *God the Son* and *Holy Ghost,* 162, &c.
Good men; their security against sin depends upon their improving their virtuous habits, 98.
Good and evil, natural; the great variety and seeming inequality of their distribution, 228, 229.
—— moral; the notion of it implies good desert, 331.
Goodness: see *God.*
Government, the formal notion of it, 37.
—— *natural* and *moral,* 47, 48.
Guilt, the idea of it in our minds always associated with that of illdesert, 331.

Habits, what, and *how* formed, 86, 87, &c.
—— how they differ from *passive impressions,* 87–91.

Habits, the great consequence of obtaining them in their *proper season,* 92, 93.
—— *virtuous* and *vicious,* the manner of their formation, 98, 100, 104.
—— *of virtue* necessary to all rational creatures, whether supposed virtuous or depraved, 100, 101.
Happiness, wherein it consists, 85, 86.
—— and *Misery,* reflections upon the means of their distribution at present, 35.
—— *present,* mainly depends upon our own behaviour, 35, 40, 44.
—— why it is not given to all promiscuously, 36.
—— why not confined to *merit,* 60.
—— *present,* not to be secured without great hazard and difficulty, 82, 83.
—— how this is reconcilable with the goodness of God[k], 82, 83.
Heathen world, the state of religion in it, 151.
History, what account it gives of the origin of religion, 176.
—— of the world, in what view it is considered in Scripture, 273, 274.
—— see *Scripture, Prophetic, Miracles.*
Hope and Fear, proper principles of religious obedience, 106, 107.
Identity or sameness, the different senses of the word, 304, 320.
—— in what sense applied to *persons,* 306, 319, 322.
—— *personal,* not *constituted* by consciousness, 320.
—— why by some thought to be so, 320.
Jews, a summary of God's dealing with them, 277.
—— their history as contained in Scripture, confirmed by known fact, 283.
—— not to be accounted for, but upon supposition of the miracles recorded in Scripture, 283, 284.
—— the circumstances of their dispersion, and yet continuing a distinct people, how they confirm the truth of revelation, 285, 286.

[h] Qy.—*Butler.*   [i] Qy.—*Butler.*
[k] Credible from hence, that this is the case too with regard to our future happiness.—*Butler.*

Ignorance in matters of *Religion*, owing frequently to men's negligence and prejudices, 244.
—— in matters of *Revealed Religion*, no more excusable than of *Natural*, 163.
—— what experience may teach us concerning our ignorance, 141.
—— of *the causes* on what the course of nature depends, 177.
—— of *the nature of our condition*, present and future[1], and of the *reasons* why we are placed therein, 233.
—— of the *manner and degrees* in which either natural or supernatural *knowledge* would be conveyed to us, antecedently to experience, 183, 184.
—— *how this* life is a preparation for a *better*, should be no objection against the credibility thereof, 94.
—— concerning the scheme of the *natural* world should teach us not to wonder at the incomprehensibleness of the *moral*, 132, 133.
—— objections drawn from our *i.* sometimes very absurd,—*when* more particularly so, 225, 226.
—— in *what* cases *i.* may serve for a satisfactory answer to objections, and when not, 134, 135, 139.
—— may be urged as a just answer to objections against the scheme of God's providence, 134, 135, 140, 141.
—— may be a satisfactory answer to objections against a *thing*, and yet not affect the *proof* of it, 140.
—— answers taken from our ignorance applied to objections against providence [m], in what sense they may be called answers, 141.
Imagination, apt to mislead us, 18.
Improvement of the human faculties in all respects is *gradual*, 90.
—— whether this circumstance does not render them more useful than if we had been born with them in their full maturity, 91, 92.
Inspiration; in *what manner* or in *what degree* it should be vouchsafed to mankind not knowable by human reason, 183.
Interest; sense of interest, what, 97, *n.*
—— in what respect it is, and in what it is not, sufficient to restrain men from criminal self-indulgence, 97, *n.*
—— in what sense it is always coincident with virtue, 108.
Irregularities in nature, whence the appearance of them arises, 202.
—— unreasonable to expect to have them remedied by occasional interpositions, 138.
Irreligion, its aggravated guilt beyond that of *other* vice, 212, 306.
—— more especially aggravated in men of high rank and character, 237.
—— not justifiable upon any pretence of want of evidence in religion, 235, 236.

Kingdom; idea of a *k.* perfectly virtuous and happy, 68.
—— see *Political.*
Knowledge, natural, the ordinary methods of improving it, 190.

Liberty; why the proof of religion from thence is omitted in this treatise, 303, 304.
—— the nature of it insufficient to account for the *Fall*, 99.
—— the constitution of the present world and our condition in it imply that we are *free*, 117.
Life: see *Future Life.*
Living Powers, what, 15, *n.*
—— death not necessarily the destruction of them, 16, 17, 21.
—— why thought so, 17.
—— their not being exercised does not imply their non-existence, 16.
—— present life has reference to a larger plan of things, not fully to be comprehended by us, 142.
Locke, Mr., his notion of personal identity examined, 322.
Locomotive powers, to what they properly belong, 24.

---

[1] Natural and moral.—*Butler.*
[m] Answers before given to objections against Providence, not taken from our ignorance only, but from somewhat which analogy teaches us concerning it.—*Butler.*

Mahometanism was not received in the world upon the foot of miracles, 255.
Man, how his nature differs from that of brutes, and wherein it agrees, 328.
Manifestation of persons' characters in this life to other intelligent creatures, what uses may be served thereby, 111.
—— this may be one use of temptations, 242.
Martyrs, primitive; what argument their sufferings afford of the reality of Christ's miracles, 258.
Matter, our being affected thereby does not prove it to make part of our *self*, 21, 22.
Means and *End;* speculative reason, antecedently to experience, is a very incompetent judge of either, 6, 8, 135, 141.
—— the distinction between them not always rightly applied by us to *Divine* actions, 204.
—— the making use of *means* for the salvation of mankind not inconsistent with the supposition of wisdom in the contrivance [n], 203.
—— prescribed by Christianity, no presumption against their wisdom, 200.
Mediator between God and man, the notion of it agreeable to the light of nature, 205, 312.
—— the appointment of a Mediator considered, p. ii. ch. v.
—— the Christian doctrine of a Mediator, in what respect mostly objected to; and the frivolousness of such objections, 222, 226.
—— see *Redemption.*
Messiah: see *Christ.*
Miracle, a relative term, 174.
—— whether the power exerted at the first formation of the world should be so called, 174, 175.
—— whether the analogy of nature affords any presumption against their reality, pt. ii. ch. ii.
—— with what *phenomena* of nature they should be compared, in order to judge whether there lies any presumption against them, 178.
Miracles, the consideration of religion carries with it distinct reasons for them, 178.
—— the primary design of them, 154, 155.
—— whether they confirm natural religion, and how, 155.
—— peculiar to the Mosaic and Christian religion, 255, 256.
—— whether any others are well attested by historical evidence[o], 262, 284, 285.
—— whether the supposition of such attestation would discredit the Scriptural miracles, 262, 284.
—— related in Scripture, how confirmed by contemporary and subsequent facts, 238, 251, 252.
—— what observable as to the *manner* in which they are related in Scripture [p], 250, 252, 253, 254.
—— recorded in Scripture, what confirmation they receive from the credibility of common history, 281, 284.
—— referred to in St. Paul's Epistles, 254.
—— what proof of their reality is afforded by the conversion of the first Christians, 256, 257.
—— Pagan or Popish, no parallelism [q] between them and those recorded in Scripture, 255.
—— *invisible m.,* what may be termed thus, 174.
Miraculous, in what respect many events seemingly brought about by natural means may justly be esteemed to be miraculous, 285.
Misery: see *Happiness.*
Moral action, whether the nature of it can be altered by virtue of a command, 194.
Moral faculty: see *Conscience.*
Moral obligations, whence the force of them arises, 140, 165, 167.
Moral precepts, see *Positive.*
Moral part of religion, why preferred in Scripture to the positive, 167, 168.

---

[n] Conformable to the whole constitution and course of nature.—*Butler.*
[o] Like historical evidence of fabulous ones, to that there is for those which are alleged in proof of Christianity, would not destroy the evidence of the latter.—*Butler.*   [p] Qy.—*Butler.*   [q] Parallel.—*Butler.*

Morality of actions depends chiefly, but not solely, upon the intention of the agent, 332.
—— depends partly upon the nature and capacity of the agent, 333.
Mysteries, as great in nature as in Christianity, 202.
Mysteriousness of the Christian scheme affords no just objection against it, 197.

Nature, light of n. insufficient, 151.
—— course of n. what, 5, 37, 207.
—— is progressive, 204.
—— with regard to intelligent beings, is carried on by general laws, 9, 137, 200.
—— (as known by experience) affords no presumption against any of the Christian doctrines, 173.
—— our ignorance of the causes, &c. on which the course of nature depends, 177.
Natural, in what sense those events may be termed *natural* which proceed from God's immediate interposition, 32, 33.
—— see *Government, Religion, Knowledge.*
Necessary existence, how attributed to God, 113, 114.
Necessity, as held by the Fatalist, does not exclude deliberation and choice, 112.
—— the supposition of n. will not account for the origin and preservation of all things, 112.
—— in what sense n. is said to be the foundation of the existence of God, 113.
—— existence of things by n. implies some operating agent, 114.
—— does not exclude an intelligent agent, nor destroy the ground of belief that we are in a state of religion, 115.
—— nor the justice of punishment for crimes, 119.
—— nor the proof of God's moral character, 120, 147.
—— nor the proof of the obligations of religion, 119, 298, 299.
—— nor the external evidence of religion, 126.
—— in what respect the opinion of n. may be said to be destructive of all religion, 129.
—— if made a principle of conduct in affairs of common life, experience would soon convince us of its absurdity, 115–118.
Negligence, no more excusable as to matters of revealed religion than of natural, 163.
—— is one source of dissatisfaction about the evidence of religion, 243, 244.

Objections; the use of shewing that the same objections lie against natural religion which are commonly urged against revealed, 294, 295.
—— though not cleared up, do not destroy the proof of religion, 245.
—— drawn from our ignorance, when more particularly absurd, 222, 223.
—— what qualifications are requisite in order to their due consideration, 246.
—— against the *argument from analogy*, drawn from the supposed small degree of influence which it is likely to have upon mankind, considered, 302.
—— against the scheme of Providence are generally mere arbitrary assertions, and receive a proper answer from our ignorance, 133, 141.
—— against the dispensations of Providence, how far we are concerned to answer them, 297, 298.
—— drawn from the seeming irregularities of the moral world, how solved by comparing them with what occurs in the natural world, 131, 134, 141, 142.
—— against the credibility of future punishments obviated, 39, 46.
—— against the credibility of a future life, drawn from our ignorance how this life is a preparation for it, 94.
—— against this world's being designed for a state of moral improvement in virtue; drawn from the frequent instances of men's improving only in vice, 105, 160, 108, 109.
—— why the matter of the Christian Revelation must be expected to appear liable to o., 184, 185, 177.
—— against the reality of the truths discovered by Christianity, drawn from their appearing un-

like the known course of nature, 173.
Objections against Christianity, drawn from the *manner* or *degree* in which the light of it is vouchsafed, why frivolous, 184.
—— against Christianity, from its supposed want of universality, 191, 192.
—————— from its mysteriousness, 197.
——— against the wisdom of it, 197.
——— drawn from the perversions of Christianity, 158.
——— against Christianity itself, as distinguished from those against its evidence, why frivolous, 180.
——— against the Scriptural doctrine of a Redeemer, 211, 226.
——— against Scripture, the common ones, their frivolousness, 184.
—————— from its liableness to be perverted, 195.
—————— as to its not answering our preconceived expectations, 187.
——— what gives particular force to objections against Christianity, when offered in common conversation, 291.
Obligations of duty, arising from the bare supposableness or credibility of religion, 237, 239.
Occasional interpositions to remedy the supposed irregularities in the government of the world, would be attended with manifest ill-effects, 138.
Omissions, when vicious, 332.
Opinion: see *Evidence*.
Origen, his hint concerning analogical reasoning, 5.

Passions, how they contribute to make our present state a state of trial, 77, 78.
——— are excited towards particular objects whether we will or no, 96, 97.
——— such bare excitement not criminal, 97.
——— always dangerous, 99-101.
——— how to be regulated, 100, 101.
——— how the fall of man may be accounted for from thence, 99.
Passive Impressions differ from practical habits, 89, 90.

Passive Impressions are less sensibly felt by being repeated, but not less apt to influence our practice, 89, 90.
St. Paul's Epistles, what particular evidence we have of their genuineness, 253, 254.
——— what distinct proof of Christianity they afford, 254, 255.
Perception may be without external objects, 22, 23.
——— our powers of *p*. different from the senses, 23.
——— ridiculous to dispute the truth of our *p.*, 327.
Person, what, 320, 321.
——— sameness of *p.* prior to all considerations of consciousness, 323, 324.
Personality, in what sense founded in consciousness, 320.
Pleasure attending the gratification of our passions, *whether*, and *how far*, intended to put us upon gratifying them, 37.
——— the distribution of *p.* in the world, in what sense it is *reward*, 47.
Political state of kingdoms, in what view taken notice of and foretold in Scripture, 275.
Positive institutions implied in the notion of a visible Church, 156, 157.
——— the great presumption of those who slight them, 170.
Positive precepts, how they differ from moral, 165.
——— whether founded in natural religion, 166.
——— when and in what cases they yield to moral, 168.
——— caution necessary when we compare *p.* precepts with moral, 167.
Practical proof, what, 126.
Practice: by what evidence matters of *p.* are often determined, 294.
——— in matters of *p.* their importance is always to be considered, 290.
Prejudices; several sorts of *p.*, 260.
——— occasion dissatisfaction about the evidence of religion, 243.
——— the folly of being influenced by *p.* arising from contempt and scorn, 271.
Present existence affords presumption of continuance, where there

appears no reason to the contrary, 15.
Presumption: see *Evidence.*
Presumptuousness, the unjustifiableness of it, 46.
Principles upon which we are apt to reason antecedently to experience, generally prove fallacious, 194, 195, 196.
—— the several *p.* of virtue, however distinct from each other, are coincident, 108.
Probability: see *Evidence.*
Probation: see *Trial.*
—— a state of *p.*, what is meant by it, and how it differs from moral government, 75.
Profaneness: see *Irreligion.*
Proof, practical, what is meant by it, 126.
Prophecies recorded in Scripture, the primary design of them, 154.
—— whether they confirm natural religion, and how, 154.
—— concerning the Messiah, how understood by the Jews before the coming of Christ, 267.
—— the question concerning the force of the argument arising from *p.* stated, 271.
—— whether their true meaning is to be determined by their apparent completion, 267.
—— the conformity between prophecies and events not merely accidental, 289.
—— though applicable to other events, might nevertheless, in the Divine intention, have had regard to the Christian dispensation, 270, 271.
—— the force of the argument from *p.* is best seen by taking them in a long series, 266, 267.
—— the obscurity of one part of a *p.* does not invalidate the proof of foresight, arising from the apparent completion of other intelligible parts, 265.
—— the force of the argument from *p.* not destroyed, though we suppose the prophets not to have understood the intended meaning of their predictions, 269.
—— the qualifications requisite to take the force of the argument arising from *p.*, 286, 287.
Prophetic History confirmed by the state of the world, and of the Christian church, 285, 288.
Prophets, not the sole authors of what they wrote, 268, 269.
Providence: see *God.*
Prudence, whether it ever requires us to act, and *when*, though there is no probability of our succeeding, 3.
—— the difficulty of obtaining *p.*, 243.
—— when a course of action may be called prudent, 301.
Public spirit, the true notion of it, 65.
Punishment, its proper notion, 38, 39.
—— why natural *p.* is in Scripture ascribed to divine justice, 128.
—— *p.* of the innocent for the guilty, whether and how far it affects the doctrine of Christ's satisfaction, 223, 224.
—— instances of vicarious *p.* in the daily course of providence, 224.
—— see *Future Punishments.*

Reason, a very incompetent judge of the conduciveness of means to their respective ends, 135, 136.
—— or in what manner God would instruct mankind, 183.
—— could not have discovered the scheme of Christianity, 172.
—— *how far r.* can judge of revelation, and in *what respect*, 180, 193.
—— is an incompetent judge of the matter of Divine revelation, 310.
—— this consideration affords no presumption against revelation, 170, 310.
—— an account of the opposition sometimes made to religion upon supposed principles of *r.*, and the folly of it, 308, 310.
Reasons of a divine command ceasing, the obligation ceases, 153.
Reasoning upon the course of nature, without attending to known facts, apt to be fallacious, 5, 8, 9.
—— upon the several possible formations of the universe, why ridiculous, 7, 8.
—— upon the principles of others, what is meant by it, 303.
—— whether abstruse *r.* be ever

necessary in matters of religion, 306.
Redemption; the scriptural doctrine of r. distinctly represented, 216.
—— how illustrated by what we experience concerning the remedies which God hath provided against temporal evils, 208, 209.
—— further illustrated by analogy, 311, 312.
—— agreeable to our natural notions, our hopes and our fears, 213.
—— the manner of its efficacy not represented in Scripture, nor discoverable by reason, 313, 314.
—— why we are incompetent judges of it, 222.
—— the rashness of some persons in determining questions concerning it, 225, 226.
—— see *Punishment, Mediator.*
Reflection, our powers of r. do not depend upon what is liable to a dissolution from death, 27, 28.
—— our powers of r. may be improved by death, 30.
—— do not depend upon our bodily powers, 29–31.
Relations, impossible for us to say how far the r. of the several species and individuals in the natural world extend, 131.
—— between the several parts of the Divine administration in the moral world, 132, 133.
Religion, its general system, 70.
—— what is implied in the notion of r., 295, 296.
—— wherein the general spirit of r. consists, 170.
—— in what view considered throughout this treatise, 303.
—— is founded in the moral character of God, 119.
—— implies a future state, 33.
—— implies our being in a state of probation, 248.
—— the importance of being influenced by r., 148.
—— the proper proof of r. and motives to it, 148.
—— the force of its obligation is not destroyed by the opinion of necessity, 120.
—— degrees of knowledge of r. different among different men, 230, 231.

Religion; why its evidence has been left at all doubtful, 238, 239.
—— such doubtfulness does not destroy its obligation, 235, 236.
—— its importance, 126.
—— an account of those who oppose it, as they suppose, on principles of reason, 308, 309.
—— the origin of r. according to history and tradition, 176.
—— the state of r. in the heathen world, 151.
—— distinguished into internal and external, 161.
—— natural r. what, 10, 11, 123.
—— is not the only object of our moral regard, 162.
—— probably owes its rise and establishment to revelation, 125, 152, 280.
—— whether it hath any external proof, 123.
—— what proof it receives from tradition, 124.
—— the great advantages which it receives from Christianity, 153, 160.
—— what credibility it receives from the miracles recorded in Scripture, 154, 155.
—— how promoted by the settlement of a visible church, 156.
—— the obligations of natural r., as inculcated in Christian countries, lie obvious to all apprehensions, 306, 307.
Religious knowledge, a general account of the different degrees of it to be found among different men, 230.
Remorse, what, 55.
Repentance, its insufficiency to expiate guilt, argued from analogy, 211, 312, 313.
—— the general sense of mankind upon this subject, 212.
—— its efficacy whence derived, 221.
Resignation to God's will, an essential part of virtue, 107, 108.
—— how the habit of it is produced, 108, 109.
Revelation necessary to explain the scheme of the universe, 67.
—— to ascertain and supply the defects of natural religion, 151.
—— the great usefulness of it with respect to natural religion, 154, 163.

Revelation, supposed to have been given at the beginning of the world, in what sense *miraculous,* 174.
—— no peculiar difficulty in supposing a *r.* to have been made at that time, 176.
—— the pretences of false *r.* imply a true one, 125.
Revealed Religion (viz. Christian), what is implied in the notion of it, 10, 11, 171.
—— the suppositions on which it is grounded, 205, 206, 212, 213.
—— a short view of its scheme, 171, 197.
—— the extensiveness of it, 197.
—— the reasonableness and the credibility of its system are two distinct considerations, 298, 299.
—— no presumption against it from the analogy of nature, 171.
—— upon what kind of proof it is to be received, 307, 308.
—— its evidence, part direct, part collateral, 250, 251, 272.
—— consists of various parts to be united into one view, 288.
—— briefly represented, 272, 287.
—— why left at all doubtful, 296, 300.
—— cannot be destroyed, 291, 292.
—— how far tradition may be admitted in proof of it, 176.
—— how the question concerning its truth ought to be stated, 183, 184, 195.
—— may be considered as wholly historical, 273.
—— unreasonable to expect to have all difficulties in it cleared, 294, 295.
—— difficulties in it are parallel to those which arise in the ordinary administration of providence, 182.
—— objections against the matter of *r. r.,* 179.
—— admit of the same answers as those alleged against the wise constitution of nature, 197.
—— the difference between its scheme and the experienced course of nature illustrated by analogy, 314.
—— the mysteriousness of *r. r.,* 197.
—— its dispensation, whether carried on by general laws, 200.
—— how far to be judged of by reason, 180, 193.

Revealed Religion, objections against its want of universality considered, 191, 192.
—— against the wisdom and justice of it, 196, 197.
—— against it as a matter of fact, 298, 299.
—— against it drawn from its abuses and perversions, 158.
—— the duties of it strictly moral, 160, 161.
—— the practice of it may be shewn to be reasonable, though we cannot evince the reasonableness of each precept, 299.
—— the rashness of treating it with disregard, 165.
—— the occasion of some men's treating it with scorn, and the sinfulness of so doing, 308, 316.
—— a brief account of its first propagation and establishment, 255, 283, 284.
—— what strength its evidence receives from the conversion and zeal of the first Christians, 259.
—— Jewish and Christian, the degrees of their evidence different at different times, 230.
Rewards and Punishments, according to the natural constitution of things, correspond to virtue and vice, 145.
Ridicule, how it obstructs men's seeing the evidence of religion, 244.
Sacrifices propitiatory, the general prevalence of them shews the sense of mankind about the inefficacy of mere repentance, 212.
—— legal, their design, 216, 220.
—— the death of Christ a proper *s.,* 216, 220.
—— the manner of its efficacy not explained in Scripture, and therefore unwarrantable in any man to attempt explaining it, 221.
Scepticism, no justification of indifference about religion, 248.
—— about the evidence of religion implies a suspicion at least of its being true, 263, 264.
Sceptics among us, their immorality and irreligion utterly inexcusable, 315, 316.
Scorn of religion, to what it is owing, 308, 315, 316.
Scripture considered in an historical view, 273.

Scripture; the great antiquity of the first parts of it, 280.
—— the genuineness of Scripture history shewn by internal evidence, 251.
—— the historical parts of it illustrated by correspondent facts, and other histories, 279, 280.
—— a summary of the history of the Old Testament as respecting the Messiah, 278, 279.
—— the observable manner in which the miraculous history is related, 251, 252.
—— confirmed by contemporary and subsequent facts, 252.
—— its not having been confuted affords a presumption of its truth, 276.
—— its claim to a considerate regard, 280.
—— how far reason is a proper judge of the contents of it, 193.
—— its meaning not always to be explained according to the common rules of criticism, 184, 185.
—— what are the ordinary methods of coming at its true meaning, 190.
—— difficulties of *S.* no argument of its not coming from God, 5.
—— the unreasonableness of expecting to have all difficulties in it cleared, 293.
—— probably contains several truths as yet undiscovered, 191.
—— the common objections against it are frivolous, 184.
—— some precepts of *S.* matter of offence, why, 194.
—— the folly of rejecting Scripture because it does not answer our preconceived expectations, 193.
—— some precepts of *S.* prescribing things seemingly unjust, how to be considered, 193, 194.
—— the chronology and history of the Old Testament confirmed by other histories, 281.
—— the Jewish history in it confirmed by known fact, 283.
—— the internal marks of its truth, 281, 282.
—— not discredited by the seeming strangeness of some incidents, nor by supposed mistakes of transcribers, 282.
—— its common history gives credit to the miraculous, 282.

Scripture; not to be accounted for without supposing the reality of the miracles therein recorded, 283.
—— its *prophetic* history confirmed by the state of the world and of the Christian church, 285, 286.
—— the credibility of its full and final completion, 286.
—— what evidence it gives to Christianity, and how to be considered, 286, 287.
—— see *St. Paul's* Epistles.
Self, indivisible, 18, 19, 20.
—— its sameness does not depend upon the sameness of our body, 21, 22.
Self-denial, the use and necessity of it, 82, 83, 93.
—— productive of resignation to God's will, 108.
Self-love, whether this principle wants to be improved, 98, 99.
Senses, what, 21, 22.
—— different from the perceiving power, 22, 23.
—— the dissolution of them implies not the dissolution of the agent which perceives, 25.
Simplicity of a living agent, what proof it admits of, 20.
Soul, its indivisibility, 18, 19.
Temptations are implied in the supposition of a future judgment, 75, 76.
—— their various sorts, 78, 103.
—— how they serve to improve our virtue, 104, 105, 241.
—— the supposition of them lessens our perception of ill desert in vicious actions, 332.
Testimony; see *Evidence.*
Treatise, this, the design of it, 10–12, 70, 71, 305, 309.
—— to whom it is particularly addressed, 314, 315.
Trinity, whence our obligation of duty to each Person in the *T.* arises, 160, 161.
Trial, state of, what is implied in the notion of it, 75, 76.
—— that we are in such a state, 145–147, 248.
—— how, in respect of our understanding, 234.
—— as to our temporal interests, 75–77.
—— as to our religious concerns, 80.

Trial, state of, as to our present and future welfare compared, 77, 79.
—— the supposition of God's moral government sufficiently accounts for our being placed in a state of t., 84, 95.
—— intended for our improvement as a qualification for future happiness, 85.
—— may be also intended for the manifestation of our characters to other intelligent beings, 110.

Vegetables, no arguing from their decay to that of living creatures, 31.
—— their identity, 321.
Veracity, our natural regard to it, 261.
Vice, what it chiefly consists in, 332.
—— does not consist merely in the intention to produce unhappiness, 336, &c.
—— the manner in which the habit of it is formed, 99, 100.
—— whether folly be a species of it, 334.
—— passion no excuse for it, 148.
—— temptations to v., various sorts, 103, 104.
—— the prosperity with which it is sometimes attended, how reconciled with God's moral government, 53, 54, 61.
—— the pleasures of it scarce worth taking into account, 148.
—— the disadvantages naturally attending it, 55, 210.
—— why not always punished, 145.
—— private, may be public benefits, and yet, upon the whole, it were more beneficial for the world if men would refrain from it, 136.
Viciousness of the world fits it to be a state of trial to good men, 103.
Virtue, its general nature the same universally and at all times, 329.
—— implies in it intention and design, 330.
—— is relative to the capacity of the agent, 332.
—— does not consist merely in an endeavour and intention to produce happiness, 335, 336.

Virtue corresponds to our notion of good desert, 331.
—— common instances of it do not raise in us any strong perception of good desert, and why, 331.
—— whether prudence be a sort of virtue, 333, 334.
—— the habit of virtue not attainable by mere contemplation, 88.
—— its habit, how formed, 99, 100, 102, 103.
—— its improvement progressive, 100, 101.
—— improved by temptation, 103, 241.
—— the advantages attending v. in this world as to internal satisfaction of mind, 56.
—— as to external advantages, 52, 56, 57, 65.
—— its tendency to improve the happiness of kingdoms, 68, 69.
—— often rewarded as such, but never punished as such, 59.
—— why not always rewarded, 145, 146.
—— its liableness to afflictions, how reconcilable with God's moral government, 53, 54, 62.
—— the restraints which it lays men under are not to be thought disadvantages, 50, 51.
—— a qualification naturally requisite to make us happy in a future state, 95.
—— whether a true esteem of moral v. be consistent with a neglect of Revelation. 152, 153.
Understanding, our probation with regard to it upon the subject of religion, 234.
Universe, scheme of it knowable only from Revelation, 67.
—— speculations about the several possible formations of it and schemes of its government, why ridiculous, 8.
Universality, objections against Christianity from its supposed want of u., how answered, 191, 192, 227, 313, 314.

World, the present fitted to be a state of discipline for moral improvement, 102, 103.
—— a theatre for the manifestation

of persons' characters to other intelligent creatures, 110.

World, the natural government of it carried on by general laws, 137.

—— the natural *w.* intended to be subordinate to the moral, 132.

—— its history in Scripture, in what view to be considered, 273, 274.

World, its period as spoken of in the Old and New Testament, 275.

Youth, the great importance of right direction in that stage of life, 42, 86, 87, 91, 92.

www.ingramcontent.com/pod-product-compliance
Lightning Source LLC
Chambersburg PA
CBHW030602300426
44111CB00009B/1076